Jimmy Carter and the Anglo-American Special Relationship

Edinburgh Studies in Anglo-American Relations

Series Editors: Steve Marsh and Alan P. Dobson

Published and forthcoming titles

The Anglo-American Relationship
Steve Marsh and Alan P. Dobson

The Arsenal of Democracy: Aircraft Supply and the Anglo-American Alliance, 1938–1942
Gavin J. Bailey

Post-War Planning on the Periphery: Anglo-American Economic Diplomacy in South America, 1939–1945
Thomas C. Mills

Best Friends, Former Enemies: The Anglo-American Special Relationship and German Reunification
Luca Ratti

Reagan and Thatcher's Special Relationship: Latin America and Anglo-American Relations
Sally-Ann Treharne

Tacit Alliance: Franklin Roosevelt and the Anglo-American 'Special Relationship' before Churchill, 1933–1940
Tony McCulloch

The Politics of Diplomacy: U.S. Presidents and the Northern Ireland Conflict, 1967–1998
James Cooper

Jimmy Carter and the Anglo-American 'Special Relationship'
Thomas K. Robb

The Congo Crisis: Anglo-American Relations and the United Nations, 1960–1964
Alanna O'Malley

euppublishing.com/series/esar

Jimmy Carter and the Anglo-American Special Relationship

Thomas K. Robb

EDINBURGH
University Press

Edinburgh University Press is one of the leading university presses in the UK. We publish academic books and journals in our selected subject areas across the humanities and social sciences, combining cutting-edge scholarship with high editorial and production values to produce academic works of lasting importance. For more information visit our website: www.edinburghuniversitypress.com

© Thomas K. Robb, 2017

Edinburgh University Press Ltd
The Tun – Holyrood Road,
12(2f) Jackson's Entry,
Edinburgh EH8 8PJ

Typeset in 11/13 Sabon by
IDSUK (Dataconnection) Ltd

A CIP record for this book is available from the British Library

ISBN 978 1 4744 0701 4 (hardback)
ISBN 978 1 4744 0702 1 (webready PDF)
ISBN 978 1 4744 0703 8 (epub)

The right of Thomas K. Robb to be identified as the author of this work has been asserted in accordance with the Copyright, Designs and Patents Act 1988, and the Copyright and Related Rights Regulations 2003 (SI No. 2498).

Contents

Acknowledgements	vi
Abbreviations	viii
Introduction	1
1. Détente, Human Rights and Anglo-American Relations	10
2. Embracing the Special Relationship, 1977–8	24
3. Stresses and Strains	64
4. Thatcher Comes to Power	89
5. The End of Détente	113
Conclusion	152
Notes	158
Select Bibliography	233
Index	239

Acknowledgements

I would like to thank the numerous archivists that have assisted in locating material for the writing of this book. The assistance offered by the various staff at the British National Archives, Kew, the British Olympic Archive, University of East London, Churchill College, Cambridge University, the modern papers section at the Bodleian Library, Oxford University, the Gerald R. Ford Presidential Library, Ann Arbor, the Jimmy Carter Presidential Library, Atlanta, the US National Archives II at College Park and the staff at the Sterling Library, Yale University, have all been courteous, professional and efficient. Without such dedicated staff then the process of writing history would be infinitely more difficult. Professor Alan Dobson first approached me about writing this book and it was with his encouragement that the final volume saw the light of day. I extent my gratitude to Professor Dobson and his co-editor of the series, Dr Steve Marsh, who have both professionally edited and guided this volume to its successful publication. The publication team at Edinburgh University Press have been the model of professionalism in ensuring the timely publication of the book.

Colleagues and friends, such as Dr James Cooper, Dr Donal Lowry and Dr David Gill, deserve a special mention for discussing this work over the past several years. Dr Lowry's expert guidance on issues related to Rhodesia helped me to better appreciate the nuances that affected the course of events. Of course, any misunderstandings or errors of fact or interpretation are a reflection on me and not Dr Lowry. Dr Cooper has provided engaging conversation about the Carter presidency and Anglo-American relations more broadly. Dr Gill has read numerous drafts of

Acknowledgements

this work at various stages of the writing process and his sharp insights and questions have resulted in a much stronger work than it would have been otherwise. Of course, it is to my family and friends that I also offer my appreciation. It is to them that I dedicate this book.

Abbreviations

Main Text

CIA	Central Intelligence Agency
CND	Campaign for Nuclear Disarmament
CTB	comprehensive test ban
EEC	European Economic Community
ERW	enhanced radiation warhead
FCO	Foreign and Commonwealth Office
FRG	Federal Republic of Germany
G7	Group of Seven
GCHQ	Government Communications Headquarters
GDP	gross domestic product
ICBM	intercontinental ballistic missile
IMF	International Monetary Fund
IOC	International Olympic Committee
IRA	Irish Republican Army
IRBM	intermediate range ballistic missile
JCS	Joint Chiefs of Staff
LDC	low developed country
MIRV	multiple independently targetable re-entry vehicle
MOD	Ministry of Defence
MP	Member of Parliament
NATO	North Atlantic Treaty Organization
NSC	National Security Council
PRC	People's Republic of China
RUC	Royal Ulster Constabulary
SALT	Strategic Arms Limitation Talks/Treaty
SCC	Special Coordination Committee

Abbreviations

SLBM	submarine-launched ballistic missile
UDI	unilateral declaration of independence
UK	United Kingdom
UN	United Nations
USSR	Union of Soviet Socialist Republics
ZANLA	Zimbabwe African National Liberation Army
ZANU	Zimbabwe African National Union
ZAPU	Zimbabwe African People's Union

Notes and Select Bibliography

BDOHP	British Diplomatic Oral History Project
BOA	British Olympic Association Archive
CAB	Cabinet Office files
DEFE	Ministry of Defence files
FCO	Foreign and Commonwealth Office files
FO	Foreign Office files
FRUS	*Foreign Relations of the United States*
G6	Group of Six
GFL	Gerald R. Ford Presidential Library
GLCM	ground launched cruise missile
JCL	Jimmy Carter Presidential Library
NAII	US National Archives II
PPP	*Public Papers of the Presidents of the United States*
PREM	Prime Minister's Office files
T	Treasury files
TNA	National Archives (UK)
USA	United States of America

Introduction

> In Britain we know how much we owe to America. We understand how close our countries are. America's cause is, and always will be, our cause.[1]

> We share a lot in common. Although our cars, or our automobiles, may drive on opposite sides of the highway, our people generally move in the same direction. And we share, or at least attempt to share, a common language. Sometimes we don't succeed. But in the most important things, we do see issues and ideas, challenges, hopes, and expectations in the same way.[2]

The above quotes mirror the romantic notions of the Anglo-American relationship which Margaret Thatcher long propagated in her writings and public speeches. Thatcher's rhetoric echoes the sentiments of another British prime minister, Winston S. Churchill (British prime minister 1940–5; 1951–5) who declared in 1946 that the English-speaking peoples shared a common heritage which obligated both countries to work together to maintain international security in the post-war world.[3] This book explores crucial aspects of the Anglo-American strategic and diplomatic relationship during the presidency of Jimmy Carter, 1977–81. Throughout this book a rather different impression of the Anglo-American relationship emerges than the one suggested by the opening quotations. Whilst the subsequent chapters reveal a relationship that was indeed characterised by strategic and diplomatic cooperation, it was also a relationship afflicted by strategic, political and economic competition and rivalry.

Several interconnected topics and questions are addressed throughout the work. Included is an analysis of both American and British policies towards Carter's international human rights agenda and efforts to improve NATO's defence posture. More specifically, the study sheds new light on Anglo-American cooperation and competition as it related to implementing a majority rule settlement in Rhodesia, the taking of American hostages in Iran and finding a joint response to the Soviet Union's invasion of Afghanistan. The subsequent diplomacy pertaining to possible economic sanctions against the Soviet Union and the boycott of the 1980 Moscow Olympic Games is also explored. The study is also concerned with what has hitherto been regarded as the most sacrosanct area of the Anglo-American 'special relationship', that being nuclear and intelligence cooperation between the two states. Special emphasis is afforded to the 1980 agreement whereby the Carter administration officially agreed to sell Trident C4 to the United Kingdom to replace its ageing Polaris force.

The study of Anglo-American relations during the Cold War has been dominated by the idea that a special relationship exists between the two countries by virtue of the close and unique cooperation undertaken between London and Washington.[4] Of course, reference to a special relationship immediately begs the questions, special in relation to what and special to whom? Commentators highlight the nuclear cooperation and intelligence sharing between America and Britain as clear examples of this special relationship in practice. No two other sovereign states cooperated to the extent that London and Washington did throughout the Second World War and subsequent Cold War in these highly sensitive areas of national security. It is these two areas that are often regarded as the central props of the special relationship.[5] Various explanations for this special relationship abound with some scholars highlighting the shared cultural bonds which morphed into a mutual understanding of how international security would be upheld following the end of the Second World War.[6] Others suggest more practical motivations explain the special relationship. As David Reynolds notes, the special relationship 'grew out of a sense of shared threat and mutual need'.[7]

Certainly, from the perspective of elite foreign policy makers in London, it was this perception of international threats and Britain's serious economic challenges which encouraged them in their efforts to sustain a special relationship with Washington. Indeed, the fighting of the Second World War had been extremely costly for the British state, which was effectively bankrupt by the end of the war. Britain had emerged victorious from the war but it had lost somewhere close to 25 per cent of its national wealth and accumulated a sovereign debt of nearly 250 per cent of gross domestic product (GDP).[8] At the end of the war the British government owed approximately $31 billion to the US Treasury alone.[9] To be sure, the United Kingdom would only repay $650 million of the total $31 billion borrowed, and would receive additional loans in the post-war period, but the British economy remained in a perilous situation.[10] The British government simply could not afford to maintain a significant military presence all over the world and could not face alone the perceived growing menace posed by the Soviet Union. Sustaining and enhancing close relations with Washington now became the cornerstone of British security policy, which would aid British ambitions of containing the Soviet Union and provide greater influence over American foreign policy. Closer ties could also help the United Kingdom win better financial terms from the United States for future borrowing and trade agreements. The Attlee government (1945–51) was successful in this pursuit as shown by the establishment of an official intelligence-sharing agreement and staff talks between the United Kingdom and United States. As Ritchie Ovendale has noted, the efforts of Ernest Bevin, British foreign secretary, 1945–51, led to the creation of 'an informal military alliance' between the two states.[11]

In sum, a special relationship was needed to shore up Britain's dwindling international power. Harold Macmillan (British prime minister 1957–63) typified this sort of thinking when he referred to Britain playing the role of Greece to the American Roman Empire.[12] Implied in such a statement is that Britain would utilise its well-practised diplomacy, its remaining global bases, along with its military and intelligence capabilities, to exercise a decisive influence over US foreign policy for the promotion of British interests. Robert Cecil, First Secretary in the British Embassy in Washington during the early years of the Cold War, explained how the special relationship was:

a means of making sure that if this little British gunboat was following in the wake of the American battleship . . . on the bridge . . . the Americans would be receiving messages from the British who had this long experience of international affairs and knew so much more about things than the Americans did.[13]

To this day such attitudes persist amongst British foreign and national security policy making elites as illustrated during one recent interview with the former head of Government Communications Headquarters (GCHQ) Sir David Omand. When quizzed by the BBC's *Today* programme about the nature of the Anglo-American intelligence relationship, Omand explained that 'We have the brains. They have the money. It's a collaboration that's worked very well.'[14]

Whether the British government ever exercised the level of influence over US policy that they sought is questionable. Regardless, as Henry Kissinger, US secretary of state 1973–7, perceptively noted, 'Whatever the "reality" of the "special relationship," Britain has tried hard to give the impression to the outside world that American policy is strongly influenced, if not guided, by London.'[15] As Kissinger appreciated, the perception of power and influence is critically important in the conduct of international affairs and thus explains why successive British governments sought to perpetuate the idea of significant British influence over US foreign policy.

For British policy making elites, maintaining influence over Washington's foreign policy became increasingly difficult as the Cold War progressed because of the obvious decline in British economic, military and international power.[16] As early as 1946, American intelligence assessments concluded that the United Kingdom was a much diminished global power and that the United States would have to be the principal world power to contain the mutual threat posed by the rise of Soviet international power.[17] Throughout the first decade of the Cold War there was a growing sense that the scales of power within the Anglo-American relationship were tilting decisively in Washington's favour. No clearer demonstration of Britain's diminished power is evidenced than during the Suez Crisis of 1956 when US political and financial pressure forced the government of Anthony Eden to withdraw embarrassingly from the military action it had undertaken against Nasser's Egypt. The disparity in American and British power was so marked that the likes of Harold Caccia, the British Ambassador to Washington 1956–61, remarked that talk of a 'special relationship' between London and Washington was an 'embarrassment'.[18]

By the 1960s, Britain's economic difficulties were so pronounced that the governments of Harold Wilson (1964–6; 1966–70) decided that crucial vestiges of Britain's remaining global power would be disbanded. The Wilson government announced in its 1967 defence review that the United Kingdom would withdraw from its military obligations that lay 'East of Suez'.[19] As such, the idea that Britain could have a decisive influence upon US global strategy became simply untenable. The advent of superpower détente, and other American 'special' relationships (with the Federal Republic of Germany, Israel and others), meant there was less scope for intimacy in Anglo-American relations.[20] These altered circumstances, however, did not prevent Wilson from promoting the idea of an Anglo-American special relationship. Whilst aware that Britain held less importance with Washington's policy makers, the British prime minister still believed he could exercise decisive influence in regards to international economic policy, promoting superpower détente, finding nuclear arms control agreements and in helping to promote a peace agreement in Vietnam. However, Wilson was largely ineffective as President Johnson by and large ignored the British prime minister on many of these key subjects. Only on the subject of nuclear weapons diplomacy did Wilson exert meaningful influence over Washington.[21]

From the 1960s onwards, 'Europe' became the solution to Britain's twin problems of economic malaise and international decline. Membership of the European Economic Community (EEC), when it eventually came at the third time of trying in 1973, proved not to be the magic elixir that its adherents had claimed it would be. Persistent economic difficulties and the humiliation of the International Monetary Fund (IMF) Crisis of 1976–7 only cemented the growing impression in American circles that the United Kingdom was no longer a first-rate ally capable of promoting global US interests. In the assessment of some senior US policy makers the United Kingdom had become a 'parasite' and a 'scrounger'. State Department officials even debated the 'British problem'. Given such assessments, it became increasingly difficult for British policy makers to sustain even the image of a special relationship between the two countries.[22]

By the time Carter assumed the US presidency in 1977, the Anglo-American relationship was no longer of first-rate importance to Washington or to international affairs more broadly. The Carter administration's decision to re-evaluate the nature of the intelligence relationship between London and Washington, which included limiting the United Kingdom's access to 'extremely sensitive intelligence material', was indicative of the diminished importance that US policy makers attributed to the Anglo-American relationship.[23] For one commentator writing in the mid-1980s, the conclusion was reached that 'since the 1970s Anglo-American relations, considered entirely by themselves, have ceased to be very important or very interesting'.[24]

Yet the period under analysis here does reveal some 'very important' and 'very interesting' matters once the Anglo-American relationship is contextualised within the framework of how superpower détente morphed into the 'Second Cold War'.[25] Moreover, as demonstrated in subsequent chapters, there were a number of significant processes that materially affected both the Anglo-American relationship and the course of international events. As argued throughout, the relationship became steadily more important to both powers and to international relations more broadly as the Carter administration progressed. This shift in perception can largely be attributed to outside factors, not least the international economic and energy difficulties confronting the United States which required multilateral solutions. The challenges to America's global position throughout the Persian Gulf and Africa coupled with the onset of the Second Cold War following the Soviet invasion of Afghanistan in 1979 further encouraged closer cooperation. London and Washington's shared perceptions of international security threats ultimately encouraged closer relations. Anglo-American relations became more important for both countries and for international relations during Carter's presidency.[26]

Yet it is also important to note that whilst the Anglo-American relationship became more important it did not necessarily lead

Introduction

to warmer diplomatic relations between the two countries. Nor did increased diplomatic cooperation always run smoothly. As seen throughout Chapters 4 and 5 in this book, Anglo-American tension, disagreement and antagonism persisted even as outside factors stimulated closer cooperation. It is the purpose of these chapters to analyse why such disagreements existed, what were their principal causes and how resolutions to these differences were found.

The recent declassification of government records in the United States has allowed for a reassessment of the Carter presidency. A central feature of this research highlights how in spite of only occupying the Oval Office for one term, Carter's presidency had a number of long-term and profound consequences for US national security and foreign policy. For instance, it was under Carter that normalisation of relations with the People's Republic of China (PRC) was established, that the Camp David Peace Accords between Egypt and Israel were signed and that the modernisation of the American nuclear arsenal began. As highlighted in one recent study, Carter's efforts to 'harden' US defence policy pre-dated those of Ronald Reagan, who is usually associated with increasing US defence expenditure and strengthening America's nuclear weapons capability.[27] And in the context of the Anglo-American relationship, Carter presided over a number of important events and agreements which had long-term consequences for both countries and for international relations more broadly. The most pertinent example is the 1980 agreement between the two governments to sell the US Trident C4 submarine-launched ballistic missile to the United Kingdom. This guaranteed that London would remain a nuclear power and helped sustain the consequent unique defence collaboration between the two countries. As Peter Jay, the British Ambassador to Washington 1977–9, contemporaneously argued:

> the quality that makes the Anglo-US relationship so crucial is defence. The defence relationship is by no means one-sided. We have received, and continue to receive, considerable American assistance in the military nuclear field which has enabled us to maintain our strategic deterrent. This reflects a degree of cooperation in military nuclear

matters which is unique between any two powers ... The Americans recognise that our contribution to the conventional forces of the Alliance remains substantial and indispensable.[28]

In addition to security collaboration Anglo-American diplomacy was vitally important in bringing about a majority rule settlement in Rhodesia, and the discourse of human rights promotion which persists to this day as a central element in American and British foreign policy was cemented under the Carter presidency.

The book makes three main interlinked observations and arguments. The first of these is that the Anglo-American relationship became steadily more important to both countries and to international relations more generally as the breakdown of superpower détente encouraged closer cooperation between the two countries.

Second, considerable cooperation between the two countries existed in this period as demonstrated most clearly with the decision in 1980 by the Carter administration to sell Trident C4 to the British government. Intelligence sharing and security cooperation within the context of the NATO alliance also continued. It is demonstrated how the long-established security cooperation central to the Anglo-American security relationship was able to largely transcend political differences and endured in spite of the decline in Britain's international status. Political cooperation was also a central characteristic of the relationship as both James Callaghan (prime minister 1976–9) and Margaret Thatcher (prime minister 1979–90) sought to promote Carter's international security and foreign policy objectives with other allies, especially with Helmut Schmidt's West Germany. By doing so, both Callaghan and Thatcher believed they could win Carter's confidence and thus shape the president's policies along paths deemed appropriate for promoting British interests. By and large such influence was fleeting and limited in its success. Whilst sustained diplomatic cooperation took place in regards to settling the question of majority rule in Rhodesia, it was largely the American opinion on how to solve the question that won through. It is this example which serves to demonstrate that London's ambition of exerting 'soft power' over Washington clearly had its limitations.[29]

Introduction

Third, the book also reveals a considerable amount of political and strategic competition and disagreement between the two countries which is generally underappreciated within the extant literature. For instance, the Callaghan government sought to persuade Carter to downplay his emphasis on promoting international human rights but to little effect. Considerable disagreement between the two countries persisted in relation to solving international economic and energy problems as both Washington and London sought to influence the make-up of joint solutions. Finally, during Thatcher's short political relationship with Carter, considerable Anglo-American disagreement affected the course of diplomacy as it related to the creation of finding mutually agreeable policies in reaction to the Soviet Union's invasion of Afghanistan. Thus, this study demonstrates that there existed levels of cooperation, competition and antagonism within the Anglo-American relationship which existing studies do not emphasise or fully explain. The chapters that follow seek to provide a more nuanced and fuller understanding of the Anglo-American relationship during the Carter presidency.

1 Détente, Human Rights and Anglo-American Relations

The era of détente

The period preceding Carter's presidency was a difficult one for the United States. Undoubtedly, the Nixon administration had accomplished a number of significant things in the international realm but with the Watergate scandal forcing Nixon to resign his office in August 1974 and America's eventual evacuation of Vietnam in April 1975 it is with good reason that Henry Kissinger termed this period the 'Years of Upheaval'. Given these circumstances, it is little wonder that the American electorate in 1976 wanted an 'outsider' to assume the presidency and to bring a fresh approach to the conduct of foreign affairs. Carter's election brought a president to the White House determined to promote a post-Vietnam foreign policy that would not be dictated solely by Cold War considerations.[1]

For the United Kingdom the 1970s was a time marked by continued relative economic decline, industrial unrest, political uncertainty and global military retrenchment. The decision by the Heath government in 1970 to endorse Wilson's East of Suez withdrawal meant that by 1977 the United Kingdom would no longer retain significant global military bases. The outbreak of the fourth Arab–Israeli war in October 1973 and the subsequent Arab oil embargo added to Britain's significant economic problems. Such were these problems that by the middle of the 1970s the United Kingdom was being described by political commentators as the 'sick man of Europe'.[2] The extent of this sickness was highlighted in 1976 as the British government had to resort to the ignominy of accepting a financial bailout from the IMF. Further damaging

Détente, Human Rights and Anglo-American Relations

British sensibilities was the fact that the British government had been treated by the IMF as 'just another' country.³

The immediate years prior to Carter's election had also been difficult ones for the Anglo-American relationship. Disagreement, antagonism and discord appeared to be the main characteristics of the relationship during the government of Edward Heath (1970–4). Anglo-American disagreement was so severe that the likes of Nixon and Kissinger even spoke about the end of the 'special relationship'. Both showed what this meant in practical terms as the Nixon administration temporarily suspended both nuclear and intelligence collaboration with the British government in 1973–4 because of ongoing political disagreements. The governments of Harold Wilson (1974–6) and James Callaghan (1976–9), whilst never quite hitting the lowest points witnessed during the Heath years, also found themselves facing the ire of Washington on a number of occasions.⁴ Nevertheless, diplomatic flashpoints were the exception, rather than the rule, for Anglo-American relations during the presidencies of Nixon and Ford.⁵ A case in point is illustrated by the decision of the Nixon administration in 1974 to approve additional assistance to the British nuclear programme. Though the Anglo-American relationship had diminished in importance, such cooperation in the nuclear field guaranteed that it would remain relevant for years to come. But when the British government sought to exploit its special relationship with Washington for its own interests during the IMF Crisis London found US support lacking. Crucially then, events during the IMF Crisis demonstrated the lack of influence which London had over Washington when it really mattered. There were limits to just how much leverage the British government could exercise over Washington and on this occasion the consequences of this limited influence were to prove profoundly negative for the government of James Callaghan.⁶ London was not oblivious to its diminished position with Washington. One briefing memorandum for David Owen (appointed foreign and Commonwealth secretary in February 1977) articulated this very point:

> During the last administration our relations with the US were generally good, due both to mutual interest and to the close relationship which Mr Callaghan and later Mr Crosland developed with

> Dr Kissinger ... But even at the height of the good relationship with Dr Kissinger, the relationship was no longer an exclusive one: the FRG now matters as much to the US as does the UK, and even US–French relations are on a firmer setting.[7]

This then was the context for the Anglo-American relationship at the beginning of the Carter presidency. The Carter administration, if not as candid in their judgement of British decline as their immediate predecessors had been, shared the same basic assessment that the Anglo-American relationship could no longer be expected to promote US interests to the degree that it once had. Rather, as far as the Carter administration viewed things, the United Kingdom was deemed an important European power within the framework of a broader democratic alliance which would tackle global problems on a multilateral basis.[8] As one report supplied to Cyrus Vance, US secretary of state 1977–80, noted in February 1977, 'The British government is beset with troubles', which meant a special relationship was difficult to sustain.[9] Vance's personal assessment of the United Kingdom mirrored this type of analysis. As he outlined for the president, Callaghan's government was faced with 'serious economic problems and mounting political problems. Trade balances are off, inflation has not been brought under control, and the Labor [sic] Party is fighting to keep itself in office.'[10] British officials clearly understood this shifting perception of the United Kingdom in Washington. Peter Jay informed London in February 1979:

> Britain is not anywhere near central to the American world vision. We are not big enough as a friend and ally to share a really large part of the US's military and economic burdens nor strong enough as an adversary to threaten seriously the key American interests, nor bad enough as a problem to demand more widespread or constant attention.[11]

Yet the Anglo-American relationship, even if it could never return to its level of importance during the years of the Grand Alliance in the Second World War, or even to the 'Golden Days' of Macmillan and Kennedy, progressively regained ground during Carter's term in office as Washington sought to re-energise its alliances in the face of mounting international challenges.[12] Following the Soviet invasion of Afghanistan (December 1979), the onset of more bellicose US–Soviet relations, the coup in Iran by Islamic fundamentalists (February 1979) and the steadily worsening US economy, cooperation between the two countries intensified. British and American policy makers undertook intensive negotiations regarding how to respond to the Soviet invasion of Afghanistan. Cooperation in NATO was given a boost as US ground-launched cruise missiles were dispatched to Britain as part of the Dual Track decision of September 1979. And the Anglo-American nuclear relationship was reaffirmed in 1980 as Carter agreed to sell Trident C4 to the British government. It is in the chapters that follow that the changing nature of the Anglo-American relationship during Carter's presidency is analysed.

Jimmy Carter

As Peter Rodman, the long-serving adviser to multiple American presidents noted, 'Jimmy Carter . . . came into office determined to avoid what he saw as the errors of his predecessors.'[13] For Carter, the biggest error of the Nixon and Ford administrations was the lack of weight afforded to human rights considerations in formulating US foreign policy.[14] Of course, Carter's presidency was not the first to be concerned with international human rights. Since the foundation of the American republic there had been a struggle between those that believed US foreign policy had to pursue realistic foreign policy objectives as opposed to those who argued that idealistic objectives should be promoted. Throughout US history there have thus been intermittent swings between individual presidents that have sought to pursue a foreign policy premised to varying degrees upon idealistic or realist motivations. As Nancy Mitchell has suggested:

> Carter did not initiate the discussion of human rights; he rode a wave that had been growing since the end of World War II and that had gained momentum in 1975 when the United States, the Soviet Union, and the countries of Europe, East and West, signed the Helsinki Accords.[15]

Whilst it was politically opportune for Carter to attach his political fortunes to the cause of human rights, his own religious and moral beliefs (Carter is a born-again Baptist and to this day still teaches Sunday-school classes in Plains Georgia) convinced him that the promotion of human rights would underpin his foreign policy.[16] As Andrew Preston has argued, religion mattered to individuals and expressions of public piety were not merely 'cynical window dressing that obscures the "real" political of strategic motives behind [US] foreign policy'.[17] Such epithets certainly applied to Carter as his conduct in office was affected by his religious beliefs as evidenced throughout his efforts to bring a resolution to the Arab–Israeli conflict.[18] Carter's religious and moral beliefs also affected Anglo-American relations. This was clearly demonstrated, for instance, in convincing the president to resolutely pursue a majority rule settlement in Rhodesia. Carter's religious beliefs also influenced his decision to not proceed with the development of the Enhanced Radiation Warhead (ERW) in 1978.[19]

Care, however, needs to be taken when analysing the extent to which Carter's religious beliefs affected the conduct of his foreign policy. First, Carter's Baptist faith explicitly separated Church and State. As one of Carter's closest advisers recalled, the president never once cited his religious convictions as a reason to pursue any course of action.[20] Similarly, one historian has suggested, Carter 'should have been the ideal Social Gospel president' but he in fact 'stringently [sought] to separate religion from politics'.[21] Second, any president faces a myriad of pressures which stem from structural forces within the international system, economic influences, military factors, domestic political pressures and bureaucratic political calculations that all have a bearing upon the course of foreign policy. Carter's religious beliefs cannot simply be applied on a reductive basis to explain his foreign policy choices. Rather, Carter's religious beliefs should be weighed as another factor when assessing his foreign policy.

The ideas that Carter developed as a member of the Trilateral Commission were important in influencing the central tenets of his foreign policy. Established originally in 1973, the Trilateral Commission brought together individuals who were keen to foster a post-Vietnam US foreign policy.[22] No longer would all aspects of US foreign policy be conditioned by concerns about the Soviet Union. It was, according to the members of the Trilateral Commission, the zero-sum logic of the Cold War that had needlessly dragged the United States into the unwinnable war inside Vietnam. A new foreign policy was required to avoid repeating such major strategic follies in the future. Matters surrounding energy, economics and nuclear proliferation would be afforded a far more prominent position within US foreign policy.[23] The key foreign policy players within the new Carter administration, including the secretary of state, Cyrus Vance, national security adviser, Zbigniew Brzezinski, secretary of defense, Harold Brown, and US Treasury secretary, W. Michael Blumenthal, had all been members of the Trilateral Commission. Now that they were in positions of power, the ideas that they had all debated theoretically could be put into practice.

Domestic political considerations further encouraged the president to adopt a new foreign policy course. The previous eight years of a Republican-held White House had seen a number of foreign policy achievements but were also tarnished by political scandal in the domestic sphere. Watergate, along with the collapse of America's position within Vietnam and the increasingly hostile opinion of the American public to the Washington establishments' domination of national politics, gave an opportunity for a Washington 'outsider' to assume the presidency.[24] Carter exploited his background as a former naval officer and southern farmer to add credibility to his outsider status. The Democratic candidate persuasively argued that he was not a member of the 'Washington establishment' in stark contrast to his election opponents of Gerald Ford, the current president and a twenty-five-year veteran of the House of Representatives, and Bob Dole, who had served in the House of Representatives since 1960. Carter utilised these factors to his advantage during both the Democratic nomination process and the presidential election campaign throughout the summer and autumn of 1976.[25]

During the presidential campaign, Carter vehemently criticised the Ford administration's lack of regard for human rights in the conduct of its foreign policy. Yet simultaneously Carter attacked the Ford administration for its apparent weakness towards the

Soviet Union which he alleged had allowed Moscow to obtain a dangerous advantage in nuclear armaments. Carter essentially latched onto many of the criticisms that were being targeted at the entire détente project and signalled his intention to take a firmer line with the Soviet Union. During one presidential debate between Carter and Ford, the Democratic nominee suggested that the president had legitimised the Soviet Union's domination of Eastern Europe.[26] In a damning critique of the Ford administration Carter lambasted:

> The prime responsibility of any president is to guarantee the security of our nation, with a tough, muscular, well-organized, and effective fighting force. We must have the ability to avoid the threat of successful attack or blackmail, and we must always be strong enough to carry out our legitimate foreign policy. This is a prerequisite to peace. Our foreign policy today is in greater disarray than at any time in recent history.[27]

Further yet, the United States had compromised its 'moral authority' and had 'been out traded in almost every instance' of US–Soviet diplomacy.[28] 'It must be the responsibility of the president to restore the moral authority of this country in its conduct of foreign policy', Carter argued. In his memoir Carter concluded that 'Our country has been strongest and most effective when morality and a commitment to freedom and democracy has been most clearly emphasized in our foreign policy.'[29]

Carter's future national security team was just as scathing of the Ford administration's legacy. Walter Mondale, who would serve as Carter's vice president, provided a damning critique of the Nixon–Ford policy of shunning multilateralism in favour of pursing narrow 'national interests' to the detriment of all other considerations.[30] He claimed soon after America's evacuation from Vietnam:

> The idea of national security has militarized our foreign policy to the point of being virtually helpless when confronted by major economic problems such as energy ... I believe the fog of national security helped to lead us into the tragic swamp of Vietnam, into the morass called Watergate.[31]

Failing to promote international human rights and to 'simply allow your national self-interest to subordinate all other values' leads to 'a Hobbesian world of evil motives and worse behaviour', Mondale asserted. As such, it was the Carter administration's intention to 'show the world a different America'.[32] According to Brzezinski, the Nixon–Kissinger détente policies were 'too compartmentalised' and needed to be 'more reciprocal'. Moreover, the Nixon–Kissinger approach to foreign policy had 'elevated amorality to the level of principal'.[33] William Odom, who served as Brzezinski's principal military adviser, noted that 'the detente policy that Kissinger had designed was based on very fallacious assumptions about the nature of the Soviet Union and East–West relationships'.[34] Carter's critique of détente was so powerful that President Ford actually banned his staff from using the word 'détente' to explain his foreign policy ambitions during the election campaign. As one journalist put it, 'détente' had become a 'dirty word'.[35]

The promotion of improved human rights may have been 'the soul of Carter's foreign policy' but this did not obviously translate into meaningful policies.[36] From the outset of Carter's administration there was a clear disconnect between the theory of advancing international human rights and how US foreign and international economic policy manifested. Indeed, even before entering the White House Carter placed important limitations upon the scope and ambition of any human rights foreign policy. As he told one audience, 'We must be realistic. Although we believe deeply in our own system of government and our own ideals, we do not and should not insist on identical standards or an identical system in all other nations.'[37] Human rights concerns would be balanced by broader geopolitical factors and finding this balance was the task of a newly established inter-agency body, the Policy Review Committee.[38] It is apparent from the minutes of the Policy Review Committee that human rights considerations had to complement broader security, economic and political objectives and that this meant a 'zealous' pursuit of the promotion of international human rights had to be tempered.[39] Illustrative of such problems was the issue of supplying armaments to US allies. In Latin America arms embargoes were enacted against Argentina for alleged human rights violations practised by the Argentine government, yet in

East Asia and the Middle East there was little change in policy in spite of human rights violations being practised by allies such as Iran, Saudi Arabia and Indonesia. Anthony Lake, the Director of the Policy Planning Staff, acknowledged this contradiction at the centre of Carter's foreign policy:

> Human rights considerations have become perhaps the dominant factor in arms transfers in Latin America ... [however] the great bulk of our arms transfers ... are to East Asia and the Middle East, and they have been only marginally affected by human rights considerations.[40]

Carter's effort to promote what two scholars have termed a 'post-Cold War foreign policy' was therefore restricted from the outset by the president's understanding of geopolitical realities.[41] Mondale retrospectively outlined that Carter's foreign policy 'reflected this twin commitment to human rights and a strong defense'.[42] It was Brzezinski, though, that articulated Carter's ambitions most clearly:

> The public clearly understands that the Carter foreign policy is derived from an affirmative commitment to certain basic human values ... Starting from that moral basis, your basic priorities for our foreign policy ... are coherent and consistent: (1) we will seek to coordinate more closely with our principal allies in order to provide the foundation for a more stable international system; (2) we will engage in a North–South dialogue in order to deal with wider human needs; (3) we will seek accommodation on the East–West front in order to avoid war and to widen trans-ideological cooperation. In addition, we will seek to halt the spread of arms, both conventional and nuclear.[43]

Carter's human rights agenda was a sincere undertaking but it also offered additional leverage through which to exercise influence against certain foreign powers. Amongst all of the president's advisers it was Brzezinski that most clearly understood this point. As he suggested to the president, the United States was 'morally justified' in promoting better human rights but it provided 'American foreign policy additional influence' because it associated 'America as a society with a vital human concern. Otherwise, America runs the risk of being perceived only as a consumption-orientated society, making us the focus both of envy and of resentment.'[44] Promoting human rights would provide the United States with greater international legitimacy which, in turn, would deflect many of the criticisms that US foreign policy encountered throughout the Third World. Given the intensification of the Cold War into the Third World at this juncture, such considerations were far from insignificant.[45]

In a sign of Carter's determination to promote human rights concerns, the president looked at ways in which transgressors could be punished, including the implementation of economic embargoes and the suspension of arms sales. All of this was a particularly sensitive point for Soviet leaders given that they were under the impression that they had a tacit understanding with the previous US administration that the internal politics of both the United States and Soviet Union were to remain outside of the purview of superpower competition. As Anatoly Dobrynin (Soviet Ambassador to Washington 1962–86) recalls, the strength of Nixon and Kissinger 'lay in their ability to approach problems conceptually and not be distracted by minor questions or subordinate fragments. The diplomatic game and the imperatives of realpolitik appealed to both of them.'[46] Dobrynin was rather less complimentary about Carter's approach to foreign policy. Likewise, Carter's emphasis on promoting international human rights was to impact the Anglo-American relationship. As shown in subsequent chapters, this was most clearly felt in regards to the issue of majority rule in Rhodesia, the ongoing strife in Northern Ireland and in relation to the Soviet Union. Anglo-American relations were to be profoundly affected by the president's desire to champion the cause of international human rights.

Nevertheless, Carter was fully aware of the difficulties that pursuing a human rights agenda would generate for his administration. The challenges posed by the need to balance human rights considerations with geopolitical calculations created intense interdepartmental feuding amongst the president's closest advisers. As Carter early into his term in office complained, the lack of uniformity in US foreign policy presented 'conflicting positions' that had already 'hurt us' with congressional actors and foreign intermediaries.[47] From the outset of the Carter presidency there was no coherent grand strategy which was to be pursued because every facet of US policy was to be individually analysed as to how much emphasis would be placed upon human rights considerations. James Schlesinger, who served as Carter's energy secretary and was a former Director of the Central Intelligence Agency (CIA) (1973) and secretary of defense (1973–5), was positively scathing about Carter's supposed naïvety in foreign policy. As he recollected:

> on substance [Carter] came, by and large, with some very clear moral convictions, and very little understanding of the obstacles represented by the established interests – lethargy, inertia, and the like. This was particularly true in international relations. Carter's greatest weakness as a President was in the field of international relations, which he approached with a degree of missionary zeal and innocence that was in some sense attractive, but was bound to be unsuccessful.[48]

Yet, as other influential advisers to the president later recounted, they never believed a 'grand strategy' could be pursued anyhow. Vance explained that it was better to deal with situations on a case-by-case basis and the concept of a grand strategy was 'baloney'. Warren Christopher, the deputy secretary of state, likewise claimed that the 'best policy was a non-policy'. Of course, this contrasts with the ideas advanced by Brzezinski who in 1979 would finally convince the president to assume an overarching grand strategy as enunciated within the 'Carter Doctrine'.[49]

Carter was also unimpressed with the fashion in which the Nixon and Ford administrations had conducted diplomacy with America's allies. During his presidential campaign, Carter blamed the Nixon and Ford administrations for the antagonism that had afflicted US–European relations in the 1970s.[50] Carter's key policy advisers were equally as unimpressed with America's alliance diplomacy. Brzezinski, for instance, noted in 1970 that US policy had led to a position where 'for Europeans, contemporary America is doubtless a less certain protector, a less committed partner'.[51] Whether or not US–European problems were generated as a result of the style of foreign policy practised by the Nixon administration is largely a moot point. In Carter's assessment, US–European friction would be lessened by the re-energising of summit conferences, personal diplomacy, and increased communication and consultation.[52]

During his inauguration Carter hinted that America's alliances would be even more important during his presidency when he declared that the United States had 'recognized limits' and it alone could not 'answer all questions or solve all problems'. Ultimately, the United States had to foster improved cooperation with its allies if US interests were to be promoted.[53] In office Carter translated this rhetoric into a firmer strategy and tasked Brzezinski with devising the course to take. Carter's national security adviser duly recommended that US policy had to 'engage Western Europe, Japan and other advanced democracies in closer political cooperation through the increasing institutionalization of consultative relationships, and to promote wider macro-economic coordination pointing towards a stable and open monetary and trade system'. It should become the 'foundation stone of U.S. policy' to establish 'genuine collaboration with these states', Brzezinski further advised.[54] Such advice resonated as Carter sought to galvanise relations with America's European allies. This enthusiasm for alliance cooperation, however, would create just as much antagonism as witnessed during the Nixon–Ford years when the European allies had supposedly been ignored. It is the Anglo-American dynamic to this process that is examined in the subsequent chapters.

Callaghan and Thatcher

On becoming prime minister, James Callaghan followed the long tradition of British Cold War prime ministers in seeking to maintain a close relationship with Washington. Much like his predecessors, Callaghan believed that this was necessary in order for the United Kingdom to sustain its unique security cooperation with Washington and to better influence US foreign and international economic policy. Such a strategy had clearly failed during the IMF Crisis but Callaghan continued to pursue the Atlanticist policies he had adopted ever since being appointed foreign and Commonwealth secretary in 1974.[55]

Callaghan's key foreign policy advisers agreed with the general approach that retaining strong links with Washington was critically important for the promotion of British interests. 'The U.S.

relationship, however one describes it, is the most crucial one for the prosperity and security of our country' was David Owen's candid assessment. And like Callaghan, Owen was to 'remain a blue-water diplomatist' and wanted 'our reach to go out from Europe across the oceans of the world'.[56] Fred Mulley, as the secretary of state for defence, consistently interacted with US policy makers and officials as he discussed the update to the British nuclear deterrent and the strategic overhaul of the NATO alliance. Denis Healey, as the Chancellor of the Exchequer, met frequently with his American counterparts to negotiate international monetary and economic reforms.[57]

British ambitions of influencing Washington were considered to rest in part upon establishing good personal relations with the most important actors within the Carter administration. These were indeed quickly established and maintained by the Callaghan government.[58] Vance, for example, would describe working with David Owen as 'both delightful and stimulating'.[59] Owen would reciprocate such assessments, recalling that 'We soon developed as close a working partnership and friendship as I suspect existed between a U.S. secretary of state and British foreign secretary.'[60] As Brzezinski recalled in his memoirs:

> President Carter soon established a good working relationship with his foreign counterparts. British Prime Minister James Callaghan, for example, displayed remarkable skill in cultivating Carter personally. In fact, I was amazed how quickly Callaghan succeeded in establishing himself as Carter's favorite, writing him friendly little notes, calling, talking like a genial older uncle and lecturing Carter in a pleasant manner on the intricacies of inter-allied politics. Callaghan literally co-opted Carter in the course of a few relatively brief personal encounters.[61]

Carter's experience with Thatcher is traditionally viewed as having been less warm.[62] As shown in Chapter 4, the president and prime minister certainly never warmed to one another on a personal level; Carter found Thatcher 'overbearing'. For Thatcher, Jimmy Carter was too indecisive and too liberal for her tastes. As one observer has noted, Carter and Thatcher were never 'kindred spirits'.[63] 'Her relationship with Jimmy Carter, though correct, was not close . . .

The two respected one another, but they did not particularly like one another', Thatcher's official biographer has concluded. It would take the election of Ronald Reagan in November 1980 before the British prime minister found a US president disposed of a similar world view.[64]

But, personal relationships, be they good or difficult, are rarely determinate in international affairs. As one former US Ambassador to London noted, 'A good relationship at the top works at the margins of decision-making, not at the centre.'[65] As a case in point, Thatcher may have agreed with Reagan's philosophical outlook but this did not prevent serious disagreements from occurring.[66] Likewise, Jimmy Carter's visit to Newcastle upon Tyne in 1977 was certainly popularly received by the British press but this did not prevent British policy makers worrying about how US foreign policy was damaging British interests in relation to European security or Rhodesia.[67] The Anglo-American relationship is largely driven by national interests, not by good personal relations. Intelligence, nuclear and wider defence cooperation are at the core of the special relationship, and are undertaken and sustained because they suit the interests of each power. As Peter [Lord] Carrington (British secretary of state for defence 1970–4 and foreign and Commonwealth secretary 1979–82) bluntly suggested in one interview, 'It's always been national interests. People like to bang on about the special relationship but it's always interests.'[68] Personal relations were ultimately subordinated to broader material concerns. And it was how these broader national interests were interpreted by each power that largely explains the course of Anglo-American relations during the Carter presidency. It is to the first year of Carter's term in office that we now turn.

2 Embracing the Special Relationship, 1977–8

A new administration

The advent of a new US president provokes apprehension in foreign capitals as diplomats and foreign leaders hypothesise how the public statements set forth by a candidate in the presidential campaign will translate into actual policies once the president-elect assumes office. Carter's election provoked a number of specific concerns for British policy makers of which the most troubling aspect had been Carter's suggestion that the United States would become involved in the ongoing difficulties in Northern Ireland. This constituted a complete break from previous presidential rhetoric concerning Northern Ireland and created considerable unease in London. Carter's stern statements about the Soviet Union coupled to his promise to promote human rights within America's relationship with Moscow caused further apprehension in British policy making circles.[1] Detailed studies of the president-elect were thus undertaken but one report supplied by Michael Palliser, the permanent under-secretary at the Foreign and Commonwealth Office (FCO), advised Callaghan that there were grounds for optimism. As the prime minister was informed in November 1976 following Carter's election victory, the president-elect was believed to hold the United Kingdom in 'special esteem'.[2] Quite what this meant in real terms was unclear but the implication was that somehow this emotional attachment could be exploited for the promotion of British interests.

Peter Ramsbotham, the British Ambassador to Washington, provided a fuller appraisal once Carter had assumed office.[3] In his estimation, Carter seemed at ease in his new role and was determined to pursue his ambitious foreign policy agenda in spite of his limited experience in foreign affairs. Ramsbotham, however, struck a note of warning, notifying London that Carter operated on a 'short fuse' and had a level of 'obstinacy' about him which he found 'mildly disturbing'. The British Ambassador provided a more detailed explanation of the president's policy objectives and how this would have a bearing upon British interests. As London was subsequently informed in March 1977, Carter had set himself a series of ambitious objectives which he would enthusiastically pursue in the opening months of his presidency. Amongst these included finding a new Strategic Arms Limitation Talks (SALT) agreement with the Soviet Union, promoting his international human rights agenda, continuing the Middle East peace talks between Egypt and Israel which had begun under the auspices of Henry Kissinger, as well as seeking to improve the military posture of the NATO alliance.[4]

Carter's national security team also came under close scrutiny in London. And on this front, the British were optimistic. Kissinger's replacement as secretary of state, Cyrus Vance, was received especially well. As the British Ambassador reported to London, 'The president has in Vance, Brzezinski and Young – the skilled operator, the ideas man and the idealist – a team whose qualities complement each other and should be able to work effectively together under Mr Carter's leadership.'[5] In an effort to establish good relations with the president's new national security team, a number of letters congratulating them on their appointments were dispatched by the British government.[6] All of this reflected Callaghan's desire to galvanise strong personal relations with Washington in order to better influence US policies which could affect British interests. Ramsbotham followed the lead set by London and arranged to be the first ambassador to meet with President Carter. Callaghan's efforts, superficially at least, had immediate results as Carter wrote to the prime minister stating that he wished to 'strengthen the ties of friendship between the people of your country and ours'.[7]

Yet beneath this surface cordiality a number of matters remained unresolved and continued to cause unease in London. From the British viewpoint there were two key issues. The first revolved around how much influence the British could now have upon Washington given Britain's diminished global power.[8] The second area of major British concern related to Carter's public declaration to emphasise human rights in the conduct of US foreign policy. For many in London, Carter's idea to promote international human rights was considered somewhat naïve and ultimately dangerous. In particular there was a concern that Carter's determination to advance the cause of human rights in his diplomacy with the Soviet Union would cause tenser superpower relations and undermine the prospects of further international nuclear arms agreements (which the British ultimately determined to be in their interest). Coupled to this, a more confrontational Cold War would threaten British economic and commercial interests were it to lead to a restriction on trade with Moscow or result in the NATO alliance having to spend more on defence. In sum, the British concluded that Carter's human rights agenda would actually contradict his stated ambition of sustaining superpower détente and lead to a far more unstable and dangerous international environment.[9]

These doubts about Carter's foreign policy further encouraged the prime minister in his quest to maintain an as close as possible relationship with the new president in order to better guide the course of US foreign policy. An opportunity for the prime minister to establish closer relations with the new Carter administration presented itself in January 1977 when Walter Mondale agreed to meet with Callaghan in London.[10] British suspicions that the new Carter administration would be unwisely idealistic in the conduct of US foreign policy were confirmed during the Mondale visit. On discussing Carter's broad foreign policy objectives, the US vice president emphasised that the 'realist' policies of the Nixon–Ford years were a thing of the past. No longer would the United States conduct its international affairs solely according to the dictates of power politics. Instead, the Carter administration was determined to promote international human rights and its interaction with other states would be conditioned by this factor. On the subject of the Soviet Union, Mondale explained that Carter would be looking to speedily conclude a strategic arms limitation agreement with the Vladivostok agreement that had been struck in 1974 under President Ford being utilised as the basis for the new treaty. From here the United States would look to push ahead with a far more wide-ranging agreement with the Soviet Union.[11]

On the subject of NATO, Mondale spelled out that the president wanted the British to support his plans for increasing NATO's defence expenditure to better face the growing superiority of the Warsaw Pact's conventional forces. However, the vice president sounded a note of warning when he told his hosts that Washington would only increase its own levels of defence expenditure if other members of the alliance did likewise. On bilateral matters, Mondale brought with him the news that the Carter administration would maintain existing defence and security cooperation with the United Kingdom.[12]

Mondale's confirmation that bilateral security cooperation would be maintained under the Carter administration calmed anxieties in London. The main reason as to why Callaghan had agreed to meet with Mondale in the first instance was to obtain official confirmation that existing Anglo-American security cooperation would be maintained by the Carter administration. At the conclusion of the Mondale meeting this notable British objective had been achieved. However, the meeting also confirmed many of the fears that British policy makers held about Carter's international policy with regards to US–Soviet relations and the promotion of human rights. Perhaps more concerning was Mondale's insistence that Carter's efforts to improve NATO would require additional resources from all members of the alliance. Given the recent difficulties with the British economy, such demands were naturally enough met with a lukewarm response.

Aside from an unfortunate report in the press, the Mondale meeting was of significance because it confirmed to the British government that Carter's foreign policy approach would differ from that of his predecessor in some quite important ways.[13] First, Mondale confirmed that Carter had begun to raise human rights concerns with the Soviet leadership and would continue to do so in the months ahead. In the weeks that followed, Mondale would prove true to his word as both Carter and Vance gave lengthy speeches that emphasised the importance that the United States attached to the promotion of international human rights. In March 1977, for example, before the UN General Assembly Carter placed the promotion of improved human rights at the forefront of US foreign policy ambitions and advocated that the UN's Human Rights Commission should take a far more robust approach to improving international human rights. As the president argued, 'Strengthened international machinery will help us to close the gap between the promise and performance in protecting human rights.' Vance would further emphasise the message a month later in a lengthy address before the Law School at the University of Georgia.[14] Even if the reality of US foreign policy under Carter fell short of these idealised declarations the fact that these statements were made forced other states, London included, to engage in the discourse of human rights promotion. As a case in point, David Owen issued a statement endorsing the Carter administration's stance on promoting international human rights even though in private British reservations about the wisdom of this course persisted.[15]

Coupled to this, it also became clear from the Mondale meeting that the Carter administration remained committed to improving NATO's force posture and would look to convince the alliance to provide the necessary additional funding to achieve this. Once again the president went on the public offensive and gave a number of speeches wherein he emphasised his determination to improve the force posture of the NATO alliance to counterbalance the Soviet Union's increasing military strength.[16] London concluded that the Carter administration was implementing its own distinctive foreign policy that coupled together traditional security concerns with the promotion of idealistic objectives. The first meeting between Carter and Callaghan in March 1977 would provide an opportunity for the prime minister to galvanise his relationship with the president and better appreciate Carter's foreign policy intentions.[17]

Callaghan in Washington

Callaghan attached enormous significance to his visit to Washington for he believed it afforded him the chance to better understand Carter's foreign policy ambitions and duly influence them in ways more amenable to British interests. The meeting would also provide Callaghan the opportunity to discuss a number of outstanding bilateral matters such as ongoing intelligence and nuclear cooperation, Anglo-American cooperation with regards to the situation

Embracing the Special Relationship, 1977–8

in Southern Africa, the proposed improvements to NATO's force posture, US SALT II objectives and US trade proposals.[18]

Callaghan arrived in Washington on 9 March 1977 and held a meeting with the press before proceeding to Blair House to convene discussions with Carter's national security adviser, Zbigniew Brzezinski. Southern Africa, reforming NATO's defence posture and ensuring the continuation of superpower détente, were all areas that Brzezinski suggested would benefit from increased Anglo-American cooperation. It appeared as if Brzezinski was proposing the types of cooperation that Callaghan sought with Washington.[19] Such positivity was, however, rather short lived. On meeting Harold Brown, the US defense secretary, complaints about Britain's lack of military spending surfaced. Brown suggested that Britain needed to reverse the policy trend of the past two decades and make an increased commitment to the NATO alliance. Callaghan took unkindly to such pressure and responded with the now almost standard British retort that the British government spent more on defence as a proportion of GDP than the other key members of the NATO alliance, America included.[20]

From here, the discussion moved on to the ongoing US–Soviet negotiations over the contents of the proposed SALT II agreement. Callaghan raised the issue of a No Transfer agreement being struck between the two superpowers and warned that such a condition could have ramifications for the continuation of Anglo-American nuclear cooperation. As the prime minister further cautioned, a No Transfer agreement could complicate the process of updating Britain's strategic nuclear deterrent and could well lead to the British government having to find additional funding for the already spiralling costs involved in the Polaris improvement project. Subtly, the British prime minister was suggesting that without US support for Britain's nuclear deterrent, there was little probability that the United Kingdom would increase its spending upon conventional forces which Washington desired. In spite of Callaghan pressing the issue, Brown spoke only in the most general of terms and refused to offer any assurances about a No Transfer agreement. This was not necessarily a slight upon the special relationship. In large part, Brown's refusal to enter into more detailed discussion reflected the fact that the Carter administration remained undecided as to what they would agree to in a SALT II treaty. Nevertheless, Callaghan was left only with a platitude that the US government would keep the British informed of any developments.[21]

The next day Callaghan met with the president in the Oval Office. None of the disagreements evident during the previous day's talks surfaced in this forum. Thus, in a similar fashion to statements made by Brzezinski, Carter emphasised how he believed that Anglo-American cooperation would be necessary for tackling a number of international problems of mutual concern. Whilst matters related to the ongoing SALT discussions provoked slight disagreement between the two sides, Carter was prepared to announce at the end of the discussions that the United Kingdom was one of the 'closest friends and allies' of the United States.[22]

Such rhetoric has encouraged commentators to conclude that Callaghan had managed by the end of his Washington talks to have 'established an ease of communication and a surface cordiality' with the new president.[23] Contemporaries shared a similar assessment. Peter Ramsbotham declared Callaghan's visit to have been 'an outstanding success'.[24] Certainly this was the impression that the Carter administration was keen to foster with their British counterparts. As Brzezinski insisted in discussion with British officials, 'The president really meant it (that a special relationship existed) [and] he was not saying it to please . . . Mr Carter regarded our relationship as historical and visceral.' Brzezinski himself 'even felt it a little'. As such, when 'Britons and Americans got together there was no need for preliminaries, they could discuss any problem without hang ups'.[25]

Whilst the talks may have been deemed a success a number of outstanding matters remained which were likely to lead to Anglo-American difficulties in the future. With regards to matters that could be classed as of secondary importance, such as the landing rights of Concorde at US airports or US–EEC trade issues, little headway had been achieved during the discussions.[26] On matters believed to be of supreme importance to British policy makers, such as the subject of nuclear weapons technology and testing, Carter's policy direction remained unclear and this generated considerable uneasiness in British circles. For example, during the Carter–Callaghan meeting the president had hinted that he was prepared to sign a comprehensive test ban (CTB) agreement with the Soviet Union which would obligate all signatories to cease the testing of nuclear weapons for a specified period of time. Whilst this was not something that Callaghan would necessarily oppose, a ban on nuclear weapons testing would have ramifications for the British government's own ongoing programme to improve the British strategic nuclear deterrent. As Callaghan made clear to Carter, the British were 'utterly dependent' on the United States for testing their own nuclear weapons.[27] In response, Carter had only offered to discuss the matter in more detail and was unwilling to provide the British with any firm details as to what the US would agree to in a CTB treaty. The president's enthusiasm for reducing the number of nuclear weapons was proving to be an added complication to the British government's already problematic upgrade to Polaris.

The discussion with Harold Brown also highlighted that the US Department of Defense would continue to exert its institutional pressure against the British government to encourage it to increase its defence spending. This was important because Carter had made it known that any further American improvements to NATO's force posture were dependent upon similar commitments being undertaken by the rest of the alliance. Moreover, the US Department of Defense was vitally important with regards to continuing to support the United Kingdom's strategic nuclear deterrent. As recently demonstrated during the Nixon–Ford years, the US Department of Defense was willing to allow this relationship to be utilised as political leverage against the British government in order to attain other US policy objectives with London. Policy makers in London had thus recently experienced just how detrimental falling afoul of the White House could be for Britain's interests. Though the Anglo-American nuclear relationship was not a one-way street, it was imbalanced in that it left the United Kingdom dependent on US goodwill for continuing to support its nuclear programme. Callaghan's discussions with both Carter and Brown simply reminded the prime minister of this fact.[28]

Callaghan's meeting with Carter was far from the overriding success that British officials at the time convinced themselves it had been. Of course a personal rapport between Carter and Callaghan had been established which both London and Washington would look to exploit over the course of Carter's presidency. Both Carter and Brzezinski had alluded to utilising the Anglo-American relationship for solving common problems in a way that had largely been absent during the Nixon–Ford years. However, such statements are easily made and whilst the president had spoken of closer Anglo-American cooperation, he had crucially been unable to explain how this would work in practice. The real litmus test for the relationship would be how unresolved issues would be dealt with in the coming months.

Burden sharing and nuclear weapons

Cyrus Vance informed the British government that one of Carter's priorities on assuming office would be to improve NATO's force posture because the alliance was not getting 'value for money'.[29] Soon after taking office, Carter began the process of reassessing current American military commitments. This resulted in a lengthy memorandum titled PRM-NSC 10.[30] PRM-NSC 10 concluded that NATO's conventional force posture had to be improved as currently there was little chance of 'conflict termination' being achieved on favourable terms. More simply put, the United States could not fight a conventional war with the Soviet Union and expect to hold back Eastern bloc forces for any reasonable length of time without having to resort to the use of nuclear weapons. Significant improvements to NATO's conventional force posture were therefore required to rectify this dangerous military-strategic imbalance. Whilst all of the major protagonists within the Carter administration agreed that improvements to NATO were required, there was no consensus as to how this should be accomplished. Essentially the debate within the Carter administration surrounded the emphasis that should be given to building up conventional and tactical nuclear forces within the NATO alliance.[31] Following internal debate within Washington, Carter brought the subject into the public domain during a speech before NATO delegates in May 1977. It was here that the president called for all NATO members to increase their existing defence budgets by a minimum of 3 per cent per annum. Later in the month, Carter spoke at the University of Notre Dame and repeated his call for NATO members to increase their defence expenditure.[32]

Carter's call for a 3 per cent increase in defence expenditure was not some arbitrary figure which he hoped NATO would agree to. In the opinion of the Chairman of the Joint Chiefs of Staff, General George Brown, members needed to increase their defence expenditure by at least 3 per cent to ensure NATO could uphold its 'territorial integrity' without having to resort to nuclear weapons almost immediately in a war with the Soviet Union. Brown and Brzezinski concurred with this thinking. Vance, whilst far more sceptical as to whether NATO's military position in relation to the Soviet Union was as unfavourable as others suggested, agreed that defence expenditure had to be increased by all members of the alliance. A presidential directive was therefore issued in August 1977 explaining that it was now official US policy to encourage all members of NATO to provide additional resources to the alliance.[33] But it was evident from the outset of this initiative that senior members of the administration, including the president himself, doubted whether this agenda would be realisable. As Carter lamented in his diary, the European members of NATO were economically weak and 'can't do much'.[34] Events would demonstrate that Carter was too pessimistic as the alliance would eventually agree to these American proposals. Obtaining this agreement, however, required lengthy and often antagonistic diplomacy within the alliance.

During his meeting with Callaghan in March 1977, Carter emphasised that he would be looking for British support in bringing about improvements to NATO's force posture.[35] Carter's proposal was met with a lukewarm response by the Callaghan government as lingering doubts, which centred on political and economic factors, existed about the desirability of supporting Carter's proposals. As Ramsbotham warned, the president was investing serious political capital in overhauling the NATO alliance and expected the British government to 'deliver' the support of the European members of NATO. This was problematic. The Treasury was less than pleased by the prospect of having to sanction additional defence expenditure when it considered existing spending to be disproportionally too high as a part of overall British public expenditure.[36] Even more importantly, the Carter administration exaggerated the degree of influence that London had with its European allies and its consequent expectations of Britain were too high. For his part, Callaghan was only too well aware of his constraints and of the dangers of failing to deliver upon Britain's long-standing claim to be an Atlantic intermediary. In March 1977 he remarked, 'I am not sure we can deliver anything for them. I am worried that they will be disappointed.'[37] If Washington reached the conclusion that Callaghan could not 'deliver' then British ambitions of decisively influencing US policy would be significantly undermined.

At the same time, Callaghan recognised that Carter had afforded him an opportunity to resolve common challenges of interest. The task then was to convince Britain's European allies to support the president's proposals, including the controversial issue of improving NATO's tactical nuclear weapons. It was the development of the ERW and whether it would be deployed within the NATO arsenal that became an enormous source of inter-allied disagreement throughout 1977–9 before the eventual Dual Track agreement was reached in September 1979. The ERW was being considered for development because military experts argued that it offered the most cost-effective way to counter the Soviet Union's conventional and theatre nuclear force superiority in Europe. In particular, the Soviet modernisation programme of its intermediate range ballistic missiles (IRBMs) demonstrated the Soviet Union's growing military capabilities.[38]

ERWs therefore had a number of benefits in terms of financial and military efficiency. First, in terms of cost, it was far cheaper to purchase ERWs then the equivalent number of conventional forces required to balance the Warsaw Pact's enormous advantage in armoured vehicles, especially heavy and medium-sized battlefield tanks. In terms of military efficiency, ERWs were ideally suited to destroying large quantities of battlefield tanks without inflicting the massive explosive damage that would result from the use of other forms of nuclear weapons. As was surmised in one briefing paper for the president, 'in battlefield use, [ERWs] would allow a desired kill radius against military personnel with less undesirable physical destruction than standard nuclear warheads'.[39]

The Soviet Union's development of the SS-20 IRBM further compounded the problem for the Carter administration. Following the US–Soviet summit at Vladivostok in November 1974, guidelines for a SALT II agreement had been reached. This agreement had crucially omitted to include American nuclear capable aircraft or short-range missiles based within Europe. There had also been no agreement that prevented either superpower from modernising their respective IRBM systems. The Soviet Union's decision to modernise their IRBMs and nuclear capable bomber aircraft did not therefore contravene any arms limitation agreements reached with the United States. Yet, Soviet improvements alarmed observers in Washington and London. Attracting the attention of NATO's intelligence and military observers were the RSD-10 Pioneer IRBM and the Tupolev Tu-22M strategic bomber, which assumed the respective monikers in NATO circles of the SS-20 Saber and the Backfire Bomber. The SS-20 was first tested in September 1975 and, following further trials, began to be deployed throughout Eastern Europe in March 1976. It was at this point that American and British analysts started to become seriously interested in the SS-20 for it provided the Soviet Union with much improved nuclear targeting accuracy and hence destructive capability. Furthermore, the SS-20 would carry three nuclear warheads as opposed to a single warhead carried by existing Soviet IRBMs.[40]

Why then was the ERW to prove so controversial? Central to the ERW debate was the fact that the Carter administration was reluctant to approve its production unless other members of the NATO alliance would agree to have ERWs deployed on their territory. This made sense on a tactical level given ERWs were designed to destroy Soviet tank columns which would be moving across mainland Europe in the event that the Cold War turned hot. For European governments, however, the prospect of allowing ERWs on their territory was domestically a politically unpopular course given that sensationalist newspaper coverage presented the ERW (or the 'neutron bomb' as it was termed) as a weapon which would kill people but leave buildings standing. It was, as the critics would have it, the ultimate capitalist weapon in that it would destroy people but protect material goods. Moreover, ERWs were interpreted by some as a signal that the West was prepared to ratchet up the nuclear arms race, abandon détente and return to a more confrontational relationship with Moscow.[41] Furthermore, as the British government well understood, opposition to ERWs in European circles reflected the traditional European (and for that matter British) aversion to planning and preparing to fight a 'tactical' nuclear war. ERWs were designated as a tactical nuclear weapon which the critics of such weapons suggested only encouraged the fallacy that a nuclear war could be fought and won.[42]

For the Carter administration, the ERW also grew into a troublesome domestic problem as Carter had run for the presidency on a nuclear arms reduction platform. Ordering the development and deployment of the ERW would contradict this and undermine his political base within the Democratic Party. As Carter appreciated, his entire foreign policy agenda, including SALT II, peace talks in the Middle East, the normalisation of relations with the PRC and a treaty with Panama to resolve access to the Panama Canal, could only be successfully accomplished with congressional support. Sparking a confrontation with Congress over the ERW would potentially undermine Carter's broader foreign policy ambitions. At the very least then, Carter had to handle congressional actors carefully and he consequently went to great lengths to explain his priorities to congressmen in order to win their support.[43]

Throughout the summer of 1977 the president weighed up the arguments for the production and deployment of the ERW. Whilst remaining undecided on the issue of deployment, the president requested that congressional funding be approved for the production of the ERW.[44] Carter, however, made it known that whilst he was ensuring that the ERW could be funded he had not actually approved its production at this juncture. Regardless of whether or not the go-ahead for the ERW would be given, Carter first required confirmation from the European allies of NATO that they would actually accept the deployment of ERWs on their territory.[45] Only once this approval had been provided would the president authorise production of the ERW. Gaining such approval would be no easy task given the growing domestic opposition within European countries against ERWs.[46] Indeed, little enthusiasm for the ERW existed within European policy making circles. In Brzezinski's assessment the European members of NATO simply wished to 'duck the issue' of how to tackle the growing imbalance in conventional and nuclear forces between NATO and the Warsaw Pact.[47]

Sterner US diplomacy within the NATO alliance was required if European support for the ERW was to be obtained. Vance encouraged the president to take such action and advised that 'We believe that the Europeans, if pressured by us, would accept a presidential decision to develop the weapon, but would breathe easier if you should cancel.'[48] And it was the Anglo-American relationship that was seen by the Carter administration as one useful avenue for encouraging NATO to accept the deployment of ERWs. Consequently, the Carter administration envisaged utilising the British government as a stalking horse with West Germany and other European members of NATO as a means of encouraging them to accept the deployment of ERWs.[49]

American thinking was misplaced for it crucially neglected that London was also unenthusiastic about the deployment of ERWs. Indeed, the Callaghan government shared many of the reservations about ERWs that their European neighbours did.[50] As the British concluded, ERWs would increase the probability of US military planners believing in the absurdity that a tactical nuclear war could be fought. Quite simply, the British government did not believe a war which involved tactical nuclear weapons could ever remain limited and believed that it would in fact quickly escalate to strategic nuclear war which would likely obliterate the British Isles. In addition, domestic political calculations were influencing London's thinking. For the prime minister, the possibility of the ERW being deployed in Britain would likely cause serious problems within the Labour Party and with his unofficial coalition partners in the Liberal Party. The left of the Labour Party, which had traditionally been sceptical about the merits of nuclear weapons, was asserting its influence, as evidenced by the rise of the Campaign for Nuclear Disarmament (CND).[51] While Callaghan had been able to compartmentalise other aspects of Britain's nuclear programme, the acceptance of ERWs on British sovereign territory would require a public statement acknowledging their deployment, not least because such a deployment could not be hidden from interested parties in the media and CND. Accepting ERWs would thus likely generate enormous political difficulties which the prime minister would rather avoid.[52]

The British remained apprehensive about the possible deployment of the ERW and looked to avoid having to give any decision to Washington. British policy makers concluded that the preferable solution was to simply play for time, which they hoped would kick the whole question of ERW deployment into the proverbial long grass.[53] As such, when Brzezinski sought to win support for the deployment of the ERW from the British government he found British officials would provide only non-committal statements and raise numerous technical questions and queries about US nuclear strategy and intentions. On discussing the matter with other European members of NATO a similar response was to be found.[54]

These ongoing negotiations within the NATO alliance encouraged the Carter administration to reassess its position on the ERW. Even though the US had been unable to get NATO to approve the deployment of ERWs, on 16 November 1977 the president gave his approval that funding for the production of the ERW should be made available. A final decision on deploying the ERW was still to be taken.[55] At the heart of the ERW controversy lay competing ideas about nuclear strategy, the nature of nuclear deterrence and the feasibility of nuclear war fighting. The subject also importantly highlighted how the Anglo-American relationship did not necessarily work in the fashion that Washington wanted. London throughout this episode resisted American pressure. Interestingly, Callaghan was on the verge of deciding to side with his European allies in opposition to US wishes even though it risked antagonising opinion in Washington. Interests and not sentiment dictated the course of British foreign policy. Yet London's decision to procrastinate would only succeed for so long. Soon Washington would demand a decision from London and Callaghan would have to give an answer to the ERW question one way or the other.

Callaghan's decision to play for time had won him a temporary reprieve and had been a tactical triumph. Ultimately, however, the question remained to be answered.

Increasing defence expenditure

As highlighted above, Carter had requested that the members of the NATO alliance should increase their defence expenditure by 3 per cent per annum. Extensive deliberation amongst British policy makers and officials in London therefore began. Whilst not unsympathetic to these suggestions, a divergence in opinion within London's policy making bureaucracy existed.[56] Given that the Ministry of Defence (MOD) had been calling for improvements to NATO throughout the 1970s, it greeted Carter's proposals positively. The critical point, however, was being able to finance these NATO improvements, and, as the MOD itself acknowledged, and the Treasury was keen to emphasise, pursing such a course would place a 'significant' extra strain upon the British economy. Such a scenario was hardly welcome given that all British ministers well remembered the economic difficulties that the United Kingdom had experienced in 1976. The economic forecasts for the immediate future hardly emboldened the Treasury to engage in additional spending either. Accordingly, when Fred Mulley wrote to his American counterpart Harold Brown in May 1977 he rebuffed the American request to undertake additional defence expenditure.[57]

Carter's proposals also sparked strategic concerns in London that the president was somehow intending to chart a more isolationist course in foreign policy that would result in the United Kingdom being strategically exposed in defending its interests against what was perceived as the existential threat posed by Soviet Communism. A lingering suspicion existed in British circles that the United States was looking for the European members of NATO to assume a greater share of the military burden in order for the United States to reduce its own commitments. Perhaps then, Carter's suggestions were part of a broader American plan to retreat from the global stage and make local actors assume a far greater burden in providing for their own security.[58]

British officials substantiated such thinking by pointing to Carter's rhetoric about seeking to significantly reduce the size of existing nuclear arsenals; the president's decision to cut back a number of strategic assets from the US defence budget (the B-1 strategic bomber was publicly cancelled in June 1977); the president's decision to substantially reduce the US navy's expenditure; and the growing impression emanating from the United States that Carter was somehow a 'weak' president that could not stand up to the Soviet Union.[59] In the face of the American public's growing apathy with foreign engagements following the debacle of the Vietnam War, there was a sense in British circles that the United States might critically reduce its European security commitments. The perennial fear of the British government that the United States could lurch back into isolationism and leave the United Kingdom alone to face foreign enemies resurfaced at this point.[60]

British assessments misjudged the Carter administration's intentions towards NATO and European security more broadly. Requesting that all members of the NATO alliance provide additional resources was not an attempt by the Carter administration to lessen America's own commitments. Rather, the president was determined to avoid the scenario whereby the United States would unilaterally assume a greater burden of the alliance's military commitments. Carter was encouraging burden sharing so as to distribute the economic consequences of increased defence expenditure more equitably throughout the alliance. Second, Carter believed that these force improvements were essential to sustain the strategic status quo vis-à-vis the Soviet Union and the Warsaw Pact. As had been outlined earlier in the administration, US policy sought to assure an 'overall balance of military power between the United States and its allies on the one hand and the Soviet Union and its allies on the other at least as favourable as that that now exists'.[61] The president was not intending to retreat from America's international obligations and security commitments. What Carter sought was a greater effort from America's allies in upholding these shared security interests.

Carter's problem was largely a communication one in that he was unable to articulate this policy clearly and convincingly to his allies. As a case in point, the British had been less than warm to the American proposals and a similar lack of enthusiasm was encountered when US officials met with their other NATO counterparts. The response of the Federal Republic of Germany was particularly cool, which caused enormous irritation in Washington. Private diplomacy was achieving little from the American perspective so the president again went on the public offensive.[62] In an address in August 1977 Carter urged all member states of NATO to increase their defence expenditure by 3 per cent per annum. Once again the response fell short of American desires but subtle shifts in the positions of London and Bonn now developed. Agreeing that President Carter would continue to push for NATO reforms to the point that a serious diplomatic disagreement would develop, Callaghan and Schmidt agreed bilaterally that they would both increase their defence expenditure by the 3 per cent per annum through 1979–85 requested of them.[63] In the end, Callaghan prioritised longer-term strategic cooperation with the United States over any short-term economic or domestic political benefits he would derive from not increasing the defence budget. Persistent US pressure had paid dividends in the end.

SALT II and British fears

On campaigning for office, Carter had spoken boldly about wishing to re-energise the stalling SALT II negotiations. Once in power, he gave further public emphasis to his desire to see strategic nuclear arsenals reduced. Walter Mondale even informed one French official that Carter wanted to reduce the number of nuclear weapons 'to zero'.[64] The president's commitment to substantial reductions in nuclear arms was sincerely held as he proposed to Anatoly Dobrynin, the Soviet Ambassador to Washington, that the United States and Soviet Union should reduce their stockpiles to 1,000 ICBMs equipped with one warhead apiece.[65] To put this into context, in 1977 it was estimated that each superpower owned in the region of 2,000–2,400 ICBMs, with the Soviet Union possessing some 5,000 warheads. The United States was estimated to have somewhere in the region of 9,000–10,000 warheads.[66]

Given Carter's appetite for a SALT II agreement he ordered a detailed study of US nuclear policy to be drawn up soon after entering office. In the interim, he wrote to the Soviet premier, Leonid Brezhnev, suggesting that the Vladivostok agreements struck in 1974 with the Ford administration would be the basis of the SALT II agreements. Carter hoped that this could be settled speedily and then further progress on arms limitations could begin in the context of a SALT III negotiation. However, his agenda became rather more ambitious and he sought more aggressive reduction targets in a SALT II agreement than had originally been agreed to at Vladivostok. On 23 March 1977 Carter thus issued a presidential directive outlining that the United States would seek 'a comprehensive agreement based on reductions to a level of about 2000 [ICBMs] and [a] resolution of the Backfire and cruise missile issues'.[67]

In London, such directives were observed closely because any SALT II agreement had the potential to have negative consequences for the maintenance of Britain's strategic nuclear deterrent. Uppermost in British thoughts was the idea that the United States would agree to a No Transfer provision in a SALT II agreement. Such fears were premised upon Soviet public declarations that made Moscow's agreement to a SALT II treaty contingent upon inclusion of a No Transfer provision. Yet, at the same time, British policy makers were supportive of Carter's overall effort to reduce the level of nuclear armaments as long as this was achieved via a multilateral agreement and in a fashion which maintained the credibility of strategic nuclear deterrence. As such, British policy makers looked for reassurances from the Carter administration that any SALT II agreement would not affect the Anglo-American nuclear relationship. London was subsequently informed that the Carter administration would not enter into any nuclear agreements which would undermine the Anglo-American nuclear relationship. Yet such assurances failed to calm British anxieties as Carter's decision to accept a non-circumvention clause in a SALT II treaty raised considerable apprehension in London that the Carter administration would agree with the Soviet Union to stop selling nuclear weapons to third parties.[68]

London maintained public support for Carter's SALT II policies but in private British fears became more pronounced.[69] Whilst not fundamentally opposed to a non-circumvention agreement, the British government wanted the United States to spell out clearly what this did and did not involve in real terms. John Hunt, the British cabinet secretary, suggested that British concerns could be placated by the United States agreeing to a clause which specifically stated it would not circumvent the agreements of SALT II rather than signing up to a general 'non-circumvention' agreement. This, as Hunt reasoned, would safeguard any future exchange of nuclear weapons between London and Washington.[70] Whilst appreciating the British predicament, ultimately the Carter administration remained unconvinced that British concerns were justified. As Washington viewed matters, the provisions of the Mutual Defense Agreement of 1958 and the Polaris Sales Agreement of 1963 safeguarded Anglo-American nuclear cooperation. British fears that SALT II would destroy the Anglo-American nuclear relationship were misguided and exaggerated.[71] 'There was no question of our accepting a no transfer provision', Vance would retrospectively argue.[72]

Perhaps so but London remained ever cautious that Carter's nuclear diplomacy would crucially undermine the Anglo-American nuclear relationship. Whilst Callaghan was always careful to publicly endorse Carter's SALT II efforts, in private he remained concerned that superpower diplomacy would hurt British interests.[73] Reassurances about US policy were again sought from Brzezinski and his staff on the National Security Council (NSC). Again, the Carter administration assured the British government that a SALT II treaty would not infringe upon the Anglo-American nuclear relationship. Such reassurances did at least convince Peter Jay, the recently appointed Ambassador to Washington, that the Carter administration was being forthright in its consultations with the British.[74] Nevertheless, when the British Ambassador informed London in October 1977 that 'there is no significant danger of the

US selling us down the river in SALT II' it did little to quell apprehensions back in London.[75] Quelling London's suspicions about US nuclear policy would prove to be one objective that the Carter administration would never quite accomplish.

Human rights and US foreign policy

Carter's decision to place additional emphasis upon the promotion of international human rights was to have profound consequences for the Anglo-American relationship. For London, Carter's new approach created two key challenges. First, as one paper provided to David Owen noted, Carter possessed an 'almost evangelical sense of international morality' which was problematic in the sense it could lead to the Carter administration pressurising the United Kingdom to 'adopt a morality based foreign policy which would not accord with either our political or economic interests'.[76] Callaghan articulated his concern candidly when he told Bernard Donoughue (the prime minister's senior policy adviser) that he was 'afraid the president was in daily communication with God' and that this would lead to Carter pursuing an unrealistic foreign policy.[77] Such concerns about the president's foreign policy gained strength throughout British policy making circles and became a key area of concern for officials within both the FCO and Treasury. Second, British officials feared that Carter's human rights agenda would encourage the president to become embroiled in events in Northern Ireland as these were coming under closer scrutiny by human rights activists.[78]

On the subject of economics, international trade was extremely important for the British economy and a not insignificant proportion of this was conducted with regimes that Washington now considered to be human rights abusers. In the estimation of British officials, if the United States sought to implement global trade restrictions against certain regimes (probably through some sort of United Nations sponsored sanctions) such restrictions would significantly harm British economic interests.[79] In addition, wider political and security concerns about the US pursuing a human rights agenda, especially in relation to the Soviet Union, abounded. British officials concluded that if the US decided to pursue its human rights concerns directly with the Soviet Union this would result in Moscow taking a less cooperative attitude in areas deemed to be of vital significance to British interests, such as a SALT II treaty, a Mutual Balanced Force Reductions (MBFR) agreement or a comprehensive nuclear test ban treaty. All told, whilst the British government had never been particularly enamoured with superpower détente, they preferred it to continual superpower confrontation and crisis, which they believed Carter's championing of human rights with Moscow would likely lead to.[80]

British officials articulated these concerns to Washington and encouraged the Carter administration to temper their human rights agenda, especially vis-à-vis the Soviet Union. British arguments were met with little sympathy in Washington. As Brzezinski made plain to British officials in September 1977, President Carter was not obsessed with the 'balance of power' and would continue to promote human rights issues with the Soviet government. This was something which the president fundamentally believed in and he would continue to do this regardless of whether Moscow appreciated it or not.[81] Vance, Warren Christopher (deputy US secretary of state) and Marshall Shulman (Vance's special adviser on Soviet affairs) all reaffirmed this line, telling London that the Carter administration would publicly speak out about ongoing Soviet human rights abuses and press their concerns during bilateral engagements with Soviet officials. More disquieting yet from London's perspective was that the Carter administration appeared to reject British arguments that other areas of US–Soviet relations which had a bearing on British interests, such as the SALT II negotiations, would be more difficult to conclude if Washington continued to lambast Moscow's approach to human rights. In essence, the Carter administration was rejecting the very notion that US–Soviet relations were as interlinked as the Nixon–Ford administrations had insisted that they were.[82]

Back in London, US arguments were met with concern by British policy makers because they rejected the idea that the Carter administration could vehemently criticise the Soviet Union's human rights record without this having some type of negative repercussion upon other areas of US–Soviet diplomacy. The failure of the two superpowers at the March 1977 Moscow summit to reach agreement on a SALT II treaty appeared to endorse British thinking.[83] Though Vance informed the British that Brezhnev had made a 'strong' statement condoning the president's rhetoric on Soviet human rights policy, the US secretary of state denied that this explained the motivation behind Soviet intransigence. Instead, it was the sheer level of cuts proposed by the United States to existing nuclear stockpiles that had frightened the Soviet leadership and accounted for the failure to find agreement. British policy makers were unconvinced by Vance's argument and as one influential official within the Foreign Office reasoned:

> The explanation of why the Russians should have rejected the American proposals in such outright terms may to some extent lie in their general dissatisfaction with President Carter's handling of US–Soviet relations. They have, of course, been stung by the president's human rights policies and perhaps saw the two SALT options presented to them as a further example of pressure tactics by the president.[84]

This was an early setback for the Carter administration and in some ways it acted as an example that linkage in US–Soviet relations was a reality. As one historian has justifiably concluded:

> Incredible as it may seem Carter believed that he could condemn the lack of personal freedom in the USSR without at the same time hurting US–Soviet relations. The reasoning behind this rather naïve expectation was that, as long as his administration denied that there was any linkage between Soviet human rights abuses and other policy matters, no damage would occur.[85]

Linkage was evidently a fact of superpower relations. Certainly this was the impression that Soviet officials liked to convey to their US counterparts at the time. And as Jonathan Haslam has shown, this was certainly the opinion that the Soviet leadership sincerely held at this juncture.[86] Linkage was a reality whether Carter would accept it or not.

In spite of their denials to their allies, key actors within the Carter administration privately accepted that the failure of the recent Moscow summit could largely be attributed to Carter's decision to emphasise Soviet human rights abuses. Lengthy discussions in Washington now took place about how to rectify the continuing deterioration in US–Soviet relations. It was now suggested that tempering US criticisms of Soviet human rights abuses would assist in improving relations. Privately, Brzezinski started to refer to 'linkages' between various aspects of US–Soviet relations which needed to be accounted for when dealing with Moscow. As Brzezinski advised the president, 'we must orchestrate our efforts so they will be mutually reinforcing and not mutually contradictory'.[87]

Yet, though Carter recognised that raising human rights concerns with the Soviet Union had compromised the chances of a speedy SALT II resolution, the president did not suddenly quieten down his rhetoric. Rather, quite the opposite occurred as Carter continued to publicly criticise the Soviet Union's human rights record during the summer of 1977.[88] At first glance this may appear a curious approach given that concluding a SALT II agreement was one of the president's foreign policy priorities. However, Carter calculated, quite rightly as events would demonstrate, that the Soviet Union was interested in seeking accommodation with the United States because this was deemed to promote Soviet interests. Because of this factor, Carter concluded that he could afford to push his human rights considerations with the Soviet Union and still find agreement with Moscow on SALT II. In Carter's estimation, the recent Soviet intransigence in relation to SALT II was a diplomatic tactic designed to achieve better terms for Moscow. Fundamentally the Kremlin desired agreement and this would be reached given time and regardless of whether or not Carter raised concerns about Soviet human rights or embraced Soviet dissidents. Yet, there was also from the autumn of 1977 onwards a subtle shift in the rhetoric on human rights and in how often this was mentioned in discussion with the Soviet Union.[89] Carter had realised that if he wanted to have a SALT II settlement concluded prior to the end of his first term in office and, quite crucially, before his re-election campaign began from the autumn of 1979 onwards, then his promotion of human rights with the Soviet Union would have to take a back seat for the time being. As one historian has noted, 'Carter ... learned the hard way what should have been obvious: that his campaign for human rights could be a huge impediment to negotiations on arms control and other issues.'[90]

Throughout this period the British government was privately encouraging this shift in Carter's thinking. Whilst London was aware that it was unlikely to be able to convince Carter to abandon his rhetoric of promoting improved human rights, a twofold strategy to influence Washington was employed. On the one hand, Callaghan instructed his officials to raise British concerns that emphasising human rights too strongly with the Soviet Union could prevent progress in SALT II and recklessly result in a more dangerous and unstable Cold War. However, in public and indeed during many bilateral conversations, the British were always careful to appear to be wholeheartedly in support of the president's human rights agenda on a philosophical level.[91]

Once again there was a clear distinction in how Callaghan handled Washington in the public and private spheres. In public Callaghan ensured that the British government supported the Carter administration. Privately the British prime minister would press his concerns in order to influence US policy along lines more amenable to British interests. Callaghan's approach nevertheless remained limited in its success. The Carter administration was aware that if it failed to deliver results in terms of a SALT II agreement, or a drastic deterioration in relations with Moscow developed, this would have profoundly negative consequences for US relations with the European members of NATO.[92] And the president had learned by harsh experience that emphasising human rights with the Soviet Union would indeed delay progress on SALT II. For Carter, reducing nuclear stockpiles was one of his central foreign policy ambitions which would have to be balanced with his appetite for promoting international human rights. It was striking this balance which largely accounted for the major interdepartmental squabbling within the Carter administration itself. Given this set of circumstances, it is likely that British influence was always subsidiary to the advice being proffered by the likes of Brzezinski and Brown in Washington.

Northern Ireland

Carter's decision to declare publicly an American interest in the ongoing events in Northern Ireland also created serious apprehension in British policy making circles. Throughout the presidencies of Nixon and Ford the United States had officially remained diplomatically silent since the 'Troubles' had erupted in 1971. Washington's official silence benefited British interests for it provided additional international legitimacy for their actions inside Northern Ireland. Behind the scenes the Ford administration was even more supportive as intelligence assessments about the activities of the Irish Republican Army (IRA) were provided to London.[93]

This official American silence was shattered with Carter's election to office. In an effort to garner Irish-American votes in the Democratic primaries Carter had briefly spoken about his sympathies for the Irish nationalist cause. Worse was yet to come as on 17 April 1976 Carter was captured by the *Economist* wearing a badge stating 'England get out of Ireland' at a Democratic rally in New York. During a speech in September 1976 Carter gave a further airing of his views when he announced that the United States could not 'stand quiet on the struggle of the Irish for peace, for the respect of human rights, and for unifying Ireland'. The Democratic Party Platform (or manifesto) even stated that 'The voice of the United States should be heard in Northern Ireland.'[94] On 27 October 1976 Carter went even further when he declared before a group of Irish-American politicians that the Democratic Party should seek to bring about a unified Ireland. Such declarations provoked an immediate response from London and serious questions were now raised as to what a President Carter would mean for British policy vis-à-vis Northern Ireland. It looked likely that if Carter was to win the presidential election then the issue of Northern Ireland would no longer be met with official silence in

Washington. The ongoing difficulties in Northern Ireland looked set to become internationalised under Carter's presidency.[95]

On Carter's assuming power, British fears that he would become directly involved in Northern Ireland were soon realised. A report provided to Congress from the Human Rights Office within the State Department in March 1977 raised concerns about the legal treatment that suspected IRA activists received from the British government. This announcement irritated British officials who sought to defend their practices in Northern Ireland.[96] Worse was to come later in the year when, following a period of intense negotiation with senior Democratic congressmen, Carter issued a statement in August 1977 that declared that the United States had a legitimate interest in seeing a 'peaceful settlement' in Northern Ireland. In order to achieve this peaceful settlement, Carter announced that the United States government would provide financial assistance to encourage such an outcome.[97]

The British government perceived Carter's actions as illegitimate US meddling in its domestic affairs. In the opinion of Roy Mason, the secretary of state for Northern Ireland, those complaining about alleged human rights abuses by British forces did not fully appreciate the scale of violence that British citizens and soldiers faced in Northern Ireland. As Mason candidly wrote:

> In this same period there were also countless acts of thuggery, beatings, maiming, threats and robberies all perpetrated in the Republican cause. This was everyday reality of life in Northern Ireland. Words can't express the disgust I felt when the people responsible for such evils bleated about the alleged erosion of their human rights.[98]

Mason's opinion captured the state of British official thinking towards Carter's interference in events in Northern Ireland. In the assessment of British policy makers, the United States had no legitimate basis to become involved in what they considered to be a domestic matter. Callaghan thus remained wedded to the concept that a devolved government for Northern Ireland would be brought into being only once it was deemed acceptable by the parties in Northern Ireland itself. Whilst the Carter administration remained committed to 'encourage [a] close constructive relationship between Ireland and the UK, especially regarding Northern

Ireland Issues', Washington had made a decision to refrain from pushing the matter more forcefully in their bilateral diplomacy with London.[99] Thus, when Callaghan met with Jack Lynch, the Irish Taoiseach (prime minister) in September 1977, the Carter administration did not seek to interfere in the negotiations. Instead the US Ambassador in Dublin simply reported the meeting to the State Department. Throughout the rest of the year a similar stance was adopted as the Carter administration monitored British efforts in Northern Ireland but did not interfere directly.

Tellingly, in bilateral communication between London and Washington the Carter administration did not broach the subject of Northern Ireland in any serious manner.[100] One speech which the president gave on Northern Ireland was described by a British observer as having been 'so watered-down that it came as a damp squib'.[101] The British had correctly understood that the president would largely leave the issue of Northern Ireland to the British to settle internally as long as London made it known to Washington that they would not tolerate US interference.[102] Carter's interest in Northern Ireland had originally been driven by his desire to win Irish-American votes in the Democratic primaries. This had been achieved and having raised the subject with the British government he could also legitimately point out to Tip O'Neill (the speaker of the House of Representatives and a leading figure in the Irish-American community) that he had tried to resolve the issue. Once the president had obtained what he wanted in the domestic sphere, his enthusiasm in Northern Ireland largely waned.

Yet the fact that Carter had involved himself in the issue in the first place demonstrated a number of important factors. First, it illustrated that the US president could play a role in settling the Troubles inside Northern Ireland, albeit one that still depended on the British government legitimising American involvement. Indeed, Carter's decision to become involved with the issues in Northern Ireland began the process of a long American engagement in resolving the problems besetting the province. Second, the British government was required to react to the pressures emanating from Washington. Even if Carter's engagement did not solve the problem, it had forced the British government to consider the opinion of Washington rather more carefully than it had hitherto.[103] Carter's involvement in the affairs of Northern Ireland may have been fleeting and largely unsuccessful but they set a precedent that subsequent US presidents followed.

Rhodesia

In 1960 Harold Macmillan (British prime minister 1957–63) gave his 'Winds of Change' speech before the parliament of South Africa whereby he declared his intention to dissolve Britain's African empire. Independence to Britain's remaining colonies would be premised upon the basis of majority rule, that is, elections based upon universal suffrage for all adults regardless of race. Independence for a number of former British colonies duly followed but within the Federation of Rhodesia and Nyasaland the issue of majority rule was so problematic that it resulted in the dissolution of the former British colony into three separate areas: Northern Rhodesia, Southern Rhodesia and Nyasaland. Following several attempts to negotiate a settlement, on 31 December 1963 the Federation of Rhodesia and Nyasaland was formally dissolved. Northern Rhodesia gained independence and now assumed the title of the Republic of Zambia. Later in 1964 Nyasaland became independent and was renamed as Malawi. After further wrangling between London and the Southern Rhodesian prime minister, Ian Smith, about the terms of independence, Smith proclaimed a unilateral declaration of independence (UDI) from the United Kingdom. On 11 November 1965, the Southern Rhodesian cabinet announced that Southern Rhodesia, now referred to simply as Rhodesia, regarded itself as an independent sovereign state. Questions relating to majority rule were now ones that Ian Smith (the new Rhodesian prime minister) and his cabinet would consider independently of London. Left to its own devices, Smith's Rhodesia would maintain the system of racial apartheid that had previously existed.

Harold Wilson's Labour government, which had come to office in 1964, was outraged by Smith's UDI. Accordingly, the British government refused to recognise the legitimacy of the new Rhodesian government and with British support the United Nations

Security Council declared Smith's UDI to be illegal. Economic sanctions were introduced against Rhodesia to encourage Smith to implement majority rule but little came of such measures. Meanwhile within Rhodesia itself, black nationalist movements sought to bring about majority rule as a programme of civil disobedience began. This programme of civil disobedience grew increasingly violent as the Zimbabwe African National Union (ZANU) declared its intention of achieving national self-determination via violent methods if necessary. The first phase of the Rhodesian Bush War erupted. Little progress toward majority rule occurred as Smith's Rhodesia, which received considerable military assistance from South Africa, proved militarily capable of subduing the guerrilla forces of ZANU's military wing, the self-declared Zimbabwe African National Liberation Army (ZANLA).[104]

The second phase of the war grew in intensity and in violence as Portugal's decision to grant Mozambique independence (1975) provided ZANLA with a sanctuary and staging area outside of the Rhodesian security forces' remit. The conflict also became increasingly internationalised as ZANU declared their sympathy for the world communist movement and received increasing military and economic assistance from the PRC. Within Rhodesia itself, Ian Smith instigated a draft to help quell the growing trouble posed by ZANLA forces. The British government's position throughout the conflict was to remain supportive of the principle of majority rule but there was a growing sense that Rhodesia could be lost to the communist bloc unless a resolution to the war could be swiftly brought about. With the increasing involvement of communist forces across Africa's growing litany of wars (Angola; Mozambique; the Congo) Washington's interest also grew throughout the period. Joint efforts by the British foreign and Commonwealth secretary, Anthony Crosland, and the US secretary of state, Henry Kissinger, produced agreement in 1976 that London and Washington would support Smith to implement majority rule within two years. After the successful implementation of majority rule, the United States and United Kingdom would ensure that the United Nations economic sanctions against Rhodesia would be lifted and the new majority rule government would be granted formal international recognition.[105] Kissinger subsequently met with Ian Smith and with the two prominent leaders of ZANU, Robert Mugabe and Joshua Nkomo, in the summer of 1976. Kissinger quickly found that the leadership of ZANU were less than enthusiastic about his proposals. British efforts to push ahead with talks stalled, leaving Kissinger to complain that 'it is difficult to imagine how incompetent the British are'. In the US secretary of state's assessment, British efforts were likely to result in 'another Angola'.[106] Regardless of Kissinger's private complaints, President Ford's election defeat to Jimmy Carter in November 1976 meant that he was out of office. It would thus be left to the Carter administration to assume the task of resolving the question of Rhodesian majority rule.[107]

Carter's interest in events in Southern Africa is explained by a series of interconnected factors that touched upon geopolitics, Cold War politics, domestic considerations and the president's own sense of morality as personified in his promotion of an international human rights agenda.[108] First, like his predecessor, Carter's concern about Rhodesia was raised by virtue of the PRC's support of ZANU. ZANU's military wing was fracturing into two distinct groups headed by Mugabe (ZANU) and Nkomo (Zimbabwe African People's Union: ZAPU). Both groups consequently sought support from their respective communist backers as the PRC backed ZANU and the Soviet Union with Cuban assistance supported ZAPU.[109] Even though Carter had deliberately sought to distinguish himself as a president that would not pursue policies solely according to the zero-sum logic of the Cold War, nevertheless he could not ignore the obvious growth in communist influence inside Rhodesia either.[110]

Second, the Black Caucus in the Democratic Party, which reminded the president that African American voters had voted overwhelmingly for his election, encouraged the president to pursue majority rule in Rhodesia more vigorously than his predecessor had. For the Black Caucus it was imperative for the United States to be seen to be supporting racial justice and democracy internationally. In essence, the Civil Rights movement was becoming increasingly internationalised and was now starting to have a direct influence upon US foreign policy.[111] As one author has noted, the 1976 general election signified 'a remarkable rise of black influence in the Democratic Party and on foreign policy'.[112]

Carter's domestic position thus encouraged him to at least demonstrate greater interest in Rhodesia and Southern Africa more broadly than his predecessor had.[113] Third, as one astute commentator has noted, Carter's own sense of morality, which was influenced by his own experiences of witnessing racial prejudice inside the United States and his religious beliefs, encouraged his pursuit of majority rule in Rhodesia.[114] Vance explained US policy thus:

> Our decision to break sharply with the policy of the past did not merely reflect concern about Soviet influence or revolutionary movements. We were committed to majority rule, self-determination and racial equality as a matter of fairness and basic human rights. If the United States did not support social and political justice in Rhodesia, Namibia, and South Africa itself, Africans would correctly dismiss our human rights policy as mere cold war propaganda, employed at the expense of the peoples of Africa.[115]

For Carter to achieve his ambition of majority rule in Rhodesia, he sought to place political and economic pressure upon Smith's Rhodesia to encourage internal reform. Along with this, Carter would place political pressure against the government of South Africa (led by John Vorster), which was Smith's most significant ally.[116] Yet in spite of his determination to bring about majority rule in Rhodesia, the president remained unwilling to place the United States at the centre of negotiations in the fashion it was assuming in relation to the Middle East peace talks. It was to London, therefore, that Carter looked to lead negotiations towards majority rule even though the president privately accepted that the United Kingdom had 'practically no remaining influence'.[117] Yet Carter concluded that with Washington's support the chances of achieving majority rule in Rhodesia would be significantly increased.

Carter was thus looking to utilise the Anglo-American relationship as a means of promoting US interests and for obtaining his international goals. He could pursue his objective of implementing majority rule in Rhodesia without having to assume the burdens of leadership. After all, Carter and his national security team were already engaged in serious and complicated diplomacy in relation to arms control and the Middle East. Allowing London to lead these negotiations, though not to dictate the content of any final settlement, would allow the president to obtain what he desired. In a fashion, Carter was looking to the Anglo-American relationship in exactly the same way that Callaghan viewed it, that is, it was a vehicle for advancing national interests but could also settle matters of mutual concern.

Andrew Young, the president's envoy to the United Nations, was tasked with leading this new American effort to bring about majority rule in Rhodesia. Young now liaised with British officials and discussed how they might jointly proceed.[118] Agreement was reached to form an 'Anglo-American consultative group' which would lead the diplomatic efforts. This was headed by John Graham (a senior FCO official) and Stephen Low (US Ambassador to Lusaka).[119] Quickly apparent from these early discussions was the fact that London would not undertake a fresh round of diplomacy which could entail new economic and political sanctions against either Rhodesia or South Africa without first securing guaranteed assurances from the Carter administration that full American support would be forthcoming. Anglo-American consultation was characterised by British procrastination. British diplomacy was deeply irritating to the president who privately complained in March 1977 that the British government had shown a 'remarkable incapacity' to resolve the issue of majority rule inside Rhodesia.[120] In the weeks that followed the president assured London that American support for firmer action against Rhodesia would be forthcoming and he urged the British government to be sterner in its diplomacy with Smith. Carter went as far as to suggest that the British government should propose to Smith that London would dispatch a British Commonwealth peacekeeping force to Rhodesia which would maintain security during the transition to majority rule in the country. Along with this, Washington requested that London support a further round of economic sanctions against Rhodesia.[121]

When Vance met with Owen on 10 March 1977 he encouraged the latter to support Carter's proposed economic sanctions, which would include a ban on selling Rhodesian chrome. The US secretary of state also urged Owen to assume a sterner stance against Smith during Anglo-Rhodesian talks. Vance's argument won through as Owen agreed that the British would support the

American proposals to implement economic sanctions against Rhodesia. Why then did Owen accede to the American request at this point in spite of knowing that Britain's economic interests would be hurt by this action? The answer rests upon a number of strategic and political calculations undertaken by Owen and the wider British government. First, with Carter so determined to pursue this sterner course of diplomacy it was decided in British circles that it would be unwise to be in opposition to Washington so early on in the new president's term of office. Second, the British government wanted the United States to take a far greater interest in Southern Africa, which Carter, in contrast to his predecessor, clearly was doing. Whilst Carter was taking a policy line which did not entirely fit with British opinion on how to advance the negotiations, opposing the president could threaten to fatally undermine Anglo-American cooperation. Furthermore, the British well understood that Carter was determined to obtain his sanctions against Rhodesia regardless of any opposition that London might generate. The British calculated it better to give the impression of influence by supporting Carter than to reveal impotence in unsuccessfully opposing the US president. As such, when Carter pushed to repeal the Byrd Amendment in Congress (which had allowed American companies to import Rhodesian chrome into the United States in spite of other sanctions against Smith's Rhodesia being maintained), London endorsed the president's actions. Finally, Owen himself was seeking a 'Kissinger style' settlement in relation to Rhodesia whereby he would lead the negotiations to a grand settlement (Vienna was touted as one location to finalise this agreement) and thereby enhance his own political stature.[122] Personal political ambition coupled to broader political and strategic calculations therefore informed the British government's decision to endorse economic sanctions against Rhodesia and to press ahead with implementing a majority rule settlement.

Having agreed to further sanctions, Owen proposed that a conference between the warring factions inside Rhodesia should be convened for the summer of 1977. At the conference, Owen believed that he could negotiate a timetable for establishing democratic elections in Rhodesia which would bring about majority rule. The Carter administration, though, was deeply sceptical as to whether Owen's plan would actually succeed. From Washington's perspective, the leaders of the warring parties were nowhere near reaching any sort of agreement and the British foreign and Commonwealth secretary had a greatly inflated sense of his diplomatic abilities.[123] Owen's proposed conference therefore threatened to create a very public and diplomatically embarrassing and damaging failure that would make it harder for the warring factions to reach a settlement in the future. Further yet, as US officials argued, the economic sanctions had not been given sufficient time to really hurt Smith and thus encourage him to be more accommodating. Moreover, given that Smith was continuing to negotiate with Bishop Muzorewa (the leader of the United African National Council and the only remaining legal black party in Rhodesia for it had renounced violent struggle) about a majority rule settlement, it seemed improbable that Smith would agree to attend such a conference at this stage.

American doubts may have had substance to them but Owen remained determined to hold the conference regardless. As one close adviser to Callaghan noted, there was a sense that Owen's enthusiasm for settling the question of majority rule in Rhodesia was governed by his own political ambitions and vanity.[124] Sensing the inevitable, and in keeping with US policy to allow the British to lead Anglo-American diplomacy vis-à-vis Rhodesia, Vance agreed that he would attend Owen's conference.[125] In the meantime the Carter administration sought to apply additional pressure on Smith via the Vorster channel. In May 1977 Mondale met with Vorster and pressed the case that South Africa had to encourage Smith to accept fundamental political reform in Rhodesia.

As expected, Vorster brushed off the American demands and pointed to the fact that Smith was currently engaged in discussions with Muzorewa about delivering majority rule. And these very talks increased British and American concerns that Smith would somehow find a compromise settlement with Muzorewa which would allow him to remain in power and uphold a system of racial apartheid in Rhodesia. Such a scenario would only likely lead to a broader Rhodesian civil war as the supporters of Muzorewa would be utilised in an effort to crush ZANU (which would never recognise a settlement that allowed Smith to remain in power).

Owen again met with Vance in June 1977 to discuss the situation and it was decided during these talks that the Anglo-American consultative group would convene with the various leaders of the warring factions in Rhodesia to see if some sort of compromise settlement could be found. On liaising with the various leaders, it was soon apparent that little appetite for compromise existed on any side. As Vance informed the president, the warring factions in Rhodesia were so far apart that there stood little chance of them reaching any settlement.[126]

The British FCO informed Washington that it would continue to apply political pressure against Smith's regime and would seek to negotiate a compromise between the warring factions in Rhodesia. No offer of a British Commonwealth peacekeeping force was to be made. And an escalation of the scale and intensity of economic sanctions against Smith was also to be avoided. As Owen made clear to Vance in April and June 1977, intensifying economic sanctions against Rhodesia (or South Africa) would have serious consequences for the British economy and could not at this point be endorsed.[127]

Carter was unimpressed with the British response and sought now to win British support for a series of political moves against Smith. As such, Carter requested British support for a United Nations resolution that would declare that Smith had to afford equality under the law to all of Rhodesia's population; for the principle of one man one vote regardless of race to be implemented; a new constitution drawn up by the British government; and for free elections to be held in the following year. If Smith failed to comply then the United Nations would implement a further round of economic and political sanctions against the government of Rhodesia. Concomitantly Carter looked towards South Africa for assistance in bringing Smith in line. Whilst the president was of the opinion that the United States would not 'push South Africa around on their own racial and political characteristics, except over a long period of time', Carter let it be known to Vorster that economic sanctions against South Africa would be enacted if Vorster did not encourage Smith to comply with the demands of the United Nations. Furthermore, the president again revisited the idea of London dispatching military forces to Rhodesia to act as peacekeepers during a transition period to majority rule and, in discussions with the leadership of the Front Line States

(Angola, Botswana, Lesotho, Mozambique, Tanzania and Zambia), the United States suggested that they would support a final political settlement in Rhodesia which saw all of Rhodesia's armed forces placed under the control of the government. When Smith learned of this, he immediately opposed it because he feared that a Rhodesian government composed of black rulers would utilise the armed forces against white Rhodesians.[128] Carter's bold rhetoric was therefore creating as many problems as it appeared to solve.

Carter's latest initiative again encountered opposition in London. First, economic sanctions against South Africa and Rhodesia would damage Britain's well-established commercial and economic interests in the region. The British government, in an effort to disguise its economic motivations, suggested to Washington that economic sanctions were unlikely to accomplish the desired outcome and so were an inappropriate form of diplomatic leverage. As Owen outlined, economic sanctions against Vorster were likely to antagonise him and lead to a more unhelpful South African position vis-à-vis Smith. The joint Anglo-American approach to the situation in Rhodesia appeared to have reached an impasse; economic sanctions appeared not to be working and Smith refused to negotiate with anyone other than Muzorewa. For their part, the other leaders of the warring parties in Rhodesia appeared little interested in attending some grand conference under Owen's auspices to settle matters either. Again it was Washington that sought bolder action as both the president and Vance urged Owen to commit to the idea of dispatching a British Commonwealth peacekeeping mission to Rhodesia to ensure the stability of the country during any transition to a majority rule government. Owen had little enthusiasm for such action and the increasing levels of violence inside Rhodesia did not encourage anyone in London to change their minds.

Again, American willingness to pursue what the British believed were overly belligerent policies created considerable apprehension in London. First, the British government did not agree that Smith was being as obstinate as the Carter administration believed. Rather, in the British estimation Smith had shown a degree of flexibility and a genuine willingness to negotiate. Second, the fact that Smith would not accept the entirety of the Anglo-American proposals could largely be attributed to President Carter's indiscreet and ill-advised decision to agree with Julius Nyerere, the president of Tanzania, that the armed forces of a post-Smith Rhodesia should comprise the black nationalist liberation forces that were currently fighting the guerrilla war against the Rhodesian security forces. On learning that this decision had been reached, the British were angered because they knew such a condition would be unlikely to be accepted by Smith at this point in time. In sum, the British did not think that Smith's opposition to certain proposals was entirely unreasonable. As Washington was well aware by August 1977, there existed a 'basic difference of view' between the United States and United Kingdom on how to transition to majority rule in Rhodesia.[129]

Agreement on how to proceed was nevertheless reached during talks between Owen and American intermediaries (including discussions with Vance and Young).[130] During these discussions, Owen largely acquiesced under American pressure to agree to present proposals to Smith that would guarantee a British model of law, a democratic constitution, and the implementation of elections which would return a government based upon universal suffrage.[131] Agreement was reached that Owen himself would lead the diplomatic efforts and he would meet with both Smith and Vorster to press for their agreement. However, if these proposals were rejected then additional economic and political pressure sponsored by London and Washington would be enacted against both Rhodesia and South Africa.[132]

Following this Anglo-American agreement, the British foreign and Commonwealth secretary and Andrew Young met with Smith in Salisbury, Rhodesia, in September 1977. It was here that the joint Anglo-American proposals were put forward. The meeting proved difficult as Smith refused to accept the proposed conditions. In the American estimation Smith's failure to accept the terms meant that the economic and political sanctions against Rhodesia now had to be increased in their severity. London informed the White House that they would support efforts to increase the severity of economic sanctions against Rhodesia in the United Nations Security Council.[133]

Carter sought to place additional public pressure upon Smith and took advantage of his tour of several African states in September 1977 to reiterate the need for a majority rule settlement. The following month in an address before the United Nations General Assembly the president again reiterated American support for majority rule in Rhodesia.[134] At the same time his administration moved to head off a possible internal settlement between Smith and Muzorewa that would allow the former to retain power and exclude the Patriotic Front (both ZANU and ZAPU) from the government. Vance felt this would 'lead to the nightmare of a black civil war'.[135] Yet decision makers in Washington also recognised that a Smith–Muzorewa agreement could attract international and British support as it would provide a veneer of majority rule in Rhodesia. Washington therefore sought to shore up British support to reject any internal settlement that did not include all of the warring factions in Rhodesia. In addition, the Carter administration again looked to implement further economic sanctions against Rhodesia to convince Smith not to agree to an internal settlement which excluded the Patriotic Front. In Washington's estimation, only an agreement that included all of the warring factions could bring about a legitimate settlement to the war in Rhodesia.

Coupled to this, the Carter administration now supported calls for the United Nations Security Council to enforce an arms embargo against South Africa to cajole Pretoria into a more cooperative attitude vis-à-vis Rhodesia. For London this was an unpopular course given the lucrative armaments contracts that existed between the United Kingdom and South Africa.[136] But once again, following American pressure, the Callaghan government was convinced to support Washington's lead.[137] Little, however, came of such diplomacy. Indeed, this joint Anglo-American diplomacy appeared to be having the opposite effect upon Smith as he pressed ahead with his negotiations with Bishop Muzorewa and publicly announced his intention to reach a settlement outside of American or British auspices. Finding a settlement to the issue of majority rule inside Rhodesia would not be achieved quickly and evidently would require firmer and more patient diplomacy from both London and Washington.

Conclusion

At the end of the first year of Carter's presidency, significant Anglo-American cooperation was evidenced in the realms of NATO alliance diplomacy and in trying to settle the question of majority rule inside Rhodesia. Of course, such cooperation did not always run smoothly but this is to be expected given that two separate sovereign states with divergent interests and political pressures were involved. Yet, Carter's decision to work closely with London demonstrated the continuing relevance of the Anglo-American relationship for international relations. It also offered London the opportunity to influence Washington's decision making, and vice versa. Carter may have taken a backseat position with regards to implementing majority rule in Rhodesia but American influence with regards to increasing the severity of sanctions against Rhodesia in the face of British opposition was illustrative of how American power allowed the president to exert decisive influence against London. Likewise, the British were unconvinced that promoting human rights best served their interests but they were compelled by the Carter administration to at least engage in the rhetoric of human rights promotion. Several important unresolved items remained to be settled in the following years, amongst which was the most divisive question for the NATO alliance, the production and deployment of the ERW. Resolving such issues would test to breaking point Callaghan's ability as a meaningful interlocutor towards the European members of the NATO alliance. It is in the subsequent chapter that these issues are analysed.

3 Stresses and Strains

New Year objectives

As the end of his first year in office approached, Carter wrote in his diary that 'With the Middle East, Rhodesia, the Soviets on SALT, European acceptance of the neutron bomb, and the general reaction to my late November trip, all seem to be good.'[1] Carter's key national security advisers shared the president's sentiments. In a lengthy overview of the president's first year in office, Brzezinski claimed that immense progress in all of the core areas of Carter's foreign policy had been made.[2] Yet as the president was all too aware, 'all this could go back again quite rapidly'.[3] Events would prove that Carter was right to feel reticent. Whilst significant progress in the Middle East talks had been made, other aspects of the president's foreign policy were beginning to falter. The issue of the ERW was already developing into a major source of US–European antagonism. The SALT II talks, which were becoming mired in technical deliberations with Moscow, were encountering increasing difficulties with congressional critics. As one adviser to Carter noted:

> It's clear even to an observer unfamiliar with all of the substantive issues involved that we're in potentially very deep trouble on this matter. I can think of nothing more damaging to the president, both domestically and internationally, than to suffer a Senate defeat on SALT. It would be an unmitigated disaster.[4]

Other areas of Carter's foreign policy were also coming under pressure not least with regards to how the promotion of human rights should be incorporated into the president's broader foreign policy.

Indeed, the president's human rights agenda had become diluted to the point that nobody was quite sure, including Carter himself, as to what the promotion of a human rights foreign policy actually entailed in practical terms. Within the administration there was a divergence of opinion as to how far it was practicable to emphasise human rights concerns in US foreign policy. Throughout the year Carter failed to provide the necessary presidential leadership that was required to enforce a coherent human rights focused foreign policy. Carter's domestic challenges were just as great, as his political opponents became increasingly successful in thwarting his legislative agenda and the 1978 congressional elections saw the Republican opposition win gains in the House of Representatives that lost the Democrats the all-important two-thirds majority (which would prevent the opposition Republican Party from overriding any presidential vetoes). All told, 1978 would be a difficult year for the Carter presidency.[5]

Anglo-American relations would prove in some ways to be no exception as differences persisted over an array of issues including improvements to NATO, the deployment of the ERW and the effort to implement majority rule in Rhodesia. Yet in other ways Anglo-American relations actually warmed throughout the year. For instance, significant progress in ensuring the continuation of Anglo-American nuclear weapons cooperation was made. During Callaghan's final official meeting with Carter at the Guadeloupe summit in February 1979 the British prime minister received personal confirmation from the president that the United States would sell the Trident C4 SLBM to the United Kingdom. Second, a broader theme emerged throughout the year whereby Callaghan continually sought to position himself carefully in support of the president during Carter's quite vigorous disputes with a number of NATO allies. Callaghan ultimately maintained this position in spite of it causing significant disagreement with European leaders (especially with Schmidt); but the British prime minister did so because Washington alone had the power and influence to reach agreements on a number of matters which were seen to be of the utmost importance to British interests (for example, on SALT II, Anglo-American nuclear cooperation, Rhodesia and Northern Ireland).[6] For Anglo-American relations the second year of Carter's presidency witnessed policy disputes on a number of specific issues but it was also marked by significant cooperation.

The British government was well informed about Carter's increasing political difficulties. Peter Jay composed a lengthy round-up of the US political scene and offered his analysis on the likely trajectory of Carter's foreign policy. As the British Ambassador noted, Carter lacked the political acumen required to effectively handle the United States Congress, which endangered his chances of achieving both his domestic and foreign policy agenda. Later in the year Jay would borrow from the Roman historian Tacitus and concluded that Carter was 'Capax Imperii'. As Jay was rather pretentiously suggesting, the president suffered from an inability to govern because he could not enforce his will or garner sufficient support from the US Congress for his policies.[7]

Jay's assessment may have been verging on the hyperbolic but it did accurately reflect how key policy makers within the Carter administration assessed their own political fortunes at this time. Walter Mondale suggested that the administration demonstrated 'inadequate strategic political thinking in the development of our foreign policy'.[8] Hamilton Jordan reflected that Carter was a victim of his own outsider status, which meant that key actors within the Democratic Party resented Carter's election and looked to actively undermine his presidency. Jordan further warned that unless the president radically addressed this issue then he would only face mounting difficulties in attaining the necessary public and congressional support for his foreign policy ambitions.[9]

The problems facing Carter in the realm of international affairs were not just personality driven. Rather, as Brzezinski suggested, the United States confronted changing structural forces in the international system that challenged American interests and national security. In stark contrast to the positive appraisal of the administration's policy achievements he had provided at the end of 1977, Brzezinski had entirely reversed his assessment by February 1978. Now Brzezinski warned the president that the United States was faced with the threat of 'strategic deterioration'. The United States confronted the possibility that its allies in Europe were threatened by serious internal problems which could even lead to indigenous communist forces in countries such as France, Greece and Portugal taking power. Such a scenario would lead to the calamity of the NATO alliance comprised of communist states! Brzezinski's analysis was even darker when it appraised the Soviet Union's position in the Third World as he highlighted recent Soviet support for Ethiopia as demonstrative of Moscow's ability and willingness to project decisive global influence.[10] Brzezinski was not alone in articulating such concerns as one lengthy study composed by the NSC in April 1978 cautioned that America's continuing economic difficulties now undermined its ability to project international power. As the paper warned, 'Although the weakened dollar has undermined neither our military power nor the basic health of our economy, foreigners may have begun to question our willingness to use our strength in pursuit of our interests and to doubt our ability to grant and withdraw benefits.'[11] An even gloomier appraisal was provided by Brzezinski a week after this report was delivered.[12]

Indeed, Brzezinski's outlook had by the end of 1978 reached a new low as he advanced his thesis that the United States was confronted by an 'arc of crisis'. Brzezinski outlined his thinking in more detail as he advanced a new national security framework for the United States. This idea was centred upon the Persian Gulf and explained how American interests were threatened from the Horn of Africa across the Persian Gulf towards the Southwest Pacific rim. As Brzezinski suggested:

> If you draw an arc on the globe, stretching from Chittagong (Bangladesh) through Islamabad to Aden, you will be pointing to the area of currently our greatest vulnerability. All at once, difficulties are surfacing in Iran and Pakistan, and they are thinly below the surface in India and are very manifest in Bangladesh, and there is reason to believe that the political structure of Saudi Arabia is beginning to creak. Turkey is also becoming more wobbly.[13]

Included in Brzezinski's analysis was a plan to improve America's military posture and to encourage the rest of the NATO alliance to follow suit. 'The trends in the military components of national power ... all favour the Soviet Union', Brzezinski warned the president.[14] One way in which to meet this challenge was for each individual member of the NATO alliance to increase its defence expenditure and to approve the deployment of new nuclear weapons (including ERWs).[15]

Given such thinking existed inside the Carter administration, Peter Jay was prudent to warn London that Carter's foreign policy objectives were at their most 'delicate'. Jay advised that it would be sensible for Callaghan to maintain his public support for the central tenets of Carter's foreign policy so as to avoid creating any misunderstandings with Washington that would only lead to undesirable consequences for British interests. However, Jay well understood that Carter would look to London for support that went beyond rhetorical declarations. Specifically, the president wanted the British government to persuade the other members of the NATO alliance to now implement their 1977 decision to increase national defence expenditure by 3 per cent per annum. The president would also look for the British government's public and private support in his efforts to reach a SALT II agreement with the Soviet Union and in his ongoing Middle East peace talks between Israel and Egypt. London's continued support in forthcoming international economic, monetary and energy negotiations would also be sought by Washington.[16] The prime minister's next visit to Washington thus afforded both the Carter administration and the Callaghan government the opportunity to discuss these issues and to influence one another's policies for their own benefit.

Influencing Washington

Callaghan arrived in Washington on 23 March 1978 for a one-day working lunch with the president. Meetings were scheduled with the key members of the Carter administration with international economic policy, SALT II, NATO security policy, Anglo-American security cooperation and the ongoing diplomacy with regards to Rhodesia all set as the major topics for discussion. International economic policy and the forthcoming multilateral conference between the members of the Group of Seven (G7) dominated the Callaghan–Carter discussion. The president attached great importance to this economic summit and he sought international cooperation for boosting economic assistance to Low Developed

Countries (LDCs) and agreement to end protectionist tariffs on agricultural and industrial outputs as practised within France, Italy, the United Kingdom and West Germany (as part of their membership of the EEC). Carter wanted Callaghan's cooperation and enquired as to whether the prime minister would be willing to allow the United States to lead the discussion at the forthcoming G7 conference. Callaghan agreed, noting that the British government had no intention of 'thrusting itself into the driver's seat'.[17]

Having accepted that the British government would cede leadership to the United States at the forthcoming summit, Callaghan instead sought to shape US policy along lines that would benefit British interests. In keeping with his earlier efforts, the prime minister urged that the United States had to resist implementing protectionist policies if it was to ensure the cooperation of the other G7 members. Encouraged by his Chancellor of the Exchequer, Denis Healey, and Harold Lever, Chancellor of the Duchy of Lancaster, Callaghan suggested that the president set bolder economic growth outputs and deficit reduction targets as well as refrain from implementing new import tariffs. No promises were made, and US Treasury Secretary Blumenthal hinted that new protectionist policies could well be introduced.[18]

Callaghan, however, continued to emphasise that international economic policies had political and security implications that had to be fully appreciated. Thus, even if something made sense according to economic theory, it was only once political and security ramifications were factored in that a final economic policy could be decided upon.[19] Quite how much influence Callaghan would have over US international economic policy would of course be the litmus test for this approach but at the very least the British prime minister was making his arguments known to the key policy makers in Washington. The intensity of these British arguments is demonstrated by virtue of the fact that the US Ambassador in London sent a memorandum back to Washington warning that Anglo-American economic relations had witnessed a 'cooling' in recent months and 'more bad news' was likely to be forthcoming.[20] Yet in a sign that British influence was making some headway with Washington's policy makers, British officials pointed to the fact that their own 'tailored' protectionist policies applied against 'super-competitive countries' (such as

Japan) were being mirrored by the Carter administration. By tailoring protectionist policies against certain countries deemed to hold an unfair advantage in terms of labour costs, the British government believed it was able to prevent the introduction of more widespread international tariffs that would hurt the competitiveness of British exports. The British approach was proving partially successful, a fact that Callaghan sought to exploit in the coming months. Subtle diplomacy with Washington was paying dividends for the British prime minister.[21]

Throughout the Carter–Callaghan discussion there had been a determined effort by Callaghan to act as an intermediary between Washington and Bonn in matters pertaining to protectionist tariffs, international monetary challenges and the levels of support that the G7 states should offer to LDCs. As Callaghan told Carter, Schmidt was intellectually opposed to providing additional economic assistance to LDCs for he believed foreign aid to be unhelpful in helping them build the necessary infrastructure required to produce long-term economic growth. However, as Callaghan further explained, Schmidt was pragmatic enough to appreciate that if Washington applied sufficient political pressure upon Bonn, then the president could obtain West German approval for increasing economic assistance to LDCs. The British prime minister suggested that Schmidt's opposition to increased LDC assistance was premised upon an honest intellectual assessment and not some narrow political interest. Because of this, Callaghan recommended that Carter should arrange to meet with both West German and British representatives to see if some agreement could be negotiated that accommodated some of Schmidt's concerns.[22] This episode again highlighted Callaghan's efforts to mediate between Carter and Schmidt and in the process become a trusted confidant to both. Callaghan hoped that achieving the trust of both actors would allow him to mitigate damaging rows between the pair and also influence policies of mutual concern to the benefit of British interests.[23]

Callaghan's approach was proving fruitful as little over a week after his meeting with Callaghan, Carter wrote to Schmidt a letter that was more accommodating to West German concerns than the British had believed was likely. As the president outlined, the advanced economies faced five serious challenges which included: maintaining long-term economic growth, balancing long-term capital outflows, securing sufficient energy resources, stabilising international trade and ensuring monetary stability. Every one of these challenges could only be met with the cooperation of the major industrialised countries. Carter therefore offered to undertake detailed discussions with Schmidt in order to see how US–West German differences could be overcome and agreed strategies established.[24] In the lead-up to the Bonn Economic Summit, which was provisionally set for July 1978, Callaghan and other British officials continued to exercise this mediating role between Carter and Schmidt.[25]

The Bonn Economic Summit would demonstrate whether Callaghan's efforts at mediating between Bonn and Washington would have meaningful results. The Carter administration's ambitious agenda for the summit would test Callaghan's mediating role to its limits as Washington sought approval for comprehensive economic agreements to tackle the myriad challenges created by international inflation, monetary instability and rising energy prices.[26] Along with this, other major US goals included a pledge to limit oil imports (and thus stabilise its price), obtaining German and Japanese agreement to monetary loosening so as to stimulate economic growth, and attaining an all-party agreement on a set of trade practices that would allow for the removal and reduction of global trade tariffs.[27] Such an ambitious agenda was always likely to cause enormous differences between the G7 members, and in the media it was reported that the prospects of the summit even convening looked slim given the obvious differences between the parties. Callaghan, however, again looked to play his mediator role between Washington and Bonn and appealed directly to the president to attend the summit. Likewise, Callaghan contacted Schmidt and requested that he also attend the summit.[28]

In spite of Carter's initial reluctance to attend the Bonn Economic Summit he was convinced that his attendance was required if he was to win the support of his fellow G7 members for his ambitious international economic policies. As the president understood, the buoyancy and vitality of the US economy was interlinked with the fate of the broader international economy and his attendance was required at the G7 to help shape international agreements for the benefit of US interests. The summit convened on 16 July 1978 and it soon became evident that Callaghan's efforts to mediate the growing rupture between Carter and Schmidt would prove unsuccessful. During the discussions, Callaghan argued that economic cooperation between the G7 members was imperative and that certain decisions would have to be approved even if they resulted in damaging domestic political repercussions.[29] The British prime minister's appeal seemed to be ignored as both the German and Japanese delegations argued that US proposals pertaining to the removal of protectionist tariffs would allow US companies to export into their markets without full reciprocity. Overcoming these divergent interests proved difficult as Carter continually went on the diplomatic assault against Schmidt who ably resisted the president's pressure.[30] Thus, by the end of the summit US ambitions had not been fully met. Schmidt was left to complain bitterly that he had come under unwarranted attack from the president. US–West German relations had hardly been improved by the Bonn Economic Summit and major outstanding points relating to international economic policy remained. The communiqué issued at the end of the conference managed to create the public impression that an 'economic consensus' had been established yet British officials privately recognised that the agreements reached contained 'little substance'.[31] This growing rift between the United States and West Germany as personified in the clashes between Carter and Schmidt would continue to exercise Callaghan in the months ahead as he remained committed to his mediator role. In spite of Callaghan's best efforts relations would, however, only further sour. There were clearly limits to Callaghan's influence on the international stage and the deep-seated differences between Bonn and Washington could not be settled by the prime minister's personal diplomacy.[32]

Nuclear politics

As shown earlier, the subject of whether ERWs should be built and deployed had created enormous difficulties within the NATO alliance. For Callaghan and Carter it was a subject that they both secretly hoped would somehow just go away. Neither would be granted his wish as in the latter part of November 1977 the subject of the ERW was given renewed emphasis when the Soviet general secretary, Leonid Brezhnev, contacted a number of NATO states proposing that all ERWs should be banned. Any decision to deploy the ERW would now have magnified ramifications for it could be viewed as an escalation in the nuclear arms race or interpreted as outright provocation of the Soviet Union and further undermine US–Soviet relations. On the other hand, by not deploying the ERW, the Carter administration could be depicted as having yielded to Soviet pressure, which would raise issues about American dependability within the NATO alliance. Brzezinski neatly captured the predicament facing the president: 'It is more likely, however, that the Brezhnev letters will mean that the Alliance will continue to be in disarray over the whole issue, thus helping to accomplish the basic Soviet objective.'[33] Events that followed would prove his prophecy correct.

Following Brezhnev's proposal to ban ERWs the lobbying for their deployment was actually increased by Schmidt, who now sensed that the Soviet Union was dangerously close to obtaining its objective of 'de-coupling' the US nuclear deterrent from the protection of Western Europe. Schmidt now wanted the ERW deployed so as to act as a clear signal to Moscow that the United States would bolster its nuclear presence in Western Europe to match Soviet developments. Yet Schmidt realised his domestic position made it politically impossible for West Germany to unilaterally accept the deployment of ERWs. To overcome this domestic opposition, the solution would be for the entire NATO alliance to agree to deploy ERWs so that Schmidt could plausibly claim to the West German electorate that he was merely pursuing the traditional West German policy of supporting NATO policy. Schmidt thus informed Washington that West Germany's approval for deploying ERWs on German territory was conditioned upon the proviso that other NATO allies would do likewise.[34]

The British government consequently came under pressure from both Washington and Bonn to accept that ERWs (or their component parts) would be deployed on British territory.[35] Fearing that rejection would spark serious difficulties with Carter and Schmidt, Callaghan reluctantly indicated that he would approve the deployment of ERWs on British soil.[36] By 17 March 1978 US officials had reached agreement with both their British and West German counterparts that a public announcement to deploy ERWs would be issued. A day later, however, Carter began to have misgivings about the decision. As one British official involved in the negotiations remembered, 'We were on the point of agreeing a formula about it in the NATO council when word came through that the president (Jimmy Carter) had prayed all night and had decided not to deploy this thing.'[37]

Why then had the president reversed his decision? First, Carter had always been troubled about the morality of developing ERWs. Second, the president remained concerned that deploying the ERW would scupper his chances of obtaining a meaningful arms control agreement with Moscow. Finally, he was also aware that approving the ERW would do immense damage among core constituencies within the Democratic Party which had supported his candidacy in 1976 because of his stance on reducing nuclear arms. For all these factors then, Carter completely backtracked. Within ten days of deciding to deploy the ERW, the president announced that it would not be deployed after all.[38]

The president's indecision infuriated his European allies. As Brzezinski retrospectively wrote, Carter 'knew that the impact of this decision would be serious'.[39] The advice offered to Brzezinski was rather more candid as he was warned that Carter's indecision gave the impression that the president was unable to make and stick to a decision, which undermined his position as the de facto leader of the Western alliance.[40] Even more alarming was Robert Hunter's report on a conversation he had held with Schmidt and Owen, who both suggested that Carter's reversal demonstrated that the president was critically weak on matters of national security.[41] Such criticism was restrained in comparison with the analysis provided by the Conservative Party shadow defence secretary, Ian Gilmour, who asserted that:

> President Carter's behaviour over the so-called Neutron Bomb has been a classic demonstration of how not to conduct international diplomacy and disarmament negotiations. There have been weeks of leaks and contradictions; and after an orgy of weakness and vacillation the wrong decision has finally been reached. Mr Carter has been scared off the Neutron Bomb by the Russian propaganda barrage.[42]

Back in Washington, the likes of Brzezinski, Brown and Schlesinger all set to work to convince the president to reconsider his decision for they were all of the opinion that the ERW would act as a useful counterweight to the Soviet deployment of the SS-20. All three therefore made efforts to persuade the president to reverse his decision and give the go-ahead for the deployment of the ERW. In the end, though, Carter rebuffed such advice and decided that the ERW would not be deployed.[43] Carter now 'decided to work out a way to cancel the idea (ERW) without giving an image of weakness to our European allies'.[44] Such efforts would, however, prove unsuccessful. The West German response was visceral as Carter was personally lambasted for demonstrating weak and naïve leadership. A much more measured response was found in London as Kingman Brewster, the US Ambassador to the United Kingdom, informed Washington that 'The British government as you know will back you whatever you decide. This is a great tribute to the strength of the bond which you have forged.' This was to prove accurate as Callaghan struck a sympathetic tone and reiterated his support of Carter's decision during meetings with American policy makers.[45]

Privately, however, the British government was rather less sympathetic. Whilst Callaghan had always been reluctant to support the deployment of ERWs, now that the Carter administration had gone to the lengths of endorsing their deployment and then withdrawing this support, the credibility of the NATO nuclear umbrella was clearly being brought into question. Callaghan's position was clear: if the NATO nuclear deterrent was credible, then why was the deployment of the ERW even being countenanced in the first place? As Owen pointed out to Warren Christopher, 'because having asked Allies to march up the hill and now down again, credibility will still be damaged no matter how well the public formulation is handled'.[46] As such, the British government enquired whether the United States could provide additional resources to NATO's conventional force capability. Such a request was predicated upon the belief that if Washington would not undertake improvements to NATO's nuclear forces to counteract the Soviet Union's conventional and nuclear weapons build-up, then additional conventional forces would have to be supplied. And given that the president was unwilling to authorise the ERW, which would have been a cheaper alternative than conventional force improvements, it was London's opinion that Washington should have to foot the bill for such improvements.[47]

The British response may not have been as damning as that of West Germany but key actors inside the Carter administration understood that the ERW episode had significantly damaged the president's standing with his fellow leaders inside the NATO alliance. More damaging yet was that the president's handling of the ERW issue provided the impression that Carter was indecisive, politically weak and his national security policy was 'all over the place'.[48] All told, the possible development and deployment of the ERW had been a damaging and embarrassing affair for the president. For Anglo-American relations the episode once again highlighted the difficulties of alliance politics.

Rhodesia

As 1977 came to an end, America and Britain had reached agreement that the basis of any political settlement inside Rhodesia had to bring about majority rule, that is, black Rhodesians would have to be granted universal suffrage and new elections would be conducted to elect a new parliament and president. Events in Rhodesia, however, would soon test the unity of London and Washington. Following negotiations between Smith and Muzorewa an agreement was announced on 15 February 1978 that a settlement for implementing majority rule had been reached. This internal settlement would become known as the 'Salisbury Agreement'. On 3 March 1978 Smith provided further details and outlined that elections to form a new government would be convened which would allow for the participation of black Rhodesians. In the interim period prior to the elections, Muzorewa, Ndabaningi Sithole and Jeremiah Chirau were to join a Rhodesian Executive Council to oversee progress.[49]

London and Washington interpreted this announcement in radically different ways. From London's perspective this marked significant progress for it suggested that Smith was committed to bringing about majority rule. The Salisbury Agreement also had the additional benefit of bringing together black nationalist leaders such as Muzorewa who had renounced violent struggle in achieving majority rule in Rhodesia.[50] This contrasted sharply with the Patriotic Front of Mugabe's ZANU or Nkomo's ZAPU that continued to use violent methods for achieving majority rule and looked to the USSR and the PRC for support in realising this ambition. Given this, London believed that Smith would never enter into a formal power-sharing arrangement with the Patriotic Front. On liaising with Smith, however, David Owen found a new cooperative attitude from the Rhodesian prime minister. Indeed, Smith informed Owen that he was genuinely committed to the Salisbury Agreement and he would attend a further round of Anglo-American–Rhodesian discussions about transitioning to majority rule in the near future. Talks with Sithole and Muzorewa further encouraged the British government to view the Salisbury Agreement positively. As such, it became the policy of the British government to 'neither condemn nor condone the internal settlement'.[51] London had therefore decided to wait until they better understood Washington's reaction before committing to any definite line of policy in reaction to the Salisbury Agreement.

The Carter administration, in contrast, viewed the Salisbury Agreement rather less positively. As Vance suggested, the majority rule measures proposed within the Salisbury Agreement had a number of clauses which would sustain the privileged position of the white Rhodesian population. For example, the Rhodesian parliament would be comprised of one hundred Members of Parliament (MPs) but not all would be elected according to the rules of universal suffrage. Thus, of these one hundred MPs, seventy-two would be elected by black Rhodesian voters (who comprised 96 per cent of the population), twenty would be elected by white Rhodesian voters (who comprised 4 per cent of the population) and a further eight would be elected by black Rhodesians who had been selected to stand for office by white Rhodesians. In sum, white Rhodesians who comprised 4 per cent of the population would elect 28 per cent of the MPs in this newly proposed Rhodesian parliament. The importance of this was evident on closer inspection of the proposed Rhodesian constitution which would only allow amendments to it if seventy-eight out of the one hundred MPs voted their approval. This meant that the make-up of the Rhodesian parliament under such conditions would allow MPs elected directly or indirectly by white Rhodesians to veto any amendments to the constitution. Fundamentally the proposed Rhodesian parliament had a structural advantage built into it for white Rhodesians. Whilst the Salisbury Agreement marked a significant departure from the existing apartheid system in place in Rhodesia, it still accorded political power along racial lines.

Second, the Salisbury Agreement lacked the support of either Patriotic Front faction. Nkomo, for instance, claimed that the Salisbury Agreement was the 'greatest sell-out in the history of Africa'.[52] With such damning rhetoric it was little surprise that the Patriotic Front continued to fight the Rhodesian Bush War. As Low, Vance and Young all concluded, supporting the Salisbury Agreement would not bring an end to the Rhodesian Bush War and it also threatened to create a broader civil war in Rhodesia between the supporters of Mugabe and Nkomo against the forces of the Salisbury Group (Chiru, Muzorewa, Sithole and Smith).[53]

The Carter administration subsequently informed London that they would refuse to recognise the legitimacy of the Salisbury Agreement. Washington reminded London that it needed to remain committed to the previously agreed Anglo-American plan that any settlement in Rhodesia would only receive their endorsement if it was truly a majority rule settlement, that is, if it brought the Patriotic Front into the final agreement in some form or another. Even though congressional pressure for lifting sanctions against Rhodesia was being applied to the Carter administration, the president refused to yield.[54] Washington had been informed by various African leaders that they would not support the Salisbury Agreement, and London's refusal to condemn it had only further illustrated to these African leaders that London was not fully committed to majority rule. Given these competing pressures, the Carter administration remained more determined than ever that their support for any Rhodesian settlement would have to be premised on a system that brought together all Rhodesians and destroyed any vestiges of political power being dictated by race.[55]

The Carter administration instructed its mission at the United Nations to issue a statement that rejected the Salisbury Agreement.

The United States now proposed that all the parties in Rhodesia come together to negotiate a majority rule settlement. London, whilst angered at Carter's decision to reject the Salisbury Agreement, again decided to support Washington's actions. As British policy makers concluded, their political influence within Rhodesia was ultimately premised upon American power which meant they had to support the fundamental tenets of American strategy regardless of their own misgivings about the merits of US policy.[56] Subsequently, joint letters composed by Carter and Callaghan were dispatched to several African leaders to convince them to support the Anglo-American plan. Smith was informed that the Salisbury Agreement would not be recognised by London or Washington. In a sign to Washington that the British government remained committed to implementing the Anglo-American plan, Owen now engaged in another intensive round of diplomacy with the leadership of South Africa and the Front Line States to support the Anglo-American plan.[57]

Anglo-American diplomacy was to achieve little as Smith refused to yield to this pressure. In fact, Smith informed both London and Washington following the talks he held with Owen and Vance in April 1978 that the measures agreed to in the Salisbury Agreement were to go ahead and he would begin the transition to a new Rhodesian government.[58] Worse news was to come as both Mugabe and Nkomo made it clear that they were unprepared to enter an all-parties negotiation with the new government of Rhodesia (or Rhodesia Zimbabwe as it was now being referred to). The attitude of the Salisbury Group also prevented progress. Muzorewa and Sithole insisted that the Salisbury Agreement had established a legitimate and democratic government that should be recognised by the international community.[59] Smith insisted that the physical security of white Rhodesians had to be assured in any settlement which the Salisbury Agreement had achieved. As Smith reminded London, incorporating the Patriotic Front into any agreement would undermine his ultimate objective of providing security for white Rhodesians in a post-apartheid state. The recent killings of white Rhodesian missionaries in the Vumba Mountains along with the shooting down of a passenger aircraft by Patriotic Front guerrillas only endorsed the view that white Rhodesian security would be fatally undermined by an agreement that brought the Patriotic Front into a power-sharing arrangement.[60]

As the guerrilla war in Rhodesia intensified in the subsequent months, Smith provided a practicable demonstration of his seriousness when he declared that the 'time has come for less talk and more action' as he sought a military end-game to the war with the Patriotic Front. In the weeks that followed, Rhodesian forces began to raid Patriotic Front forces that were stationed in bordering states which led to increased guerrilla and civilian casualties. The Rhodesian Bush War was now threatening to spill into neighbouring territories resulting in a wider and more violent conflict.[61] As one British official reported in September 1978:

> It does not augur well for the holding of all-party talks with a reasonable prospect of success. It seems likely to me that, while ZANU will continue to pay lip-service to the need for an all-party meeting, they will hedge their acceptance, and play their hand, in such a way as to make it very difficult for anything constructive to emerge if talks are held.[62]

Carter was increasingly frustrated with the predicament and privately noted in his diary in September 1978 that the 'best solution is probably for Smith to give Rhodesia back to Great Britain'.[63] Whilst a revealing statement in and of itself, others within the Carter administration were increasingly concerned that American involvement in Rhodesia should not become overextended. Since the outset of Carter's involvement in Rhodesia, it had been a consistent element of American policy to 'lead from behind'. There was to be no meaningful change in US policy at this point in spite of these latest diplomatic setbacks. Indicative of such concerns was the advice proffered by Brzezinski: 'If you can't then don't.' As Brzezinski implied, if the United States could not reach a settlement then they should not try to push too hard because it would only generate increased resentment in the Front Line States against the United States for having failed to deliver on their promises. Second, if the British government supplied peacekeepers which subsequently came under attack from Patriotic Front forces, would US assistance be forthcoming? Would military action against the Patriotic Front lead to increased Soviet and PRC support for their respective clients? Aware that these scenarios would create numerous challenges for US interests, diplomatic efforts coupled to economic and political sanctions would remain the basis of Carter's approach to achieving a majority rule settlement in Rhodesia.[64]

Yet the British government was fully conscious that its limited political influence with the actors inside Rhodesia meant that it was unable to deliver the types of results that Washington desired. Britain's diminished influence was evidenced during Callaghan's visit to a number of the Front Line States in September 1978. Whilst the meetings had gone far better than the prime minister had anticipated, Callaghan informed Washington that he had been unable to make any discernible progress in helping implement majority rule in Rhodesia.[65] London feared that a failure to implement the Anglo-American plan successfully would lead to the Carter administration accusing the British government of sabotaging or delaying progress for they remained secretly committed to supporting the Salisbury Agreement. As Jay informed London, 'US policy towards Rhodesia could become an issue with mass opinion if, as Dr Brzezinski put it to me, white nuns were daily being raped on national TV by black soldiers with red stars on their caps.'[66] Additional pressure from Washington to resolve the situation was therefore expected in London. Jay reported back to London:

> Since then, there has been an unmistakable trace of schadenfreude in [Brzezinski's] reactions to the failure of US–UK policy to make some more headway. He and his deputy talk, sometimes recklessly, about the Americans washing their hands of Southern Africa. I do not believe for a moment that he contemplates this as a sensible policy for the US, if only because of the dangers of the geo-political signals which it would send all over the world. It is, rather, his way of trying to bring home to the State Department and us the need, as he sees it, for us to put more direct pressure on the Front Line States and the Patriotic Front, using sticks as well as carrots to reach a settlement, and to resist Soviet and Cuban encroachment into the area.[67]

The British government concluded that further negotiations with Smith would now have to be undertaken, not least as a means of appeasing the United States and preventing Rhodesian differences spiralling into other facets of Anglo-American relations.[68] Thus, to provide a demonstrable sign of Anglo-American unity, Peter Jay and David Newsom, the under secretary of state for political affairs, met with Smith, Sithole and Muzorewa in Washington in October 1978. It was here that both American and British diplomats argued that the Salisbury Group had to bring both factions of the Patriotic Front into the majority rule negotiations.[69] As the Anglo-American delegation made clear, the Salisbury Agreement would not be recognised. Carter was even more explicit during one public address which followed these talks when he declared:

> What we want is to have democratic elections in Rhodesia with an established constitution based on democratic principles. We want anyone who desires, to run for public office, and we want the people in Rhodesia, black and white, to be able to vote on an equal, one person one vote basis, to choose their own leader.[70]

Fresh talks between all the parties were therefore required to bring about a settlement that would implement majority rule.[71]

In an effort to now overcome this impasse the British government analysed a number of possible courses of action. The options even included dispatching British armed forces to Rhodesia as part of a UN peacekeeping mission to guarantee the security of white Rhodesians in an attempt to reassure Smith that white Rhodesian security would be guaranteed in a majority rule Rhodesia that included Patriotic Front participation. Such a step, though encouraged by Washington, was something that Callaghan was unwilling to sanction, not least because of the quite unknowable challenges that would face British peacekeepers.[72] Thus, when the South African foreign minister, Frederik Botha, suggested to Owen that 100,000 peacekeepers could be parachuted into Rhodesia to install stability, the British foreign and Commonwealth secretary replied that this 'kind of operation was out of the question'.[73] Military action was quite simply anathema to the British government. Callaghan therefore decided on a less risky course of action and dispatched Cledwyn Hughes, the Labour Party chairman, as a 'special envoy' to the region in December 1978. Callaghan also met with Nyerere and requested that he place pressure upon the leaders of the Patriotic Front to enter negotiations.[74] American pressure on London was clearly encouraging the Callaghan government to engage in a renewed round of diplomacy and to hasten progress towards a majority rule settlement that included the participation of the Patriotic Front.

The British further analysed what additional pressure they could apply to Smith in order to convince him that he should attend an all-party conference. London looked at the possibility of implementing a broader economic embargo against South Africa with a view that under such pressure the South African government would convince Smith to attend the talks. London believed that with the Shah of Iran's recent overthrow from power, South Africa's main source of oil would be curtailed by the new Iranian regime. An oil embargo applied to South Africa could now perhaps lead to the desired political outcome. The British also looked at inducements they could offer to the various factions to bring about agreement. These included improving existing levels of development aid, providing a British contingent to any UN peacekeeping force, ensuring the supply of oil to the new government of Rhodesia and offering to help white Rhodesians with emigration costs.[75] But it quickly became apparent that British intervention was producing little diplomatic progress. Carter was made aware that Hughes's intervention had probably hindered negotiations for his arrival had only antagonised all parties in the Rhodesian negotiations. British efforts at persuading the Front Line States to place pressure upon Mugabe and Nkomo to enter negotiations appeared to make little headway either. Thus, on 19 December 1978 Callaghan informed Carter that the Hughes mission had to all intents and purposes failed.[76]

By the end of 1978 little progress had been made as both Mugabe and Nkomo refused to attend an all-party conference and the Salisbury Group asserted that they remained the legitimate government of the newly named Rhodesia Zimbabwe. Meanwhile, Rhodesian security forces were stepping up their efforts to militarily defeat the Patriotic Front. Given the events in Rhodesia, Carter remained suspicious that London would look to support the Salisbury Agreement and in preparation for the forthcoming Guadeloupe summit (February 1979), Carter and Vance decided that they would remind the prime minister to continue to urge the leaders of the Patriotic Front and the Salisbury Group to attend an all-party conference. Pressure was therefore being placed on London to continue to support the American policy that an acceptable majority rule settlement would have to include the Patriotic Front.[77]

Over the course of the next weeks little progress was made as the British government remained unable to convince the parties to come together for all-party talks. The dispatch of a British Commonwealth peacekeeping force was again mooted but London rejected this course fearing that British forces would become targets for the Patriotic Front.[78] With Smith pressing ahead with his referendum of white Rhodesians to decide whether or not to create a new Rhodesian constitution, which would be followed by elections on 20 April 1979 (which would allow certain black leaders to stand but excluded the Patriotic Front), London looked on powerless, unable to implement a majority rule settlement that all parties in Rhodesia could agree upon. All Callaghan could offer was to publicly reiterate that 'The referendum of the White electorate held in Rhodesia on 30 January has little significance in terms of the acceptability of the regime's constitutional proposals to the people of Rhodesia as a whole.'[79]

By the time Callaghan left office the situation in Rhodesia was perhaps even more unstable than the one he had inherited on becoming prime minister. Nevertheless, a number of significant advances had also been made. First, Callaghan had exploited America's growing interest in the question of majority rule in Rhodesia to ensure that American power supported British diplomatic efforts. Of course, this support came at a price, especially in terms of freedom of action. Consequently, the British government had to yield to American demands on occasion, most notably having to reject the Salisbury Agreement as the basis of a legitimate majority rule settlement which London had initially welcomed. Yet Callaghan's diplomatic hand was also weakened by his unwillingness to undertake sterner measures against Smith in the form of more comprehensive economic sanctions. The prime minister's outright rejection of deploying British military forces to act as peacekeepers further limited the effectiveness of his diplomacy. Because of these decisions, London's already weak diplomatic position undermined Callaghan's ability to influence a transition to a majority rule settlement that would be acceptable for all of the parties involved.

America's influence was similarly limited by virtue of Carter's unwillingness to undertake bolder measures towards solving the Rhodesian majority rule question. Whilst Carter was happy to suggest that London commit military force to Rhodesia, there was never any question that Washington would do likewise. The unwillingness to utilise US military power inherently limited the effectiveness of US diplomacy. Nevertheless, given that both London and Washington rejected the Salisbury Agreement and remained insistent that a majority rule settlement had to include all factions in Rhodesia, the internal settlement could never establish international legitimacy. Indeed, the unity of the Anglo-American position ensured that a legitimate settlement to the question of majority rule in Rhodesia would have to include the Patriotic Front. This was a notable achievement for it established the parameters by which any final majority rule settlement in Rhodesia would be recognised as legitimate by the international community. Carter and Callaghan may not have resolved the question of majority rule in Rhodesia but by the time Callaghan left office they had established the framework by which any final settlement would be judged as legitimate.

The Anglo-American nuclear agreement at Guadeloupe

The British update to Polaris via the Chevaline project had been quietly, if expensively, moving ahead. However, the point had now been reached where a decision on replacing Polaris with an entirely new system had to be made. Following deliberation on the options for replacing Polaris, Callaghan concluded that a submarine-based strategic nuclear deterrent was the preferred choice. Accordingly, the British prime minister would raise the possibility with the president of whether the United States would sell the latest American SLBM system, Trident C4, to the United Kingdom.[80] An opportunity to do this would be afforded at the forthcoming

Guadeloupe summit where the four leaders of France, the United Kingdom, the United States and West Germany were set to meet on the island of Guadeloupe in January 1979 to discuss matters of mutual interest.

It was during the summit that Callaghan personally raised the subject of purchasing Trident C4 with Carter. The level of secrecy which surrounded this discussion is evidenced by the fact that there was no record of the conversation created at this point. In a further illustration of the exclusive nature of the conversation, Owen informed Foreign Office posts that he did not 'yet have details or even [the] gist of [the] Guadeloupe discussions'.[81] It was only once Callaghan faced a no-confidence vote in the House of Commons and was fearful that he would be ejected from office at the end of March 1979 that he hastily arranged for an 'official record' of the president–prime minister private agreement to be created.[82]

Meeting with the president in his private beach hut in Guadeloupe, Callaghan raised the subject of purchasing Trident C4 as a direct replacement for Polaris.[83] Carter responded far more directly and positively than Callaghan had believed likely. A 'private agreement' between the president and prime minister was struck to sell the British government Trident C4 if a formal request for its purchase was made. That Trident C4 was a system that comprised multiple independently targetable re-entry vehicles (MIRVs) which could potentially create difficulties for the United States in the context of their SALT II negotiations would not, the president assured Callaghan, prevent its sale to the United Kingdom.[84] As Callaghan informed his key cabinet colleagues:

> I put it to Carter that the option which on present information I would favour as being most likely to meet our requirements was the Trident C4 Mirved missile; would he be willing in principle to make this available to us on a financial basis which would be within the limits of what we could afford? In reply Carter reaffirmed his support for the maintenance of an independent British deterrent . . . and said he was very ready to consider letting us have the Mirved C4 if this was what we wanted and that he thought it should be possible to work out satisfactory financial terms. He agreed to my suggestion that I should send over to Washington a small team to talk about this.[85]

In spite of the protestations made in the subsequent memoirs of key Labour policy makers that no decision was taken by the Callaghan government to replace Polaris, it is apparent from the private documentation now open to scrutiny that the prime minister was personally determined to purchase Trident C4.[86] Problems with the Labour Party election manifesto, which had stated that 'We have renounced any intention of moving toward a new generation of strategic nuclear weapons' explain why Callaghan was so careful in obtaining an agreement to purchase Trident C4 with 'no commitment'.[87] This 'no commitment' clause was a condition which Callaghan continually emphasised in his communication with his cabinet colleagues and with the United States.[88] At any rate, it was believed that any opposition from Healey or Owen would be overcome easily given that they had both approved the continuation of the Chevaline programme and were both politically invested in sustaining Callaghan's premiership.[89] Evidence that a decision to purchase Trident C4 was gaining political momentum is demonstrated by the fact that talks now began between British and American personnel on the technical details of Trident C4 replacing Polaris.[90] In a further sign of Callaghan's determination to purchase Trident C4, the prime minister, in a break with protocol, ensured that his successor, Margaret Thatcher, would have access to his private papers on matters related to the replacement of Polaris. This quite remarkable act was undertaken to ensure that his successor would be well briefed about the private agreements that had been reached with the United States so that a fully informed decision on replacing Polaris could be made.[91] Whilst no formal agreement had been reached to replace Polaris with Trident C4, Callaghan had put in place the necessary groundwork to ensure that any successor to him as prime minister had the option available to them if they so desired.

This episode reveals a number of interesting points about the nature of the Anglo-American relationship during Callaghan and Carter's short time in office together. First, it endorses the viewpoint that good personal relations are important in helping to reach agreement.[92] Such was the ease of the Carter–Callaghan relationship that it allowed for the prime minister to raise the subject of purchasing Trident C4 on a personal basis and without an official record of the meeting being kept. This was important because the private agreement appeared to be sufficient for both sides to proceed with further technical discussions. By the time Callaghan left office, he had ensured that any successor government had the opportunity to replace Polaris with Trident C4 if it so desired.

Callaghan's tenure as prime minister would soon come to an end. Facing increasing troubles with a number of trade unions which had forced a three-day working week upon government services and mounting rebellions within the House of Commons with the dissolution of the informally agreed Lib–Lab pact, Callaghan faced a no-confidence vote in his leadership. He narrowly lost the vote and was forced to call for a general election. The result was a political disaster for the prime minister as Margaret Thatcher's Conservative Party swept to power in May 1979. It is to Margaret Thatcher's first years in office that we now turn.

4 Thatcher Comes to Power

Thatcher in office

During her tour of the United States in 1977 Margaret Thatcher had met with Jimmy Carter, when she clearly did not endear herself to the president. Such was the tone of the meeting Carter left with the impression that Thatcher was both hot-headed and 'overbearing'.[1] Overbearing or not, US policy makers understood that Thatcher was likely to be the next British prime minister. Events would bear out such an assessment as Callaghan's political predicament was made increasingly untenable as he faced mounting industrial crisis throughout the country. In January 1979 the oil tanker drivers of Texaco Oil Company voted to go on strike, which was followed by further strikes from the road haulage union and then union strikes from public transport and water works employees. In an effort to preserve resources, the British government announced a 'three-day week'. Callaghan's visit to Guadeloupe in February 1979 and his handling of the waiting press at Heathrow, where the prime minister brushed off suggestions that Britain faced a 'crisis', hardly helped matters. When asked by one reporter, what was his view on the 'mounting crisis in the country at the moment?' Callaghan responded by stating that 'you're taking a rather parochial view at the moment, I don't think that other people in the world would share the view that there is mounting chaos'.[2] Bernard Donoughue far better understood the political implications. As he privately recognised at the time, a picture of Callaghan 'basking in the Caribbean sun' would not 'look good when Britain is frozen and coming to halt'.[3] This was indeed how one newspaper interpreted matters as it exclaimed on its front page: 'Crisis, What Crisis?' Callaghan's inability to solve these mounting challenges led to the passing of a vote of no confidence in the House of Commons which forced the prime minister to dissolve Parliament and call for an immediate general election. For Callaghan the result was a political disaster as Margaret Thatcher swept into office on 4 May 1979 with a solid forty-three-seat parliamentary majority.[4]

In certain sections of the press it was suggested that Thatcher's election victory was not particularly welcomed by the Carter administration. Advisers close to Thatcher suggested that such speculation was the work of either Peter Jay or Hamilton Whyte (David Owen's press secretary) in an attempt to discredit Thatcher's election chances.[5] Where the origins of the stories were a moot point as such reports were indeed accurate. As Carrington remembered out of office, the impression he gleaned from Washington was that the Carter administration believed Thatcher was a 'sort of right-wing baboon' that would be impossibly difficult to work with.[6] In contrast, Callaghan had proven capable of working well with the Carter administration and had always supported the central tenets of Carter's foreign policy in public. In contrast, Thatcher could be a more troublesome partner especially given the fact that she had been candid in expressing her distaste for superpower détente and had been critical of the Anglo-American plan for Rhodesia. Superpower détente had come in for special criticism from Thatcher during her time in opposition. In 1975, for example, she had claimed that the signing of the Helsinki Accords was analogous to the Munich Conference of 1938 where the British and French governments had agreed to cede a portion of Czechoslovakia to Hitler's Germany.[7]

In Thatcher's estimation détente was both an immoral and, more importantly, dangerous policy to pursue because détente was premised upon the assumption that long-term cooperation with the Soviet Union was possible. This was fatal misjudgement in Thatcher's opinion because it overlooked the fact that the Soviet Union was an expansionist power that sought to bring about a permanent revolution of the working classes. The Soviet Union therefore posed an existential threat to liberal democracies such as the United Kingdom. Moreover, in Thatcher's judgement, détente had led the Western powers into a false sense of security and had allowed the Soviet Union to obtain a dangerous military advantage. As Thatcher stated before the Conservative Party conference in October 1978:

> The Soviet Union, through its Cuban mercenaries, has completed its Marxist takeover of Angola; Ethiopia has been turned into a Communist bastion in the Horn of Africa; there are now perhaps 40,000 Cubans in that continent, a deadly threat to the whole of Southern Africa. And as the Soviet threat becomes stronger, so the Labour Government [has] made Britain weaker.[8]

Such rhetoric was not merely for public consumption in order to accrue political advantages. In private, the prime minister was even more alarmist about the Western position vis-à-vis the communist bloc. During one conversation with the out-going Supreme Commander of NATO, Alexander Haig, she claimed that the West had in the previous five years slipped from a position of 'equivalence to inferiority'. In discussion with Helmut Schmidt she advanced a similar type of argument.[9]

How the new prime minister's rhetoric would translate into actual foreign policy therefore concerned Washington. Kingman Brewster, the US Ambassador to the United Kingdom, was thus tasked with providing more details about Thatcher and her likely foreign policy trajectory. Brewster quickly supplied Washington with his analysis, noting that the new prime minister was a 'cooler, wiser, more pragmatic person now than the Opposition leader [Carter] met in May 1977'. Lord Carrington's appointment as foreign and Commonwealth secretary was particularly welcomed. As Brzezinski wrote to the president, this was 'one of the most encouraging signals Mrs Thatcher could send us at the start of her stewardship'.[10] As Jay accurately informed London, Carrington's appointment had been welcomed with 'real pleasure' and 'some relief'.[11]

For his part, Carrington intended to act as a calming influence upon the prime minister and prevent her from charting British foreign policy along any radical new course. Since Thatcher had replaced Edward Heath as the leader of the Conservative Party in 1975 Carrington had privately expressed his concern with the style and substance of her leadership. 'What are we going to do after she gets in[?]', Carrington asked Lord Hailsham. 'All we can do is see she is surrounded by adequate advisors', was the response.[12] Carrington took the advice and as he remembered out of office:

> Margaret Thatcher evinced at times a distrust of the Foreign Office, a determined attitude that it didn't stick up for Britain and was softly conciliatory when the reverse was needed. I found that this sentiment was never far from the surface, and could erupt in impatient hostility unless ably countered – and sometimes even then. I knew that I would need as much patience and firmness as I could command.[13]

Indeed, Carrington was determined to influence Thatcher away from her more confrontational tendencies and was, given Thatcher's own inexperience in foreign affairs, able to achieve this ambition to great effect. As Douglas Hurd recollected, Carrington relied upon his 'seniority and natural mastery of international problems in which the prime minister knew she was inexperienced ... By limiting himself to foreign affairs he maximised his influence.'[14] As shown later in the chapter, Carrington's influence was decisively brought to bear as it pertained to bringing about a majority rule settlement in Rhodesia and to ensuring British support for Carter's arms control policies.

Doubts about Thatcher persisted in US circles not least with regard to her personality. As US policy makers hypothesised, Thatcher's 'driven personality' did not make for an easy partner and could lead to her questioning and even challenging the central tenets of Carter's foreign policy. Her inexperience in foreign affairs and tendency to speak candidly could lead her to antagonising and complicating relations with allies and foes alike.[15] Specifically, US policy makers feared that Thatcher would assume a less accommodating attitude to the question of majority rule in Rhodesia and would take a far more hostile attitude to the SALT II negotiations.[16] The Carter administration was right to be concerned as Thatcher immediately began to question whether the United Kingdom should support some of the international treaties that the president was seeking to create (such as the SALT II and the CTB treaties). Carrington, however, quietly persuaded the prime minister to support US ambitions. As Carrington appreciated, Washington would press ahead with these agreements regardless of London's objections, thus meaning that opposition would only damage Anglo-American relations and provide no meaningful counter-benefit.[17]

Thatcher's election therefore created apprehension in US policy making circles but such concerns should not be exaggerated. The coming to power of any new political leader naturally provokes a degree of apprehension for it alters the political status quo. Carter also realised that he would have to work with Thatcher for the foreseeable future so he sought to quell newspaper speculation that he did not welcome her election. The president therefore personally telephoned the new prime minister to congratulate her on her election victory. As Carter well understood, personality differences would have to be placed to one side. More importantly, the Carter administration suspected that Thatcher's rhetoric vis-à-vis the Soviet Union was largely designed for party political consumption. Accordingly, it was suggested that Thatcher's foreign policy would likely differ from Callaghan's only in 'tone' rather than in substance.[18] Cyrus Vance's visit to the new prime minister, scheduled for the final week of May 1979, therefore afforded the Carter administration the opportunity to personally acquaint themselves with the new British government.

On 23 May 1979 Vance met with Thatcher at 10 Downing Street where a general tour d'horizon of international affairs was conducted. Noteworthy from this first encounter was that on most subjects, Thatcher carefully stuck to her pre-prepared briefing material and emphasised that she was committed to the previous British government's position of supporting Carter's core foreign policy ambitions.[19] The subject of SALT II, however, sparked keen discussion between the two sides. Knowing that the US and Soviets were close to announcing a SALT II treaty (this would be signed in Vienna by Carter and Brezhnev in June 1979), the British prime minister took this opportunity to seek clarity on the treaty's content.[20] Thatcher enquired as to whether SALT II would allow the Carter administration to improve the quality of US nuclear systems to counterbalance what she perceived to be the Soviet Union's growing quantitative and qualitative nuclear weapons advantage. She also sought clarification on how SALT II would affect the Anglo-American nuclear relationship as she reminded

Vance that a non-circumvention clause could prevent the United States from supplying the United Kingdom with nuclear material and thus undermine London's ability to maintain its strategic nuclear deterrent.[21]

Thatcher's complaints about SALT II were hardly the most original given that successive British governments had made similar arguments for the past decade. But her lengthy criticism forced Vance to mount a sustained justification of current US policy. As such, the US secretary of state explained how the president would never allow the Anglo-American nuclear relationship to be undermined by agreements reached with the Soviet Union. Vance also explained at great length how the Carter administration was ensuring that the Soviet Union could not obtain the qualitative advantage in nuclear weapons that Thatcher feared was possible because of the president's modernisation programme of the US strategic nuclear arsenal. All told, the president had endorsed a modernisation programme that would require a $30 billion investment in the US nuclear arsenal which Vance believed would ensure that the Soviet Union could not possibly obtain a qualitative nuclear advantage. It was at this point that Lord Carrington injected himself into proceedings. Evidently sensing the growing antagonism generated by Thatcher's criticism of current US nuclear weapons policy, Carrington assured Vance that the United Kingdom would fully support the upcoming SALT II agreement in public and in private discussion with America's allies.[22]

This episode is revealing at a number of levels. In some ways the British government was indeed promoting US efforts in relation to SALT II as Thatcher would go on to publicly endorse the president's policies. Privately Thatcher also sought to quell potential opposition from the likes of Helmut Schmidt who was the most vocal in publicly criticising SALT II. Ironically Schmidt's criticism echoed similar concerns that Thatcher felt. Yet her decision to publicly and privately support SALT II was premised upon the calculation that regardless of how 'imperfect' the treaty might be, it was necessary to support it for a number of important reasons. First, the Carter administration had 'pressed' London to support SALT II so the consequences of not doing so risked a major political spat with Washington. Such a scenario was believed to be unwise at a point when Thatcher was establishing herself in government and when the British government was itself engaged in discussion with Washington about finding a successor system to Polaris. As London concluded, it was imperative to avoid any political rupture with Washington and unduly endanger the Anglo-American nuclear relationship. As one British official reminded his colleagues, if President Carter was to be 'disappointed' with Britain's position over SALT II, there would likely be 'repercussions elsewhere'.[23]

Second, the British government had a realistic appreciation of its influence over Washington and understood just how much importance Carter attached to the successful ratification of the SALT II treaty. British policy makers understood that their opposition to SALT II would not stop the Carter administration signing the treaty, and knew that the mounting difficulties between Carter and the US Senate over the wisdom of its ratification was something from which London could not possibly derive any benefits. Indeed, the Carter administration appreciated just how difficult the successful ratification of SALT II would be, with one administration official noting that 'The selling of the SALT agreement, any SALT agreement, is going to be the toughest foreign policy challenge to this Administration, tougher even than the Panama Canal Treaties.'[24]

Given that British opposition would not prevent the SALT II agreement, Thatcher was convinced that it was wiser to instead derive any political benefits that could be attained by encouraging its successful ratification by the US Senate and in winning over sceptical allies such as Helmut Schmidt. Along with this, London believed that it was better to protect specific British interests (such as ensuring that a non-circumvention clause did not prevent the sale of a successor system to Polaris) instead of engaging in some broader philosophical discussion about the merits of SALT II per se. More to the point, the Carter administration recognised Thatcher's concern about the growth in Soviet theatre nuclear weapons and now redoubled its efforts to implement the Dual Track policy whereby arms limitation agreements with the Soviet Union would be sought at the same time as deploying additional nuclear weapons to Europe.[25] Even though Thatcher's rhetoric differed from Callaghan's, fundamentally the British position of endorsing Carter's SALT II policies whilst seeking to defend specific British interests remained the same.

Following the talks with Thatcher and Carrington, Vance met with Francis Pym, the new British defence secretary. It was here that Vance raised the issue of how Thatcher's publicly stated ambition of reducing public expenditure would affect the previously agreed position of the British government to increase defence expenditure by 3 per cent per annum. Pym assured Vance that this remained official government policy but such assurances were contradicted when Vance met with Geoffrey Howe, the Chancellor of the Exchequer.[26] As Howe unequivocally informed the US secretary of state, there could be 'no sacred cows' when it came to reducing British public expenditure. Defence expenditure much like everything else would be analysed and appropriate cutbacks would be undertaken. As Howe further explained, his information indicated that the British government spent more as a proportion of its GDP on defence than the United States, West Germany or France. Given this and coupled to the bleak economic outlook facing the United Kingdom, the British government would have to reduce its existing levels of defence expenditure.[27]

At the end of his visit to London, Vance could be reasonably content with the discussions he had held with the senior policy making actors within the Thatcher government. Whilst Howe had suggested British reductions in defence expenditure were likely to be forthcoming, Thatcher, Carrington and Pym had provided equivocal support for maintaining Britain's existing commitments. Only time would tell which position would win through but the Thatcher government's budgets for 1979 and 1980 left defence expenditure largely untouched pending a broader defence review. At this point in her premiership Thatcher had decided to prioritise defence expenditure over implementing her broader economic agenda.[28] Anglo-American differences over SALT II had been apparent during the Vance talks but again Thatcher and Carrington had reiterated that they supported the Carter administration's ultimate objective of securing a SALT II agreement with the Soviet Union. Importantly, Thatcher promised Vance that she would only make public statements in support of SALT II, a promise she honoured in the coming months. In all other areas of concern for Anglo-American relations Vance had received the consistent message that Thatcher would continue to pursue the same levels of cooperation as experienced under Callaghan's government. In sum, Brewster had been correct to predict that Thatcher's foreign policy would differ from Callaghan's largely in terms of 'tone' rather than substance.

The British government could also be reasonably satisfied with the outcome of the Vance talks. Thatcher had questioned the US secretary of state about US nuclear policy and had been reassured that the president was undertaking a serious modernisation programme of the US strategic nuclear arsenal that would maintain the existing strategic nuclear balance. Moreover, by advancing her concerns, the British government had received a number of assurances from Vance that Anglo-American nuclear cooperation would not be undermined by the signing of the SALT II treaty. This assurance was followed by a personal letter to the prime minister from the president himself in which he asserted that he would not allow the SALT II treaty to infringe upon Anglo-American nuclear cooperation.[29] Quite how useful such assurances would prove in the future would of course be another matter but at the very least the British had got the president and his secretary of state on the record promising to safeguard the nuclear relationship. Such assurances were of course far from ironclad but they could be exploited usefully sometime in the future.

The Washington Summit

Soon after she took office Thatcher looked to arrange an official visit to Washington, which was finally set for December 1979. Prior to this Thatcher had met with Carter at the Tokyo Economic Summit in June 1979, where the new prime minister had followed her briefing material closely and reiterated her support for the Anglo-American alliance.[30] In sum, the first Carter–Thatcher meeting had been largely uneventful but the prime minister had made a better impression on Carter than she had during her meeting in 1977.

Carter reflected in his diary: 'Margaret Thatcher is a tough lady, highly opinionated, strong-willed, cannot admit that she doesn't know something. However, I think she will be a good prime minister for Great Britain.'[31] Thatcher's Washington visit, however, would be rather more important, not least because there was a growing sense in London that Carter's presidency was in serious trouble. As British officials observed, international and domestic difficulties were making it increasingly probable that Jimmy Carter would be a one-term president. As such, Carter would look to exploit the Thatcher visit to guarantee London's support on a number of major international subjects.[32] The most important of these related to the taking of US hostages in Iran. As Thatcher was advised, Carter would look for her continued public support and would likely also propose that the British government endorse economic and political sanctions against Tehran (partly as a punishment against the Ayatollah but also as a means of helping to convince Iran to release the US hostages). Thatcher's visit would also be exploited by the president to demonstrate that he was not a 'lame duck' but was in 'command of affairs' and engaged in negotiations with one of America's principle allies.[33] Thatcher's forthcoming visit therefore assumed greater importance because of international events and because it could potentially be exploited for domestic political benefit by both parties.

Yet it was readily apparent that the British government was far from enthusiastic in supporting US plans for implementing sanctions against Tehran. Whilst Thatcher was sympathetic to the president's predicament, she remained unconvinced that Britain's interests were best promoted by supporting economic sanctions against Iran. During initial talks in London between Thatcher and Vance no agreement could be found as to what economic sanctions should be pursued against Iran. When Vance proposed that the British government should freeze Iranian assets held in British banks, Thatcher immediately opposed such action. As she reasoned, such measures had only ever been undertaken during a 'time of war'. As such, the broader economic ramifications of such action had to be analysed in much greater depth before she would agree to support such a move.[34]

British opposition to American plans was predominantly motivated by a desire to safeguard significant British commercial and economic interests. London, for instance, was a critical hub in the international financial system. Exploiting this was central to Thatcher's economic reforms at the start of her term in office as she sought to expand the financial services industry within the city. Seizing or freezing assets held by foreign states in British banks would severely undermine this broader policy ambition. More specifically, implementing these dramatic actions against banks based in the United Kingdom could encourage a capital flight away from London and significantly damage British financial interests.[35]

Implementing Vance's suggested actions therefore appealed little to British policy makers. Yet outright rejection of the Carter administration's request would potentially engender a rift with Washington. In order to camouflage these self-interested commercial and economic motivations guiding British policy, the prime minister cited a number of legal problems which would prevent her from being able to support American economic sanctions against Tehran. As Thatcher consequently argued, she could not actually authorise the freezing of Iranian assets held within British banks without first passing emergency legislation through Parliament. Such arguments appeared unconvincing to the US secretary of state. Vance challenged Thatcher's position and suggested that sources within the British Treasury had actually indicated that the prime minister had the existing legal authority to freeze foreign-held assets. Carrington interjected at this point and reiterated that the British government had 'no powers at present' to undertake the type of action that Washington was requesting. Who was factually correct was a moot point as Thatcher appeared unwilling to undertake the proposed American measures. The scene was now set for a diplomatic showdown in Washington where the Carter administration would look to win British support for enacting sanctions against Tehran.[36]

On arriving in Washington on 17 December 1979, the British prime minister held meetings with key Carter administration policy makers, senior senators and congressmen, and media representatives. On liaising with a number of US senators, Thatcher went on the charm offensive and followed her briefing advice very closely. As Thatcher told the senators, 'The special relationship was indefinable, but it existed and it gave the Americans the right to be able to count on Britain.'[37] Senator Javits (R-New York) responded in likeminded fashion as he told the group that 'There was much talk of a special relationship between Britain and the United States. This special relationship did exist: between the peoples of Britain and the United States. In a crunch, they understood each other and shared the same ideals.'[38] Thatcher looked to exploit this sentimental rhetoric by emphasising that she supported the SALT II treaty and hoped that the Senate would ratify it. She also highlighted how the United Kingdom stood steadfastly behind the United States in trying to solve the Iranian hostage situation.

Behind the highfaluting rhetoric Thatcher was quietly promoting her argument that nothing should be hastily undertaken against Iran in retaliation for the taking of the American hostages. As she informed her hosts:

> It was very frustrating for a great nation to have to move slowly and steadily, particularly when it was swept by a wave of anger. But when one was in power, one had to concentrate on the objective and she was sure that the United States was following the right course and would succeed in the end.[39]

Closely following her briefing material, Thatcher urged influential policy actors in Washington not to implement economic sanctions against Tehran. Subtly then, the prime minister was attempting to exercise influence over Washington's decision makers and encourage a cautious approach in dealing with Iran. How much influence Thatcher exercised, however, would be shown to be rather limited when the president authorised in April 1980 a series of economic sanctions against Iran and a rescue mission of the American hostages without first consulting with the prime minister.

Rhodesia and Northern Ireland were also discussed during this meeting as Thatcher thanked the senators for their public support in condemning terrorism in Northern Ireland and in praising the

Lancaster House agreements. But Thatcher also showed a sharper side to her personality as she made it clear that she would not countenance the idea that 'Ulster' did not belong to the United Kingdom. As she told the senators, including Tip O'Neill who was present:

> Ulster was a part of the United Kingdom because that was the way its people wanted it. They had voted very strongly in that sense in a referendum in 1973. So long as there was terrorist violence, the Army must stay and the British Government's aim must be (1) to beat terrorism and (2) to bring about more political progress in the Province.[40]

The British prime minister had been none too subtle in asserting that the question of Irish sovereignty was not a subject to be debated between the British and American governments.[41]

Following these discussions Thatcher met with Paul Volcker, the Chairman of the Board of the US Federal Reserve System. It was here that Thatcher sought to raise a number of British concerns about US monetary reform and the possibility of economic sanctions against Iran. Thatcher raised the question as to whether the United States was planning to introduce some dramatic changes to US monetary policy. Volcker denied that this was current American planning and he explained that there was simply no 'Holy Grail' in which to solve common monetary problems.[42] Further discussion about monetary supply and tackling inflation was conducted which once again demonstrated how the transnational interchange of ideas worked at a practical level. Solving common economic and political challenges that faced both the United States and United Kingdom was a key feature of Thatcher's talks in Washington.[43]

It was, however, the subject of possible economic sanctions against Iran which Thatcher was most interested in raising with Volcker. In a similar fashion to her discussions with Vance on this subject, disagreement quickly materialised. The British prime minister reiterated her earlier position that the imposition of economic sanctions risked precipitating a global economic recession. As Thatcher reasoned, freezing or seizing Iranian assets held by British financial institutions could lead to a serious run on Western banks. At the very least then, the British government would require detailed discussion with Washington about the likely ramifications of undertaking economic sanctions against Iran prior to London committing to such action. At the heart of Thatcher's argument then was the notion that economic sanctions against Iran could have damaging long-term repercussions for Western interests and this fact had to be fully appreciated when deliberating the action to be taken against Tehran.[44] Thatcher persistently counselled caution in her advice to Washington on how to overcome the hostage crisis.

Following this, Thatcher had a long discussion about the strategic position of the Western alliance vis-à-vis the Soviet bloc with Harold Brown, the US defense secretary. The meeting started warmly as Brown complimented the British prime minister on her continuing support for the Western alliance. Thatcher reciprocated by reminding Brown that the United Kingdom was fully supportive of the Carter administration's theatre nuclear force modernisation programme and had publicly and privately championed the ratification of the SALT II treaty. The meeting moved on as Thatcher enquired as to American assessments about current levels of Soviet defence spending. Brown explained that he believed that current levels of Soviet expenditure would slow down because of the economic challenges and labour shortages that Soviet planners faced. Yet, in spite of this, Brown estimated that the Soviet Union would spend somewhere in the region of 13 per cent of its GDP on defence over the course of the next twenty years.[45]

Disagreement between Brown and Thatcher soon emerged when discussion moved to the subject of the Soviet Union's actual foreign policy intentions. Brown suggested that the Soviet Union's growing conventional force capability was probably designed to safeguard against a future invasion. Thatcher openly disagreed, claiming that the Soviets 'surely did not expect to be invaded now'.[46] It was again Carrington that interceded to prevent an escalation of Anglo-American differences as he diplomatically suggested that given the known ill health of Brezhnev, a leadership succession loomed on the horizon. As such, the Soviet military bureaucracy would exploit its position to increase Soviet defence spending during this time of uncertainty in the Communist Party's leadership. Given this expected period of political uncertainty in

Moscow, Carrington suggested that the NATO alliance should better streamline its own defence procurement and production efforts.[47] As was often the case throughout the Cold War, the American and British governments disagreed about how best to respond to what both governments perceived as a common threat posed by Moscow. But that open disagreement was allowed to occur during bilateral meetings was testament to the closeness of relations between the two countries' political leaders.

Following her meeting with Brown, Thatcher met with the president and engaged in a general discussion about international affairs.[48] It was also during these talks that Carter sought British support for his newly emerged national security strategy as articulated within the Carter Doctrine.[49] British approval for stationing new tactical nuclear weapons on British territory was sought. The president also asked for permission to expand America's military presence on Diego Garcia. Following on from Harold Brown's earlier point that increased British military support was required globally, the president suggested that the United Kingdom should look at ways in which to increase both its political and military presence throughout the Persian Gulf. Thatcher demurred and pointed out that there were obvious economic challenges facing her government which prevented her from agreeing to such proposals. Given the economic and political difficulties confronting Thatcher, the president's hope of obtaining British agreement to reverse forty years of ever shrinking global military power was always fanciful. Carter, however, would achieve his ambition of obtaining British agreement to expand the US presence on Diego Garcia.[50]

The issue of Britain's strategic nuclear deterrent was also raised in this bilateral meeting. As the minutes of the meeting note, 'The president and prime minister agreed on the importance of maintaining a credible British strategic deterrent force and US–UK strategic cooperation.'[51] Similarly, the discussion about Diego Garcia demonstrated that the Anglo-American intelligence 'special relationship' would be continued under the new political leaders. Mutual interests clearly transcended any political and personality differences that may have existed.

The majority of the Carter–Thatcher discussion was indeed largely amicable. The exception to this, however, was the subject of the United States supplying the Royal Ulster Constabulary (RUC) with revolvers. It was the recent decision by the United States government to suspend sales of revolvers to the RUC which generated disagreement between Carter and Thatcher.[52] The issue of Northern Ireland, which had from the beginning of the Carter presidency been a thorn in the side of Anglo-American relations, thus once again surfaced at this point. But in a similar fashion to her predecessor James Callaghan, Thatcher was able to compartmentalise this point of disagreement and prevent it from affecting other aspects of the relationship. Thatcher therefore raised her complaint that the suspension of arms sales to the RUC was unwarranted and moved the conversation forward. Indeed, when Vance was set to visit London in February 1980, the British opted not to raise the issue again as British policy makers had rightly concluded that further discussion was unlikely to result in a change of US policy.[53]

At the end of Thatcher's visit to Washington a concerted effort from both sides was made to present a public image that both leaders had reached significant agreement on how to proceed over a number of common international challenges. Public statements of continued Anglo-American solidarity were issued with Thatcher making a deliberate point of informing the news media that the British government was committed to supporting America's position towards the Iranian hostage situation.[54] As Thatcher told the press on the White House Lawn, 'At times like these you are entitled to look to your friends for support. We are your friends and do support you. And we shall support you. Let there be no doubt about that.'[55] Carter's remarks were verging on the obsequious when he declared that 'Madam Prime Minister, you've exhibited greatness in the form of assuming responsibility; not only to deal with important and difficult domestic issues ... but in searching for ways in which you can meet the challenges of the international world.'[56] Such warm words evidently had some effect as one Washington insider told Nicholas Henderson, the British Ambassador to Washington, that the meeting between Thatcher and Carter had been 'the best he had attended'.[57] Another senator had suggested to Henderson that no British leader had made such an incredibly positive impression upon the key policy makers in Washington as had Thatcher. Henderson himself noted that the prime minister had made a 'remarkable impact' during her visit to Washington.[58]

Behind the rhetoric there had also been a number of agreements reached between the two sides. Thatcher had received the president's tacit approval for continuing the Anglo-American nuclear relationship which would involve the sale of Trident C4 to the British government. The United States had obtained British agreement to expand their presence on Diego Garcia. Common agreement had also been reached on updating NATO's theatre nuclear weapons and on the necessity of moving forward with a SALT III treaty. In addition, Carter had had the opportunity to appear before the American media as engaged in international negotiations with one of America's principle allies. The rhetoric of a 'special relationship' served as useful political capital for both Carter and Thatcher. Of course, disagreement also existed. Perhaps the most obvious and pronounced was with regards to Northern Ireland but the British government privately accepted that the American sale of revolvers to the RUC was probably not going to happen as long as Carter inhabited the White House and Tip O'Neill remained as the Speaker of the House. The possibility of Iranian sanctions, however, brought the two sides into opposition. Thatcher had taken a subtle approach in warning against hasty action for fear that this would spark some major economic crisis. Both sides had therefore achieved enough during Thatcher's visit to Washington to feel reasonably content.

Rhodesia

By the time Callaghan had left office in May 1979 the Anglo-American plan for implementing majority rule in Rhodesia had reached an impasse as Smith continued to press for international recognition of the Salisbury Agreement and the Rhodesian Bush War continued. A successful transition to majority rule in Rhodesia in the near future looked doubtful. On the surface, Thatcher's election only contributed to the complexity of the Rhodesian situation given that there was no guarantee that she would continue to endorse the Anglo-American plan for implementing majority rule. Within the Conservative Party itself, the question of Rhodesian majority rule was an exceptionally divisive one. Carter's own involvement in settling the majority rule issue had never been particularly welcomed. One Conservative MP, Lord Hailsham, spoke for many deemed on the right wing of the party, when he suggested that Carter would 'give away' Rhodesia to the forces of international communism.[59] From Washington's perspective, there was a concern that Thatcher would come under the influence of the right wing of her party and thus withdraw her support for the Anglo-American plan and instead support the Salisbury Agreement and provide Smith with vital international legitimacy.[60] On the subject of majority rule, the Conservative Party manifesto of 11 April 1979 was vague enough to convince Washington that Thatcher's election would see a radical departure in British Rhodesian policy. As the Conservative Party manifesto stated, 'a lasting settlement to the Rhodesia problem' had to be 'based on the democratic wishes of the people of that country'. The Carter administration feared that the Thatcher government would interpret the election of Muzorewa in the recent Rhodesian parliamentary elections as having represented the 'democratic wishes' of the Rhodesian people. If such recognition was afforded to Muzorewa's election, Washington feared that the guerrilla campaign of the Patriotic Front would in fact escalate to a broader Southern African war which could involve the participation of South Africa and the Front Line States.[61]

Thatcher's election certainly complicated Anglo-American cooperation over Rhodesia as the British prime minister requested that Washington reassess its position towards the Salisbury Agreement. By reopening this question, Thatcher was asking that the Carter administration completely reverse its current Rhodesian policy. More concerning yet was that Britain's reinvigorated enthusiasm for the Salisbury Agreement would provide encouragement for the president's critics within the US Congress. The passing of the Case–Javits Amendment had led to US observers being dispatched to Rhodesia to monitor the forthcoming multiracial elections. As an additional condition of the Case–Javits Amendment, the president would be required to make a 'determination' as to whether or not Smith's regime had allowed 'free and fair' elections. If Smith was considered to have done this, then economic sanctions against Rhodesia would be lifted. In the assessment of the Thatcher government, these 'free and fair' elections had taken place in May 1979 when multiracial elections had been undertaken and had led to Muzorewa becoming prime minister. As Carrington announced before the House of Lords, 'There had been a fundamental change inside Rhodesia' which had seen 'an election in which every adult man and woman [had] been able to cast a vote.'[62] Within the US Senate, Jesse Helms (R-North Carolina) agreed with Thatcher's interpretation of events and began the process of passing legislation to immediately end sanctions against Rhodesia.[63]

The British fully understood that this domestic pressure against the president could be exploited to bring about a change in US policy towards Rhodesia.[64] Carrington therefore proposed that Carter should make a presidential determination outlining that the conditions set by the Case–Javits Amendment had been substantially met by virtue of the fact that elections had been decided by universal suffrage. Moreover, Smith had been succeeded by Muzorewa as prime minister. Given these changed circumstances, the British government now suggested that economic sanctions against Rhodesia should be lifted temporarily and could then be permanently withdrawn in six months' time as long as Smith abided by the terms of the Salisbury Agreement.[65]

Carter remained unconvinced and refused to recognise the legitimacy of the recent Rhodesian election for a combination of factors centred upon domestic political calculations and concerns about 'realpolitik and the peculiar influence of race'.[66] As Vance explained to Carrington, the lifting of sanctions at this juncture would provide a mixed signal to Smith that Washington and London were not prepared to push forward with majority rule that included membership for the Patriotic Front (both ZANU and ZAPU). Without their inclusion there existed little probability that the Rhodesian Bush War could be brought to an end, and the continuation of the war would only ensure that ZANU and ZAPU would receive additional support from their communist backers. Ultimately, Washington made the hard-headed calculation that Muzorewa could not bring an end to the Rhodesian Bush War and thus stem the tide of growing communist influence in the region and prevent a broader war from breaking out. Second, the Carter administration did not believe that the recent Salisbury Agreement had been 'free and fair', nor that the new Rhodesia Zimbabwe constitution could be considered democratic as it afforded political advantages for white Rhodesians. Racial discrimination would continue to persist under the new Rhodesia Zimbabwe constitution which Carter refused to legitimise. Third, by ending economic sanctions at this juncture, the Carter administration believed that it would signal to the Front Line States that the United States was not fully committed to racial equality in Rhodesia and would thus endorse the propaganda emanating from Moscow that the United States was both an imperialistic and racist power.[67]

Domestic politics also influenced the president's decision to oppose the Salisbury Agreement. First, those advocating a change in US policy within Congress were mainly Republicans and with the US general election little over a year away, now would be an inopportune time to be seen to be yielding to Republican pressure. Second, the Black Caucus within the Democratic Party continued to lobby the president to remain committed to achieving racial equality in Rhodesia. At a time when relations between the White House and congressional Democrats were already seriously strained the president was reluctant to provoke further controversy with Democratic supporters. Finally, the president was already under criticism from core supporters within the Democratic Party who alleged that he allowed his foreign policy to stray too far from the human rights agenda he had been swept into office proclaiming.[68] For all of these reasons, then, the Carter administration rejected the British notion that Rhodesia Zimbabwe could be recognised by the United States or that economic sanctions should be lifted. On 7 June 1979 Carter delivered an unequivocal message: 'I am absolutely convinced that the best interests of the United States would not be served by lifting the sanctions.'[69]

Accepting that Washington would not recognise the Salisbury Agreement, and appreciating that the Rhodesian civil war was continuing to threaten to spiral into a broader Southern African war, London called for all of the warring factions to meet at Lancaster House under British auspices. As Carrington explained in his memoir, a settlement in Rhodesia which would end the civil war there would have to 'command sufficient internal assent'.[70] In other words, Carrington needed to convince the Patriotic Front to lay down its arms and recognise the political legitimacy of a new Rhodesian government. For this to be achieved, the Patriotic Front would have to be included in the new government. Carter's uncompromising stance, when coupled to the positions of several African states, highlighted to London that a solution would have to be found that would be accepted by all sides, including one acceptable to both factions of the Patriotic Front.[71] It was now Carrington's task to convince all of the factions in Rhodesia to attend British-sponsored talks to negotiate a final majority rule settlement.

It was, however, by no means guaranteed that all parties would attend such talks as each side continued to blame the other for the ongoing war in Rhodesia. Sections of opinion within the British FCO believed that Mugabe would probably never attend a conference. Even if he did, he would be unlikely to negotiate 'seriously for an agreement' because he was confident of achieving his aims by continuing with the guerrilla war. As the British reflected, Mugabe did not have the ability to defeat the Rhodesian security forces in the field but he probably reckoned that he could inflict sufficient levels of casualties against the Rhodesian security forces to ensure that the new government of Muzorewa would sue for terms. On the other hand, others within the British policy making bureaucracy suggested that there were grounds for optimism given Mugabe's own position vis-à-vis Nkomo. It was speculated that if Nkomo entered into agreement with the Salisbury Group, it would ostracise Mugabe and leave him both politically and militarily isolated. Also, South Africa had privately informed London that if Mugabe continued with his guerrilla campaign following an internationally legitimised settlement to the question of majority rule in Rhodesia, it would likely lend its military power to the new Rhodesian government to crush Mugabe. In sum, the British were fully aware that Mugabe's attendance at the talks and his acceptance of a final majority settlement was vital if the Rhodesian Bush War was to be prevented from spiralling into a broader Southern African war. Following extensive efforts on the part of both the British and American governments, all factions agreed to attend the Lancaster House talks. It was here that Carrington chaired long and intense negotiations about transitioning to a mutually acceptable majority rule settlement. Carrington's skilful handling of the negotiations encouraged cooperation as the Lancaster House agreements emerged which set up a new constitution for Rhodesia Zimbabwe and mandated new elections which could be contested by all political parties.[72]

Ostensibly the United Kingdom was to remain neutral in the forthcoming Rhodesian elections but beneath the surface London desired Muzorewa's United African National Council to emerge victorious. In London's assessment, Muzorewa's decision not to take up arms against Smith's regime demonstrated a level of wisdom that was lacking in the alternative candidates. More important still, Muzorewa was believed to be the most 'pro-Western' of the candidates. Both Mugabe and Nkomo were viewed as Marxists who would ruin Rhodesia's economic vitality and would also be susceptible to Soviet manipulation.[73] In the minds of British policy makers, considerations about Rhodesia's future well-being and broader Cold War concerns were the key factors behind London's decision to support Muzorewa's candidacy.

Again, however, Anglo-American disagreement emerged as Washington alleged that London's support for Muzorewa only encouraged Mugabe and Nkomo to break the delicate ceasefire that existed inside Rhodesia. Vance put these points to Carrington in January 1980 but the British were dismissive of the US secretary of state, claiming that he was not 'well briefed' on events.[74] Indeed, the British were now concerned that Washington's interference would actually encourage Mugabe and Nkomo to return to arms. Such an eventuality could lead to white Rhodesians having to flee to South Africa or to encouraging direct South African involvement in fighting the Patriotic Front.[75] In spite of these concerns elections were conducted in Rhodesia. The outcome was a sweeping victory for Mugabe's ZANU. Rhodesia was now formally accorded its independence from the United Kingdom and on 18 April 1980 Mugabe was instated as the country's new president.

From London's perspective there was a general sense of relief that this imperial hangover was finally over. But within the Thatcher government there was a clear sense of regret that Mugabe had won the election. Yet, as the prime minister was aware, the realities of power meant that London had to accept this outcome. 'Truth to tell, I think most people, whatever their politics, were now relieved that the business was over', Carrington reflected.[76] All that Thatcher could do was to lament in her memoir:

> It was sad that Rhodesia Zimbabwe finished up with a Marxist government in a continent where too many Marxists mal-administer their countries' resources. But political and military realities were all too evidently on the side of the guerrilla leaders. A government like that of Muzorewa, without international recognition, could never have brought to the people of Rhodesia the peace that they wanted and needed above all else.[77]

The Carter administration, in contrast, believed that Mugabe's election was a victory for democracy and the promotion of international human rights. Carter was less concerned with Mugabe being a declared Marxist. Indeed, Carter publicly announced that he believed Mugabe would no longer be a 'Marxist and hater and enemy of the United States' and would now become 'one of our strong and potentially very good and loyal friends'.[78] Carter's decision to recognise Mugabe as the legitimate head of the new government of Zimbabwe demonstrated a unique approach to handling the Cold War in the Third World. Carter's policies were dictated by a strong moral compass, that is, it was right to afford Rhodesia independence and this should be done according to the will of the people. Broader Cold War calculations about potential Soviet, Cuban or PRC influence of course informed the president's thinking but it did not dictate his policy towards the question of majority rule in Rhodesia in the fashion it had with other presidents. Carter believed that his efforts in bringing about majority rule in Rhodesia could serve as a model for America's handling of similar situations in the future. As Carter told congressional Democrats:

> What we've seen lately in Rhodesia, soon to be Zimbabwe, the institution of a Democratic government under the leadership of Great Britain, supported by us and others, that will bring majority rule there and add a sense of dignity to people who have too long been subjugated by racial discrimination. We hope to spread that concept, based on our own principles, to others who've suffered too long.[79]

The British government was far less satisfied with how the majority rule question had been settled. Both the Callaghan and Thatcher governments would have preferred a Muzorewa victory and had been prepared to support the Salisbury Agreement. Carter's reluctance to support this, however, convinced London that another majority rule settlement which eradicated all vestiges of racial discrimination would have to be pursued instead. Ultimately, the dynamics of power, both within Rhodesia and within the Anglo-American alliance, meant that Carter's wishes and those of the Rhodesian people won through. As Peter Jay remembered, Carter's coming to power brought with it an American president determined to settle the question of majority rule inside Rhodesia.[80] For better or worse, Carter achieved largely what he wanted in relation to Rhodesia, which was to establish a government that was formed according to the popular will of the Rhodesian people. By the time Carter left office this had been accomplished. But the conduct of this diplomacy also revealed the uneven nature of the Anglo-American relationship. Throughout the entire process it was Washington that pursued a majority rule settlement that included the participation of the Patriotic Front even though this did not sit comfortably in London. Ultimately, American power allowed the president to pursue a path that he believed both promoted US interests and tallied with his ideas about racial equality.

5 The End of Détente

Introduction

Zbigniew Brzezinski remembered that the 'Christmas of 1979 was grim and full of foreboding'.[1] For the president, things would not improve as 1980 turned into a political disaster. Domestic and international circumstances conspired to make Carter's re-election chances remote by the time he faced his Republican challenger Ronald Reagan in November 1980. Stagflation afflicted the American economy as the Reagan candidacy asked the pertinent question of 'can we afford 4 more years [of a Carter administration?]'[2] Whether Carter's handling of the American economy was as poor as his detractors claimed was a moot point for, as US Treasury Secretary W. Michael Blumenthal perceptibly noted, Carter was perceived to be a 'weak and indecisive economic leader'.[3] As Blumenthal warned:

> Like it or not, we have failed to convince the public that the president is a strong economic chief, leading and influencing events rather than reacting to them. That's why he gets little credit for the positives and more blame than he deserves for the problems.[4]

International events only further undermined Carter's re-election chances. The ongoing Iranian hostage situation was exploited by Carter's critics as an example of a president hopelessly unable to protect American citizens abroad. Détente collapsed following the Soviet invasion of Afghanistan in December 1979. Carter's flagship nuclear arms limitation treaty, SALT II, stalled before the US Senate. The Sandinistas took power in Nicaragua in a sign that in

America's 'backyard' Carter could not even prevent communist advances. Carter's difficulties with America's key allies continued as relations with West Germany and France bordered upon open antagonism. His difficulties were compounded by the challenge of Edward Kennedy to run as the Democratic nominee for the presidency in November 1980. Managing to just secure the Democratic nomination, Carter was soundly beaten in the general election by Ronald Reagan. It is with justification that the final year of Carter's presidency is depicted as one of 'crisis'.[5]

Anglo-American relations were to be crucially influenced by these various international and domestic factors. American and British views pertaining to the Soviet Union's invasion of Afghanistan in December 1979 differed so much that it prevented any coordinated response being pursued. Likewise, Anglo-American cooperation in relation to the Iranian hostage situation was extremely disjointed. This chapter therefore explores these aspects of the Anglo-American diplomatic relationship and illustrates the disagreement and apparent lack of cooperation between the two countries. Yet, for all of the differences in these areas, the Anglo-American nuclear relationship was renewed as Carter agreed to sell the United Kingdom the Trident C4 SLBM system to replace Britain's ageing Polaris fleet. And for all of the private disagreement between the two countries, Thatcher was also careful to remain supportive of the president in public. By analysing this period, a far more complicated and competitive Anglo-American relationship appears than is suggested within existing accounts.[6]

Afghanistan

Prior to the Soviet invasion of Afghanistan in December 1979 superpower détente was already close to breaking point. Events in Afghanistan would therefore kill the remaining vestiges of détente and usher in a return to a more confrontational and militaristic superpower rivalry. Importantly, Washington had reached the conclusion that the pursuit of idealist goals in foreign affairs now had to be more heavily nuanced by considerations dictated by power politics. As Brzezinski reflected:

> The last phase of Carter's foreign policy involved the shaping of a new balance between the priorities of power and of principle. The higher recognition of the centrality of power in world affairs emerged gradually through intense internal debates sparked largely by the impact of Soviet expansionism and the crisis with Iran. The result was a tougher policy vis-à-vis the Soviet Union, a major effort to shape a new regional security framework for the Middle East, and a sustained commitment, which paralleled during 1979 the deterioration in US–Soviet relations, to forge a broader relationship with China.[7]

The subsequent Carter Doctrine (the name given to this hardening of Carter's foreign policy) was thus formally adopted. Consequently, members of the NATO alliance were more forcibly encouraged to support the deployment of new theatre nuclear weapons. A modernisation of America's own nuclear arsenal was now undertaken which was underpinned by a marked increase in US defence expenditure.[8] The Soviet invasion of Afghanistan solidified these changes to US national security policy. As one scholar has argued, 'détente had been in retreat throughout the late 1970s, but from 1980 it was effectively dead and a revived Cold War was proclaimed and planned for'.[9] Planning for and fighting the Second Cold War would now come to dominate US foreign policy as newspaper commentators speculated on the hardening of Carter's grand strategy.[10] As one commentator suggests, there was a 'return' to 'militarism' in American Cold War strategy'.[11] This somewhat simplifies the changes to Carter's national security policy but there was certainly now a greater emphasis upon improving America's military position in relation to that of the Soviet Union.[12]

Soviet interest in Afghanistan had steadily grown throughout the latter half of the 1970s, and in 1978 Noor Mohammad Taraki seized control of Kabul for the Afghan Communist Party. Taraki's rule was far from universally popular as insurrection in Herat led to attacks on Afghan communist forces which resulted in the brutal killings of Soviet advisers that were present in the city. Taraki requested military and economic assistance from Moscow to help quell the growing rebellion against his authority. The Soviet leadership demurred but Taraki's removal in a coup orchestrated by his second in command, Hafizullah Amin, tipped the balance in the Soviet Politburo for intervention. As the Kremlin was aware, Amin was secretly meeting with the US chargé d'affaires in Afghanistan, J. Bruce Amstutz, and senior Soviet policy makers concluded that Amin was undertaking a strategic turn towards the United States or, worse yet, that Amin was in fact secretly working for the CIA to help undermine Soviet interests throughout central Asia. After a series of lengthy discussions, the Soviet leadership decided to take a more forthright approach to securing Soviet interests in Afghanistan. Thus in October 1979 the Kremlin ordered Soviet forces already stationed in Afghanistan to begin the process of isolating the Afghan capital, Kabul. Communication lines to the capital were severed and over 25–27 December additional Soviet forces entered Afghanistan and occupied key government buildings. As the Soviet leadership explained to the Politburo, 'In accordance with the provisions of the Soviet–Afghan treaty of 1978, a decision [had] been made to send . . . the Soviet Army to Afghanistan.'[13]

Soviet forces performed their task efficiently as the Tajbeg Palace to where Amin had retreated was stormed. In the ensuing chaos Amin along with his family were killed. By the morning of 28 December 1979 Soviet forces had secured the majority of government buildings and exercised control over Afghanistan.[14] Washington and London had grown increasingly suspicious throughout the summer of 1979 that some sort of Soviet intervention in Afghanistan was likely to occur in the near future.[15] Though they were suspicious of Soviet intentions towards Afghanistan, the actual invasion came as a surprise to both Carter and Thatcher. On learning of the Soviet invasion, Carter's moral sensibilities were outraged. The president exclaimed to his closest advisers that the Soviet Union was 'raping' Afghanistan.[16] He went on to inform reporters that Soviet actions in Afghanistan constituted a 'grave threat to peace'.[17] Strategically, the president was equally as concerned for he believed it was the Soviet Union's objective to 'overthrow the existing Afghan government'.[18]

Such action was 'an extremely serious development'[19] and demonstrated a 'major new development in Soviet policy'.[20] It appeared from Carter's perspective as if the Soviet Union was 'executing a grand strategy to reach the warm waters of the Persian Gulf and encircle Western oil supplies'.[21] Soviet occupation of Afghanistan would provide Moscow with a 'deep penetration between Iran and Pakistan, and pose a threat to the rich oil fields of the Persian Gulf area and to the crucial waterways through which so much of the world's energy supplies had to pass'.[22]

Opinion in London was rather more mixed than that being publicly and privately expressed in Washington. For Michael Alexander, serving at this time as the prime minister's principal secretary for foreign affairs, Soviet actions reflected 'weakness' on Moscow's part. Given this, the invasion of Afghanistan was something not worth losing 'too much sleep' about. 'If the Russians were prepared to bleed themselves white in Afghanistan, good luck to them' was the advice he provided to Thatcher.[23] The prime minister did not view matters in such relaxed terms. For Thatcher the Soviet invasion of Afghanistan was a 'watershed' in international affairs which demonstrated the expansionist desires of the Soviet Union. As she reflected, 'I was less shocked than some by the invasion of Afghanistan. I had long understood that détente had been ruthlessly used by the Soviets to exploit western weakness and disarray. I knew the beast.'[24] With the prime minister interpreting matters so dramatically she looked to work jointly with Washington in fashioning a suitable response to Soviet actions. Finding the ideal response, however, would prove extremely difficult, so much so that by the middle of the year there remained little Anglo-American agreement on how to best respond to the Soviet Union's invasion of Afghanistan.

Carter initially limited his reaction to the Soviet invasion of Afghanistan to providing public condemnation of Moscow's actions. In an interview given to ABC news, the president accused the Soviet leadership of ordering the murder of Amin and violating international law. Carter followed this by writing personally to Brezhnev, protesting against Soviet actions and requesting that Soviet forces leave Afghanistan. Privately, however, the president well understood that Moscow would not leave Afghanistan willingly. As Carter appreciated, Soviet actions in Afghanistan simply reconfirmed that the Brezhnev Doctrine, which dictated that Moscow would uphold the territorial integrity of the communist world, remained the leitmotif of Soviet grand strategy.[25] The task then for Carter was to devise a strategy which would both encourage the Soviet Union to leave Afghanistan and ensure that Moscow would not replicate similar invasions of non-communist controlled areas of the world.

As 1980 began, a meeting of the Special Coordination Committee (SCC) was held in Washington to discuss the US response to the Soviet invasion of Afghanistan. Representatives from the Department of State, Department of Defense, CIA, JCS, White House and NSC were all present at this meeting. Following long discussion, the conclusion was reached that the Soviet Union had all but secured its position in Afghanistan. The best recourse was to undermine the Soviet position, which could be achieved by supporting the Afghan rebels that were fighting against Soviet forces. Such a course, however, was problematic given that the Afghan insurgency was clearly outgunned on the battlefield and was heavily reliant upon the assistance it received from Pakistan. In turn, Pakistan relied upon continued US military and economic support. It became apparent that if the Afghan insurgency was to stand any hope of undermining the Soviet position then additional assistance would have to be provided by Pakistan. In order to meet these additional burdens, the Pakistan government would look to Washington to cover the costs involved. Following further deliberation, the president agreed to provide additional support for the Pakistan government with a view to 'indirectly' assisting the Afghan insurgency.[26]

The Carter administration also looked at various ways in which they could 'punish' Moscow for its actions in Afghanistan in an effort to signal to the Kremlin that there would be broader consequences of their altering the geopolitical status quo. Washington surveyed a list of options which included withdrawing the SALT II treaty and imposing economic sanctions against Moscow. In an ironic sense, the Carter administration was following the methods of 'linkage' and 'leverage' as practised under the Nixon–Ford administrations which it had been so critical of during the 1976 election. The SALT II treaty, which was at this point awaiting ratification by the US Senate, was seen as the most useful tool to apply pressure against Moscow. Carter, sensing that the Senate would not ratify the agreement at this moment anyhow, delayed calling for a vote on SALT II ratification.[27]

Yet Carter opted against abandoning the SALT II treaty completely because he concluded that, even in spite of the Soviet Union's actions in Afghanistan, the treaty would ultimately be in the best interests of the United States. Carter remained wedded to the concept of nuclear arms limitation in spite of Moscow's actions in Afghanistan. As the president made clear to journalists, 'It's obvious to me that the SALT treaty is in the best interest of our country.'[28] And in a letter to members of the Senate, Carter suggested that a SALT II treaty was vital for America's 'own national security and the peace of the world'.[29] As such, the president privately informed Moscow that he would seek the ratification of the SALT II treaty once the 1980 election was over and the political hostility towards the Soviet Union inside the United States hopefully would have died down.[30] There remained important limits to the actions Carter was prepared to undertake against the Soviet Union at this juncture. As one scholar has noted, 'The basic motivations that had triggered the pursuit of SALT I a decade earlier, in essence, persisted.'[31]

As US–Soviet relations continued to deteriorate, the pressure upon Carter to undertake more robust action against the Soviet Union mounted. Moreover, the president remained concerned that if the Soviet Union believed it could 'get away' with its action inside Afghanistan then it may replicate such behaviour elsewhere. Deciding on a viable course of action remained hotly debated within the Carter administration and interdepartmental feuding reached volcanic proportions.[32] Vance argued that the administration should remain committed to the maintenance of superpower détente and could not allow incidents such as the Soviet invasion of Afghanistan to usher in a return to superpower confrontation and crisis. As Vance outlined, it was imperative to maintain a 'balanced policy toward the Soviet Union' and the United States had to 'avoid violent swings between trust and hysteria' in its dealings with Moscow. As such, the president's public condemnation of Soviet actions would suffice. If further action was to be undertaken, then this should be limited to political actions, such as temporarily withdrawing the US Ambassador from Moscow or passing a UN Security Council vote which requested the Soviet Union's withdrawal from Afghanistan.[33]

Vance's call for a limited response was first challenged and then ultimately defeated by the advice offered by Brzezinski. As the US national security adviser argued in a lengthy memorandum to the president, the Soviet Union's action in Afghanistan was a decisive moment in international affairs. Regardless of what actually motivated the Soviet Union's invasion of Afghanistan, the fact remained that this action had 'changed the strategic situation in the region; and we must take steps which will restore a balance'.[34] Brzezinski further argued that there was also a credibility issue at stake for the United States in the sense that the Soviet Union could not be allowed to invade sovereign states and expect its relationship with Washington to remain unaffected. Accordingly, the United States needed to respond with a 'sustained' and 'regional' effort. Whilst there was no need to 'freeze the US–Soviet relationship any further', Brzezinski suggested that efforts to improve relations with Moscow should not be undertaken either.[35] Emphasising his advice, Brzezinski wrote to the president suggesting that:

> These are painful and difficult issues. We will never know whether any of this could have been averted, but we do know one thing: if we do not respond in a timely fashion, the consequences of an inadequate response will be even more horrendous because our vital interest in the Middle East will soon be directly affected.[36]

Brzezinski's advice only added to the growing chorus inside and outside the White House that was calling for the president to respond more forcefully against the Soviet Union. Carter, however, remained unconvinced as to the type of action that he should undertake but gradually came to the conclusion that the purely political actions advocated by Vance would not suffice. Whilst agreeing to pursue a UN Security Council vote to call for a Soviet

The End of Détente

withdrawal from Afghanistan and approving the idea of potentially recalling the US Ambassador from Moscow, the president looked to also implement economic and political sanctions against the Soviet Union. Yet, as the president deliberated his response, it was becoming obvious to all that if sanctions against Moscow were to have a meaningful impact, then they would need to be enacted by a large multinational alliance.[37] London therefore soon found itself under pressure to support the president's proposals.

In London, Thatcher and her national security advisers watched developments in Washington, Moscow and Afghanistan closely. Thatcher agreed with the assessment that Soviet actions in Afghanistan threatened Western security interests. As the prime minister suggested to the president in January 1980, the Soviet Union would continue with a policy of expansion if the Kremlin believed it would go unopposed.[38] Coupled to this, the United Kingdom had long-established security, commercial and political connections with a number of states in central and Southeast Asia. British policy makers feared that Soviet moves in Afghanistan perhaps foreshadowed further Soviet expansion throughout the region. The repercussions of Soviet actions were viewed as threatening British interests much closer to home in the sense that the Kremlin could perhaps be emboldened by its actions in Afghanistan to pursue similar tactics when confronted with problems in Europe. Carrington warned the prime minister: 'the manner of the change is unprecedented and could have extremely serious repercussions. I think it is important that the West's response should be robust, lest the Russians are led to believe that such tactics pay off.'[39] On 8 January 1980, a meeting of the British cabinet was convened where a British response was discussed in detail. As the notes of the meeting recorded, those present had to decide whether any response against the Soviet Union should be 'limited to an expression of political disapproval, or be wider in scope and perhaps painful to the United Kingdom'. Regardless of the eventual course taken, the cabinet had to formulate a strategy whereby any measures against the Soviet Union would be 'enough to deter the Russians from repeating elsewhere the action they had taken in Afghanistan'.[40]

Whilst determining the actual specific measures to take against the Soviet Union, Thatcher, in an effort to signal to Moscow that similar actions to those in Afghanistan would not be tolerated in Europe, complained at length to the Soviet Ambassador to London about Soviet behaviour. The British prime minister followed this up in a damning letter to Brezhnev.[41] Publicly, Thatcher's response was equally as resolute as she lambasted Soviet actions and warned of the need to seriously reappraise Western policy vis-à-vis the Soviet Union. During one speech before the House of Commons, Thatcher's advice was clear:

> The invasion of Afghanistan and the exile of Professor Sakharov leave no room for illusion. They seriously weaken the basis for the fruitful conduct of East–West relations. They are deliberate acts of policy by the Soviet Government. Afghanistan is a symbol and a warning. It is not just a far distant country, which we can ignore because we face no local crisis in Europe. This is not the first time that the Russians have used force to invade a neighbour, used it massively, swiftly and callously in a pattern that bears the Soviet hallmark. It is not the first time that they have claimed to have been invited in by a Government who, on closer inspection, turned out not to exist, or whose leaders they subsequently killed. But it is the first time since the world war that they have sent tens of thousands of soldiers, backed by tanks and helicopter gunships, into a country outside the Warsaw Pact; an Islamic country, a member of the non-aligned movement, and a country that posed no conceivable threat to their country or their interests.[42]

It is this type of rhetoric which has led previous historians to conclude that Thatcher provided 'vigorous' support to Washington in responding to the Soviet invasion of Afghanistan.[43]

Yet on examining previous classified material, we learn that privately the prime minister was rather more reticent about what exactly the United Kingdom could or, more importantly, would do in response to the Soviet invasion of Afghanistan. Discussing British options with her foreign and Commonwealth secretary, Lord Carrington, Thatcher agreed that certain political actions could be undertaken. London, for example, refused to recognise the new Afghan government and continued to publicly condemn

Soviet actions. In the United Nations the British government supported Washington's efforts to obtain a UN Security Council statement condemning Soviet actions. And British missions abroad were instructed to make Soviet diplomats as 'uncomfortable' as possible in their dealings with the British.[44] Following further discussion with the Carter administration, London agreed to follow the American lead and increase British military and economic support for Pakistan and in turn assist in indirectly supporting the Afghan insurgency. Along with this, Thatcher confirmed that she would support the creation of an Anglo-American working group within NATO which would study ways in which the alliance could bring pressure to bear against Moscow.[45]

But the British government's response was far more limited than Washington desired. This is explained by a number of interlinked factors. First, any British response was complicated by its imperial legacy within the region. For instance, the British understood that the likes of Pakistan, India and Bangladesh would likely soon recognise the new regime in Afghanistan because they had 'to do business' with their neighbour. Accordingly, the British government would face political pressure from these allies to recognise the new Afghan regime and, more importantly yet, would find its own commercial and economic interests within the region undermined by continuing to refuse recognition.[46]

The prime minister was also aware that economic sanctions applied against Moscow were unlikely to produce meaningful policy consequences unless they were undertaken by a broad multilateral alliance. Yet it is important to recognise that economic sanctions had not been completely ruled out by Thatcher at this stage. Rather, she would only support economic sanctions if significant multilateral support for such action could be established.[47] Strategic factors also influenced Thatcher's decision making. Indeed, London remained deeply concerned that the United States could over-react to events in Afghanistan to the point that it would precipitate a crisis with Moscow which could escalate out of control with unknowable ramifications. Central then to Thatcher's response was ensuring full consultation with Washington in order to advocate that a measured and inherently limited response should be taken against Moscow.[48]

Thatcher had assumed the classic position of her predecessor Cold War prime ministers in that she counselled patience and looked to convince Washington not to pursue overly bellicose policies towards the Soviet Union which London believed US policy makers were more naturally inclined to pursue.

As London deliberated its response, the Carter administration moved ahead with its efforts to acquire international support for the imposition of economic sanctions against Moscow. Yet these efforts were already encountering difficulties as major allies such as the United Kingdom, West Germany and France all made their opposition known. Such a response did not sit well in Washington. As Carter complained in private, the European reaction had thus far been 'very weak'.[49] Yet from the perspective of European capitals, the imposition of economic sanctions against Moscow could have extremely severe consequences. The economic self-interest of the European powers at this point triumphed over common security concerns that they shared with Washington.

Nor was Washington immune to the effects that economic sanctions would have upon its own economic interests. Indeed, the domestic implications of pursuing economic sanctions against Moscow were keenly considered by the president, not least because 1980 was a general election year. As Carter was made aware, banning the export of certain agricultural products to the Soviet Union would hurt the economic interests of American farmers who held serious political power in the mid-western states which would be so vital in deciding the victor in the forthcoming presidential election. As Walter Mondale suggested to Carter, the United States had to be 'strong and firm' but that did not have to include the president having to 'commit political suicide'.[50] Carter's task then was to formulate a set of proposals which would be able to obtain international support but at the same time would neither inflict too much economic damage on America's allies (which was essential if support was to be obtained), nor hurt American economic interests too much (again vital for Carter's own political position). Domestic political calculations and alliance relations were threatening to undermine the prospects of sanctions even being applied against the Soviet Union.

In the weeks that followed, obtaining this international support for economic sanctions became the central task of the Carter administration. And it was to the British government that Washington looked for support. Warren Christopher was dispatched to London and met with Thatcher on 14 January 1980. Here, Christopher informed the prime minister that the United States would begin an embargo on the sale of meat and soya products to the Soviet Union. A ban on the sale of high technology would also be sought in the forthcoming weeks.[51] Thatcher's response was tentative and she tellingly refused to offer British support for these proposals during her discussions with Christopher. Following further deliberation it was evident that there was very little British enthusiasm for supporting these American proposals, largely because they would seriously harm British commercial and economic interests.[52]

Following further analysis in London, British officials concluded that the imposition of economic sanctions would hurt the Western economies more than it would the Soviet Union. Détente had proven to be economically bountiful to the UK Treasury and further study in London highlighted the severe negative consequences that pursuing an economic embargo against Moscow would have for British commercial interests. It was estimated, for instance, that an embargo on selling high technology would mean a loss of about 1 per cent of total British exports.[53] Such estimates did not even take into consideration possible Soviet retaliation, which the British government believed could include the suspension of Soviet oil sales. Such action was likely to push the barrel price of oil significantly upwards. Other Soviet counter-measures could include the suspension of gold, platinum and industrial diamond exports, which would hurt Britain's industrial production at a time of acute sensitivity in Britain's economic recovery.

In sum, Thatcher and her principle advisers were fully aware that any possible economic sanctions would have very real detrimental consequences for the British state. Worse yet, such economic pain would provide little political or strategic compensation as economic sanctions would not induce the Soviet Union to leave Afghanistan. Nor would economic sanctions deter Moscow from pursuing its interests in Europe by military means; the British believed that the Kremlin was deterred by the threat of force, not economic sanctions.[54] Ultimately, Thatcher was unable to establish a coherent strategic response towards the Soviet Union. Thatcher's indecision is illustrated by the following comment she made to Schmidt: 'There must be some penalty for a nation doing what the Soviet Union has and be seen to be some meaningful penalty but it isn't easy to work that meaningful penalty out. It isn't easy to decide exactly what that penalty shall be.'[55] As the British Ambassador to Moscow, Curtis Keeble, recollected, 'the problem with which the Soviet leadership confronted us that December was one of the oldest problems in international relations – the deterrence of aggression'.[56] So it would prove as the British government found itself at loggerheads with Washington over how to respond to the Soviet invasion of Afghanistan.

Defending British economic and commercial interests appeared to be Thatcher's main ambition instead of trying to establish a coordinated response with Washington in order to punish Moscow for its transgressions in Afghanistan. Yet British policy was not entirely motivated by the cynical pursuit of defending British economic and commercial interests. Rather, London was willing to accept a degree of economic pain on the proviso it led to political or strategic advantages vis-à-vis Moscow. London had therefore to calculate whether undertaking the proposed American sanctions was worth the potential economic costs involved. This is important to note because Thatcher's unwillingness to sign up to economic sanctions was not simply driven by economic calculations. Rather, the prime minister was prepared to countenance economic sanctions against Moscow if this would encourage a change in Soviet behaviour. The challenge then was for Carter to devise such an approach which London believed it could endorse.[57]

Accordingly, in London the Thatcher government concluded that it could not support the implementation of economic sanctions against Moscow at this time. Ultimately, British policy makers believed that economic sanctions would have little discernible impact upon Soviet policy towards Afghanistan or in relation to Europe. As one lengthy memorandum to Thatcher outlined, the Soviet Union was an ideological power which sought, through various avenues, a permanent revolution of the working classes which would then be directed from Moscow. Given this ideological mindset, the Kremlin would always look to safeguard existing communist influence and given that Amin's Afghan government appeared to be flirting with the idea of leaving the communist camp, it was to be expected that Moscow would take steps to ensure the maintenance of communist influence in Afghanistan. Given the nature of the largely closed Soviet economy, economic sanctions could not therefore be expected to bring about a meaningful alteration in Soviet foreign policy.[58] As the memorandum was implying, any economic sanctions against Moscow would be a futile act because they would not encourage the desired political outcomes.

Yet Thatcher had not entirely ruled out the possibility of implementing economic or broader political sanctions against Moscow. What is clear, however, is that the British prime minister would not agree to undertake any action hastily and, moreover, wanted economic sanctions to be coordinated within the framework of a broad alliance. Thatcher now informed Washington that if she was to undertake political punishments against the Soviet Union, such as cancelling the forthcoming visit of the Soviet foreign minister, Andrei Gromyko, to London or withdrawing the British Ambassador to Moscow, then the rest of the NATO alliance would have to undertake similar action. At the heart of Thatcher's response was the attempt to ensure that the British government did not find itself out of kilter with its allies in respect of being perceived as either too bellicose or too weak in its response. Striking this careful balance was central to the British government's reaction at this time.[59]

In Washington the Carter administration found itself under increased domestic pressure to pursue a more vigorous course against Moscow. On meeting with a number of political advisers the president was urged to be 'even more forceful' in responding to the Soviet invasion of Afghanistan.[60] Edward Kennedy, challenging Carter for the Democratic nomination for the presidency, was vocally criticising the president for his supposedly inept handling of US foreign policy. Carter's Republican opponents went even further when they alleged that Carter's weak foreign policy had emboldened Moscow to the point that the Kremlin believed it could invade its neighbours without facing serious retribution.[61]

This domestic pressure against Carter only encouraged him to remain committed to implementing political and economic sanctions against Moscow. The British government, which had earlier been reluctant to pursue such sanctions, now found itself under increased US diplomatic pressure to agree to the measures. Brzezinski was thus dispatched to London to liaise personally with Thatcher, where he was instructed to press the American case. Again though, the British reiterated their earlier position that their support was contingent upon other countries supporting these sanctions. British resistance to American calls for action was a consistent and growing political nuisance for the president. The Carter administration nonetheless remained convinced that London had to agree to such measures if any meaningful punishment against Moscow was to be enacted. Moreover, if London could be won over it was believed other countries would do likewise and follow Washington's lead. In the forthcoming weeks a sterner line with London would be pursued to overcome Thatcher's continuing reluctance.[62]

Secretary Vance's visit to London in February 1980 gave the United States the opportunity to win this required British support. Again little agreement between the two sides was to be found. Whilst Thatcher indicated that she was prepared to take a 'bold' and 'strong' response to the Soviet invasion of Afghanistan, she also warned that NATO's response could be a '9-day wonder' which would 'dwindle after six months'. Given such circumstances, it was preferable for the United States and United Kingdom to avoid undertaking sanctions against Moscow. Vance assured the British prime minister that Carter's intention was to create a multilateral response against the Soviet Union but it was telling that the US secretary of state could not guarantee that Washington could bring about this multinational support which London deemed vital if it was to support the imposition of economic sanctions against Moscow.[63] Thatcher's clever rhetoric had allowed her to present the image of solidarity with Washington but she had avoided making any firm commitments. The British prime minister had assumed a wait and see policy whereby the United Kingdom would not commit to any action until a multilateral response had crystallised.

Back in Washington, the deterioration of US–Soviet relations only encouraged Carter to listen to the views of Brzezinski and to assume a firmer position against the Soviet Union. Central to this was increasing the US defence budget, improving the levels of defence cooperation within the NATO alliance, and implementing a series of economic and political sanctions against Moscow.[64] It was to the NATO alliance that Washington looked for support for this new approach against the Soviet Union. It never materialised, however, as both France and West Germany publicly announced that they would not support Washington's proposed economic sanctions against the Soviet Union. Carter could not even secure NATO-wide agreement for its members to attend a NATO summit where a unified response to the Soviet Union's invasion of Afghanistan would be discussed. With Carter failing to win approval from Giscard and Schmidt, the pressure on Thatcher to support Washington's policies therefore mounted.[65] In an effort to win London's support, Carter dispatched a scathing letter to the prime minister:

> To be frank, I am concerned about the impression of disarray in the West and the fact that leaders of the Soviet Union may draw dangerous conclusions from it. You know that there is a sense of deep disappointment in the United States over the European response to date to developments which in the first instance threaten European security more directly than our own. I personally cannot accept the concept of a divisible détente which insulates our European allies' relations with the Soviet Union from the response required to Soviet aggression.[66]

Nicholas Henderson reinforced the impression that American patience with London was wearing thin. As he warned from Washington, 'American opinion is turning nastily against the Allies' and whilst 'originally the UK was largely exempt from this criticism', this could 'no longer be the case'.[67]

This American pressure created considerable concern in London that a more serious Anglo-American confrontation would soon materialise. As a cabinet member within the Heath government, Thatcher had first-hand experience of how US–European quarrels could seriously hurt British interests, as most obviously demonstrated during Kissinger's 'Year of Europe' scheme in 1973. Key advisers to the prime minister also well remembered the detrimental consequences that broader US–European disagreements could have for the United Kingdom. Avoiding a serious diplomatic dispute with Washington remained an important aspect of British policy at this stage.[68]

Consequently, Thatcher sought to quell this simmering US–European quarrel and urged the president to avoid insisting upon a NATO conference. Instead, a NATO response could be agreed at a less public forum which would allow policy to be analysed and agreed to without the added pressure that an international conference brings with it. The British government looked at ways in which pressure could be applied to the Soviet Union that could be supported by the entire NATO alliance. Few options materialised as London well understood that they were essentially powerless to remove the Soviet Union from Afghanistan. Economic sanctions were perceived to be too costly and would not win approval from West Germany or France and thus threatened to create a very public fracture within the NATO alliance.[69] Accordingly, all Thatcher could suggest was that the relaxation of East–West tension would now have to end. A long-term build-up of Western forces would be required that would convince 'The Soviet leaders . . . that they cannot continue to enjoy détente in East–West relations while flouting it in the Third World.'[70] Platitudes aside, Thatcher could offer nothing of substance in the short term which would alleviate the domestic pressure against the Carter administration or reverse the Soviet occupation of Afghanistan.

London, however, came under sustained pressure from Washington to respond positively to American proposals and over the next several months this was a continual feature of US policy towards London. Harold Brown pursued the matter vigorously in discussion with Thatcher in June 1980. During follow up discussions with his opposite number, Francis Pym, Brown again pushed the argument that the United Kingdom had to agree to economic

The End of Détente

sanctions against Moscow. By August, this sustained US pressure had achieved some success as the British government agreed to limit sales of high technology to the Soviet Union. Eventually British opposition was worn down by concerted American pressure. Yet British agreement remained limited as London continually sought to negotiate with Washington what should and should not be included in the economic sanctions against Moscow. The definition of 'high technology' was suitably elastic that British industry was able to keep selling significant amounts of material to the Soviet Union.[71] In sum, even though Washington had secured agreement from London to implement economic sanctions against Moscow, the delay in achieving this and the limited intensity of the sanctions meant this was a pyrrhic diplomatic victory for the Carter administration. As the president had outlined to the American people during his inaugural address, there were clearly limits to American power and influence.[72] As this episode revealed, this applied to handling American allies: even those that shared a special relationship with Washington could not be easily cajoled into following Carter's lead.

The Moscow Olympics

Implementing economic sanctions against Moscow was only one element of Carter's response to the Soviet invasion of Afghanistan. Political punishments were also sought and the Carter administration investigated whether they could establish an international boycott of the forthcoming summer Olympic Games which were set to be held in Moscow. Walter Mondale was particularly enthusiastic about an Olympic boycott and wrote to the president soon after the Soviet invasion of Afghanistan: 'I hope we would really go after the Olympics – I don't see why that is sacrosanct.'[73] The president agreed. Yet Carter also understood that for a boycott to achieve maximum political effect it required the support of as many other nations as possible.[74] Winning support for a mass boycott became Carter's objective and on 20 January 1980 the president announced that US athletes would not attend the Moscow Games if Soviet troops remained in Afghanistan. In a message to the United Kingdom and other countries, Carter ratcheted up the rhetoric:

> I regard the Soviet invasion and the attempted suppression of Afghanistan as a serious violation of international law and an extremely serious threat to world peace. This invasion also endangers neighbouring independent countries and access to a major part of the world's oil supplies. It therefore threatens our own national security, as well as the security of the region and the entire world.[75]

Soon after this message Washington officially requested London's support in organising a mass boycott of the forthcoming Moscow Olympic Games.

This American request placed the Thatcher government in a quandary. Whilst the prime minister personally supported a boycott of the Olympic Games she was actually unable to legally prevent the participation of British athletes at the Games. British participation hinged upon the decision of the British Olympic Association. The prime minister would have to win the British Olympic Association's support if she was to follow Carter and boycott the forthcoming Olympic Games.[76] Moreover, the prime minister would support a boycott of the Olympic Games only if the president was able to ensure that 'other Allies did likewise'.[77]

This is not to say that the British prime minister would not do her part to establish this multinational alliance that would boycott the Olympic Games. Thatcher was determined to create such an alliance and set about achieving this task in the following weeks. Such enthusiasm was driven by her genuine desire to see Moscow punished for invading Afghanistan but this type of punishment had the additional benefit of not actually having the costly side effects that pursuing economic sanctions against Moscow would have for British interests. Thatcher looked to garner international support for establishing an alternative venue for the Olympic Games. Following extensive deliberation she decided that Montreal should be the alternate host of the Games and immediately began to lobby international leaders to support her plans. Speaking with Helmut Schmidt, Thatcher argued that the Soviet Union's actions in Afghanistan contradicted the 'Olympic Spirit' and the Games should be moved to Montreal. Schmidt's response was evasive and indicative of the lukewarm support that existed throughout the Western alliance for boycotting the Moscow Games.[78] If a successful mass boycott was to be established, then more creative diplomacy was evidently required from both London and Washington.

Whilst Thatcher continued to seek support for changing the venue of the Olympic Games, Washington continued to apply political pressure on the prime minister to announce Britain's withdrawal from the Moscow Games. Carter wrote to Thatcher and suggested that she needed to apply pressure against the British Olympic Association to convince it to boycott the forthcoming Games. As the president outlined, he did not have the authority to prevent US participation in the Games but his appeal for a boycott to the US Olympic Association had provided fruitful results. The prime minister should follow suit and, Carter assured Thatcher, similarly positive results would be forthcoming.[79] This American pressure encouraged the prime minister to contact Sir Denis Follows, the Chairman of the British Olympic Association. Sir Denis, however, would likely prove to be a difficult patron given he had already publicly stated that British participation in the Olympic Games should go ahead.[80] Thatcher wrote to Sir Denis and requested that he approach the International Olympic Committee (IOC) to suggest that the Games be moved from Moscow. If the IOC refused, Thatcher asked Sir Denis to instruct British athletes to boycott the Moscow Games.[81] Sir Denis was to disappoint the prime minister. In a polite but firm letter to Thatcher, Sir Denis informed the prime minister that it was impossible to organise an alternative venue for the Games at such short notice. However, he promised to pass the prime minister's letter on to the other board members of the British Olympic Association for further consultation.[82] Further deliberation did not result in Sir Denis altering his position as he again wrote to Thatcher informing her that the British Olympic Association did not feel it had sufficient grounds in which to advocate moving the Games away from Moscow. Second, Sir Denis made it clear that he would not advocate for a boycott of the forthcoming Games. In a follow-up letter to the prime minister, Sir Denis again reiterated this position.[83]

All of this was deeply irritating for the prime minister but legal avenues to override Sir Denis's opposition were now explored. For instance, Thatcher was informed that the British government could block the visa applications of British athletes who were set to travel to Moscow to compete in the Games. She decided against such action, however, concluding that this would likely create tremendous legal and political problems which she would rather avoid. More to the point, the prime minister believed that her actions would be challenged in the High Court and any visa denials would probably be reversed. Such action would not only be politically costly but also likely unsuccessful. As Thatcher well understood, she was to all intents and purposes powerless to move the Olympic Games from Moscow or even prevent British participation in them. As she informed the Australian prime minister, Malcolm Fraser, the best she could do now was to publicly advise British athletes not to participate in the Games.[84]

In spite of Thatcher's political predicament, Carter remained determined to win London's support to boycott the Olympic Games. During Vance's visit to London in February 1980 the US secretary of state pressed the prime minister on the Olympic boycott. The response was not what Washington desired as Thatcher explained in great detail that whilst she continued to support the president's ambition of boycotting the Olympic Games, she could not actually prevent British participation. Furthermore, Thatcher subtly indicated to Vance that British attendance at the Games was probable given the fact that the British Olympic Association had indicated that they would proceed with their plans to participate in the Moscow Games. All that Thatcher could offer was her ongoing pubic advocacy of an Olympic boycott.[85]

Learning of this news, Carter called for another meeting of the SCC to discuss the proposed Olympic boycott. Conscious that few American allies would endorse a boycott of the Games, they agreed that America would be better placed lobbying for an alternative venue to be established. American officials now lobbied

The End of Détente

the IOC to move the Games from Moscow to Montreal. In order to win support, Carter issued a public declaration that the Soviet Union had until 20 February 1980 to withdraw its troops from Afghanistan or the United States would boycott the forthcoming Olympic Games. As the Carter administration was aware, time was of the essence, so it was decided that Ambassador Brewster was to contact Thatcher directly to encourage her to continue to pressurise the British Olympic Association to agree to attend the alternative Games in Montreal. But Carter's hopes of achieving major international support to move the Olympic Games were shattered when the IOC announced that they would not countenance moving the Games from Moscow. A boycott of the Games was therefore the only option now open to the president.[86]

Achieving a mass boycott of the Moscow Games looked remote at this point as the president was informed that key European allies such as Britain, France and West Germany all looked set to attend the Games. In addition, a preliminary meeting between the United States and the European members of NATO had proven unproductive. Indeed, during this meeting the British had taken away the impression that Washington was threatening to be less cooperative in other fields of US–European interaction if a coordinated response in boycotting the Olympic Games could not be found.[87] British discussions with their European allies only further demonstrated that there was no consensus within the Western alliance. By the end of February 1980 the British government had concluded that there existed little possibility that a mass boycott of the Moscow Games would be achieved and that British athletes would likely attend the Games. Indeed, this was confirmed when the British Olympic Association publicly announced on 20 March 1980 that British athletes would attend the Games.[88]

In an effort to quell suspicion in Washington about London's lack of support for the Olympic boycott, Thatcher provided a number of public and private assurances that she would continue to advocate that British athletes boycott the forthcoming Olympic Games. Thatcher intensified her campaign to convince both the British Olympic Association and individual athletes not to attend. Contrary to the claim in her memoir that British athletes 'were left free to make up their own minds' about attending the Games, previously classified documentation reveals that a far more assertive position was taken by the British government to convince British athletes not to attend.[89] For example, in an effort to obtain political leverage over the British Olympic Association the prime minister asked Land Rover, the automobile manufacturer, to withdraw its sponsorship from the British Olympic team. Such action resulted in a considerable reduction in the level of sponsorship provided to British athletes but would still prove too little incentive to change the decision of the British Olympic Association to send a team to the Games.[90] Officials working on behalf of the Thatcher government also lobbied individual athletes not to attend.[91] And in last-ditch effort to convince the British Olympic Association to boycott the Games, Thatcher dispatched another letter to Sir Denis Follows:

> The Games will serve the propaganda needs of the Soviet Government. There is no effective palliative, such as cutting out the ceremonies. I remain firmly convinced that it is neither in our national nor in the wider Western interest for Britain to take part in the Games in Moscow. As a sporting event, the Games cannot now satisfy the aspirations of our sportsmen and women. British attendance at Moscow can only serve to frustrate the interests of Britain.[92]

Such efforts proved unpersuasive as the British Olympic Association continued to maintain that it would send its athletes to the Games. And so it did, as a full British team were in attendance when the Games began on 19 July 1980. Sir Denis Follows had essentially 'outplayed Mrs Thatcher' and successfully resisted all of the political pressure exerted against the British Olympic Association to ensure British participation in the Games.[93]

Douglas Hurd reflected that trying to organise a boycott of the Olympic Games was 'the most foolish task' that he had ever been 'entrusted to as a minister', saying:

> I knew little about the world of athletics, but enough to realise from the start that neither administrators nor athletes were likely to abandon for political reasons an occasion in which they had already invested so much work and ambition.[94]

Events proved Hurd correct as the United Kingdom along with seven of the EEC Nine attended the Games. The United States along with West Germany boycotted the Games. The Western alliance presented an image to the international community at large that it was unable even to coordinate a boycott of the Olympic Games. Worse yet, the partial boycott did not significantly reduce the spectacle of the Games. The attendance of so many of America's key allies at the Moscow Games highlighted Carter's lack of influence over the alliance and provided a further example of his unsuccessful alliance diplomacy. Carter had, as one commentator suggested, 'dropped the torch' in handling the Olympic boycott.[95]

Iranian hostage crisis

Following the Shah of Iran's overthrow in February 1979, he had been admitted to the United States for medical treatment. The Iranian revolutionaries, under the direction of Ayatollah Khomeini, demanded that the Shah be returned to Iran to stand trial for his alleged crimes during his years in power. Following months of wrangling and heightened instability in Iran, the Khomeini regime had lost patience with Washington. In an effort to coerce Washington into deporting the Shah, the Khomeini regime orchestrated the takeover of the American Embassy in Tehran in November 1979 and subsequently kidnapped American personnel based at the Embassy. The Carter administration was now faced with the predicament of American citizens being held captive and publicly paraded before the television cameras in a sign of America's powerlessness to protect its own citizens.[96]

For Carter the hostage situation quickly turned into a domestic nightmare as his political opponents attacked his handling of the crisis. Edward Kennedy, contesting the Democratic nomination for the presidency, even accused the president of 'leading the country into war' and none too subtly alleged that the Soviet invasion of Afghanistan and the taking of American hostages in Iran were the president's fault.[97] As the Iranian hostage situation dragged on throughout the rest of the year it became a growing international and domestic burden for Carter. 'It is a crisis for your presidency, for the hostages and for our country's image around the world', Hamilton Jordan warned the president.[98] The Anglo-American relationship would prove just as frustrating for Washington as the Thatcher government failed to provide the type and level of support which the president desired. It is to this episode that we now turn.

Throughout the entire Iranian hostage crisis, uppermost in Carter's mind was achieving the timely and safe release of the American hostages. As Carter later claimed, his disinclination to utilise military force to resolve the hostage situation was influenced by the twin concerns about the hostages' safety and his conviction that the utilisation of force would likely lead to the deaths of innocent civilians which he found morally difficult to justify.[99] Negotiating the safe release of the hostages remained Carter's preferred course of action for the time being. Initial diplomatic efforts did not, however, look promising as a United Nations mission to Iran headed by Kurt Waldheim was, in the president's words, 'a complete failure'.[100] In the assessment of Hamilton Jordan, Waldheim had been 'apologetic, defensive and at points obsequious' in his discussions with the Iranian Revolutionary Council, which only undermined American efforts to convince the Ayatollah to safely release the American hostages.[101] The president looked for political support internationally and he naturally turned to London. Rhetorical support was forthcoming as Thatcher provided a series of damning speeches whereby she condemned the kidnappings and urged the release of the American hostages. Similarly, in private communication the prime minister assured the president of her full support.[102]

Anglo-American solidarity was evident in the public sphere, so much so that Carter retrospectively reflected that Thatcher 'was strong and wholly supportive' of his handling of the Iranian hostage crisis.[103] This was certainly the case publicly but privately Anglo-American diplomacy was much more complicated. Over the course of the following weeks it became evident in Washington that the Thatcher government would not support more vigorous action against Tehran. Thatcher herself concluded that economic sanctions would only fuel the increasingly anti-Western rhetoric emanating out of Tehran and increase the probability that the American hostages would be physically harmed. Military action, such as implementing a blockade of Iran, would lead to similar consequences. A hostage rescue mission was deemed incredibly risky if not impossible to successfully accomplish. Diplomacy between Washington and Tehran was reminiscent of the dialogue of the deaf. As one analyst noted, 'How does a born-again Christian deal with a born-again Moslem?'[104] As Thatcher privately recognised, the options available to Carter left him in 'an impossible position'.[105]

The imposition of economic sanctions, which were at that time being proposed by the United States in the United Nations Security Council, especially troubled London. Mirroring concerns in relation to the debate about economic sanctions against Moscow, the British government feared that such action would actually hurt the Western position more than it would damage Tehran. As a tool of coercive diplomacy London believed economic sanctions would not actually convince Tehran to release the American hostages. Following a meeting with Lord Carrington, Thatcher instructed her foreign and Commonwealth secretary to assume the position that if the United Nations failed to approve the current economic sanctions against Iran then the United Kingdom would not support their implementation on an Anglo-American basis.[106]

Events in Afghanistan, however, convinced Thatcher that both the United States and United Kingdom could improve relations with the Ayatollah and help lead to the successful release of the American hostages. With Afghanistan bordering Iran, and Moscow having invaded Afghanistan to ostensibly quell the rise of Islamic fundamentalism, London believed that this would convince the Iranian regime that it had to avoid risking the ire of Moscow. Intelligence reports at the beginning of 1980 indicated that Soviet forces were indeed taking up positions on the Afghanistan border with Iran. Consequently, if the Iranians were made aware of this fact, they would seek allies to signal to Moscow just how costly an invasion of Iran would be.[107] The FCO was informed: 'The prime minister has expressed particular interest in using the crisis [in Afghanistan] to get the Ayatollah to come closer to the Western point of view.'[108] Central to this task then was convincing the Carter administration that the Soviet invasion of Afghanistan actually provided an opportunity to repair relations with Tehran.

Thatcher was to be quickly disappointed. On meeting with Warren Christopher, the prime minister learned that Washington did not see how the Soviet invasion of Afghanistan could be utilised in relation to the Iranian hostage situation.[109] Instead, Christopher focused on winning British support for a series of economic sanctions to be implemented against Tehran. This placed Thatcher in a difficult predicament for she personally sympathised with the president's position but fully understood that economic sanctions would hurt British interests and kill any immediate hope of improving relations with Tehran. More to the point, she believed that economic sanctions would have little effect in convincing Tehran to release the American hostages. Thatcher therefore carefully reiterated her support for the president but also made it clear that such support did not at this point in time extend to implementing economic sanctions against Iran. Instead, the prime minister again suggested that Washington had to exploit the recent invasion of Afghanistan to their advantage vis-à-vis Tehran.[110]

These two competing ideas as to how to successfully release the American hostages spilled over into in the broader international arena as both London and Washington undertook efforts to convince their mutual allies to support their respective approaches towards Tehran. A rivalry between London and Washington was therefore emerging at this point. Washington sought international support for implementing economic sanctions against Iran; London, meanwhile, sought to convince these same states that they should seek to negotiate the release of the American hostages by convincing Iran that the recent invasion of Afghanistan meant that Tehran required friendlier relations with the West. To make her case, Thatcher discussed the predicament with Helmut Schmidt and informed him that Carter's proposals would not work and could not, for legal reasons, actually be implemented by the British government. Schmidt, also conscious that the proposed sanctions would hurt significant West German economic interests, agreed with the prime minister's position.[111] The

The End of Détente

decision by Thatcher and Schmidt not to support Carter at this point crucially undermined the president's efforts to impose multinational economic sanctions against Iran, demonstrating Carter's political weakness vis-à-vis his most important allies and highlighting the complexity of alliance relations.

As this diplomacy continued, Vance met with Thatcher in February 1980 where he requested that London support the proposed economic sanctions against Iran. It was during this meeting, however, that Vance revealed a number of important developments that had occurred bilaterally between Washington and Tehran. Vance informed Thatcher that contact with Iran indicated that Tehran would release the American hostages on condition that a commission would be established that would produce a study on the Shah's time in power. Vance explained how this would work:

> When the document was complete, the Commission would meet the Revolutionary Council in Tehran and tell them that before the document could be taken back to New York [to the UN], the hostages would have to be handed over to the custody of the Iranian Government and lodged either in a hospital or in the foreign ministry with Mr Laingen. The Commission would not return to New York until the hostages had been handed over. Once the hostages had been handed over, the Commission would return to New York and communicate the preliminary document to the Secretary General. It would be published within two days. The hostages would be released by the Iranian Government on the day that the document was published.[112]

Vance was hopeful that this approach would lead to the successful release of the hostages and even predicted that 'the hostages might be released within about two weeks'.[113] As history informs us, Vance was wrong to have been so optimistic at this stage as the American hostages remained captive in Iran for nearly another year. In Washington the pressure on Carter to resolve the hostage situation was mounting from all directions. Media coverage of the hostage crisis was particularly intense as nightly television and newspaper comment turned sharply critical of Carter's handling of the crisis. As Jody Powell recalled in a rather bitter lament, journalists were 'busy . . . kicking Carter's teeth in every time he opened his mouth'.[114]

Unfair or not, the media coverage accurately reported the growing division amongst the president's advisers on how to solve the hostage situation. Indeed, the State Department was invested in a diplomatic solution whereas others within the administration were calling for a more forthright approach, namely economic sanctions followed by a rescue attempt. This split in the administration was personified in the ever deepening feud between Vance and Brzezinski. Their bureaucratic rivalry had steadily worsened during the previous three years but would come to its finale in 1980 as Brzezinski's advocacy of a harder line both towards the Soviet Union and in responding to the hostage situation in Iran triumphed. In large measure Brzezinski's line of argument was successful because the president himself had grown increasingly frustrated with what he saw as the State Department's 'inertia' and the almost 'total lack of initiative or innovation' in policy creation or execution.[115] The institutional rivalry between Vance and Brzezinski was finally settled with the national security adviser emerging victorious. As Madeleine Albright (US secretary of state 1997–2001), who at the time worked for Brzezinski's NSC, laconically noted, 'the only time the NSC and State Department worked together well was when Henry Kissinger was in charge of both'.[116]

By March 1980 the president was contemplating whether or not to authorise a rescue attempt of the hostages. More serious military proposals, such as introducing a naval blockade or the mining of Iranian waters, were also being considered. But undermining all of these military options was the simple fact that none would actually deliver what the president wanted, namely the safe return of the American hostages. The rescue mission was the 'best of a lousy set of options', Harold Brown suggested.[117] Vance, fearful that any military moves would likely lead to the hostages being murdered in retaliation, argued that diplomatic efforts should persist. As Vance had told Thatcher in December 1979 'the consequences of any other course of action [other than continued negotiations with Tehran] both for the hostages and for everyone else could only be very grave'.[118] Vance's influence with the president was, however, waning.

The End of Détente

On 8 April 1980 Carter announced that the United States was formally severing diplomatic ties with Iran and would implement a series of economic sanctions. Yet, as Warren Christopher recounts, whilst this 'seemed to us the right approach . . . others in government . . . had something more dramatic in mind'.[119] In fact the president had concluded that negotiations would not result in the safe release of the American hostages. 'We could no longer afford to depend on diplomacy. I decided to act', Carter remembered.[120] Following further deliberation, and advice from Brzezinski, Brown, Stansfield Turner (director of the CIA), David Jones (chairman of the JCS) and Vice President Mondale, the president authorised Operation Eagle Claw. This would involve the infiltration of Iran by US Army Rangers who would attempt to free the hostages.[121]

Operation Eagle Claw was given the go-ahead even though Vance urged the president to abandon the mission. Such was Vance's opposition to the proposed mission, he offered to resign his office if the operation was given the go-ahead. Carter concluded that the rescue mission was worth attempting even if it led to Vance's resignation and on 24 April 1980 the operation began. However, it soon encountered difficulties. In keeping with Vance's warning that during such operations 'something always goes wrong', one of the eight helicopters being utilised in the mission encountered technical trouble.[122] A second helicopter flew into a sandstorm, which caused it mechanical difficulties. A third helicopter then suffered problems and on the advice of the commanding officer, Colonel Charles Beckwith, the president aborted the mission. Magnifying this calamity was the fact that on leaving the mission area a helicopter collided with one of the C-130 refuelling aircraft with the loss of eight American personnel.[123] All that Carter could do now was to lament in his diary that 'The cancellation of our mission was caused by a strange series of mishaps, almost completely unpredictable.'[124] Given the ramifications of the failed rescue mission, it is little wonder that Carter remembers the day of 24 April 1980 as 'one of the worst of my life'.[125]

All London could do was express sympathy with Carter's predicament. The prime minister wrote in her retirement, 'I felt America's wound as if it were Britain's own; and in a sense it was, for anyone exposed to American weakness increased ours.'[126] Maybe so, but platitudes aside there was to be little meaningful British action in support of the United States. Only following 'pressure' from Washington did Thatcher agree to limited sanctions against Iran.[127] Tellingly, these sanctions were only enacted on 23 April 1980, one day prior to the hostage rescue mission, which suggests that the Carter administration did not expect the sanctions to lead to the release of the American hostages.[128]

The Carter administration had originally decided not to provide London with prior notification of the American rescue mission. However, British military personnel stationed in Oman had detected US aircraft landing in the area and began to raise questions as to the American military activity in the region (London guessed correctly that this was a build-up to a hostage rescue). Fearing that if London probed this matter further it would raise unwarranted attention as to American intentions vis-à-vis Iran, the president ordered Warren Christopher to personally visit the prime minister and to inform her of the impending mission. Christopher arrived in England and met with Thatcher and Carrington at the prime minister's country residence at Chequers. When confronted with his information, Thatcher and Carrington wished Christopher good luck and informed him that the British would cease communication as to why US planes were moving through Oman.[129]

This episode is revealing in that it demonstrates both the diminished importance of the Anglo-American relationship and its continued relevance. If it had not been for a British officer in Oman witnessing the American military presence, the Thatcher government would have remained oblivious to the US rescue mission. This demonstrates that Washington did not believe the British significantly important to warrant prior notification. This was quite a marked fall given that even during the Nixon–Kissinger years when Washington had routinely ignored London, the Nixon administration had usually informed London about any major military undertakings it was planning.[130] Britain's diminished importance in the last decade had obvious ramifications for the amount of communication it could now enjoy with Washington. And with the British government excluded it could not advise Washington on other courses of action. In essence, Britain's international decline meant that the opportunity to influence the US government was now much diminished, which undermined the traditional idea in British elite policy making circles that London could 'guide' US foreign policy. There was a political and strategic cost to dwindling international influence which the US hostage rescue mission ably demonstrated.

Efforts at further mediation throughout the summer of 1980 failed to release the American hostages. The Iran–Iraq war which erupted in September 1980 was seen as something which could be exploited to help release the hostages. In particular, Iran's military relied upon American hardware that had been sold to Iran during the Shah's rule. Thus, Iran would require replacement parts and material for the damage sustained in the increasingly violent war with Iraq. Exploiting such reliance, however, proved ineffective as the Iranian leadership accused the US government of in fact provoking Iraq's attack against Iran. Consequently, it would not be until Carter left office on 31 January 1981 that the hostages were finally released.[131] The entire episode had poisoned Carter's last year in power and contributed to his heavy defeat by Ronald Reagan in the November 1980 election. The level of support offered by London to the Carter administration throughout the hostage crisis disappointed and irritated policy makers in Washington. Walter Mondale recalled that the Iranian hostage situation:

> exposed the difficulties of international cooperation against an extremist threat. Our ability to press for a peaceful, effective resolution with the radicals turned in part on the willingness of other Western nations to help us bring pressure on Iran, and we never got the cooperation we needed.[132]

As Warren Christopher reflected, America's allies had very publicly distanced themselves from the hostage rescue effort.[133] Indeed, London had ensured that its support for the Carter administration was limited to public speeches of sympathy. Again then, Thatcher was strong on rhetorical support but was less forthcoming in providing material assistance.

Trident agreement

This chapter has thus far examined the American and British responses to moments of international crisis. As shown above, considerable disagreement existed between the two governments. Yet, considerable cooperation between the two countries continued simultaneously. In the realm of nuclear weapons cooperation the two countries reached agreement in the summer of 1980 for the United States to sell the British government Trident C4 as a replacement for its ageing force of Polaris SLBMs. It is to this decision which the chapter now turns.

During Thatcher's premiership, matters related to Britain's nuclear weapons were dealt with by an exclusive group of ministers within the British cabinet. Membership of the 'Restricted Ministerial Meetings' included Peter Carrington (foreign and Commonwealth secretary), Francis Pym (defence secretary), Geoffrey Howe (Chancellor of the Exchequer) and Willie Whitelaw (home secretary). Thatcher's approach to British nuclear weapons policy followed a tradition set by Clement Attlee (prime minister 1945–51) whereby an exclusive group of ministers within the cabinet would discuss nuclear-related matters. A group named 'MISC 7' was established and it was here that deciding on a successor system to Polaris was deliberated.[134]

That Thatcher accepted Britain needed to find a successor system to Polaris was never seriously questioned. For the prime minister, Britain's possession of strategic nuclear weapons was intrinsically linked to upholding Britain's international security. Thatcher accepted the argument that 'NATO's strategy is above all one of deterrence, in which the possession of nuclear weapons plays a key part. If we ever have to face using them, the strategy will have failed in its prime purpose.'[135] The MOD advised the prime minister that British possession of nuclear weapons was vital because:

> Britain commits all its nuclear capability to NATO in conformity with concepts of collective deterrence worked out in [the] joint forum of the Nuclear Planning Group. The decisive consideration in favour of a British capability that is ultimately independent is the contribution it makes to NATO's strategy of deterrence and thus to our own national security.[136]

Along with such considerations, the British government deemed it essential to retain an 'independent' strategic nuclear weapons capability not least because it could act as an insurance policy against the United States 'backing down' in a nuclear confrontation with the Soviet Union and leaving the United Kingdom to fend for itself against the Soviet behemoth.[137] As the MOD outlined to the prime minister:

> A Soviet leadership – perhaps much changed in character from today's, perhaps also operating amid the pressures of turbulent internal or external circumstances might believe that at some point as a conflict developed the determination of the United States might waver ... The nuclear strengths of Britain or France may seem modest by comparison with the superpower armouries but the damage they could inflict is in absolute terms immense. (A single Polaris submarine carries more explosive power than all the munitions used in World War II). An adversary assessing the consequences of possible aggression in Europe would have to regard a NATO defence containing these powerful independent elements as a harder one to predict, and a more dangerous one to assail, than one in which nuclear retaliatory power rested in United States hands alone.[138]

It was this type of argument that Thatcher accepted and that informed her decision to obtain a successor system to Polaris. Updating Britain's strategic nuclear weapons capability was never in question. The only thing to debate in Thatcher's mind was the preferred successor system.[139]

There were several viable choices available for replacing Polaris. The MOD explained the options open to the prime minister in a long briefing memorandum where the possibilities included the creation of some sort of Anglo-French system, the introduction of a new air-launched force, the building of a land-launched system or purchasing a new SLBM system (such as Trident C4). Following extensive deliberation the Thatcher government endorsed Callaghan's earlier decision that Trident C4 was the preferable replacement for Polaris for it provided the most credible deterrent at an acceptable financial level.[140]

Callaghan had already obtained a 'private agreement' with Carter to purchase Trident C4 but its sale was now complicated by a number of interrelated factors, not least the perennial concern within British circles that the Carter administration would allow the Anglo-American nuclear relationship to be undermined by Washington's ambition of finalising a SALT II agreement with Moscow. British fears were based upon the fact that President Carter appeared to be reneging on his October 1979 assurance that he would react in an 'affirmative' manner which was 'fully in keeping with our traditional relationship of close cooperation in the strategic nuclear field' to any British request to purchase a successor system to Polaris.[141] In December 1979, however, Carter informed Thatcher that whilst he remained committed to providing a 'positive response' to any British request for a successor system to Polaris, he would delay giving his approval until the successful Senate ratification of the SALT II treaty. Evidently, the British were justified in their concern that broader US geopolitical and domestic factors could negatively infringe upon the Anglo-American nuclear relationship.[142]

In the weeks that followed there was a growing suspicion in British circles that the Carter administration was 'stringing along' London. By this it was implied that the Carter administration would continue to discuss the possibility of selling the British various successor systems but would not actually publicly commit to any such sale for fear of complicating the ratification of SALT II (on agreeing a sale of nuclear weapons technology the president and the prime minister had traditionally exchanged a letter announcing the sale publicly). Little wonder that Thatcher would describe this as a period where 'troublesome and annoying complications' began to affect the Anglo-American nuclear relationship. Throughout the spring and summer of 1980 it became an overriding priority for the British government to obtain a public commitment from the Carter administration to sell London a successor system to Polaris.[143]

British suspicions about Carter's intentions would prove largely irrelevant as over the course of the summer of 1980 the ratification of SALT II languished amidst the fallout from the Soviet invasion of Afghanistan. British fears that SALT II would fatally undermine the Anglo-American nuclear relationship never materialised.[144] As Vance retrospectively argued, the decision to sell Trident C4 to the

The End of Détente

British government demonstrated that the Carter administration 'would not allow SALT to hobble our traditional defense cooperation with our NATO colleagues'.[145] Harold Brown thus wrote to Francis Pym confirming that the United States would sell Trident C4 to the British government contingent, first, on the fact that the 1963 Polaris Sales Agreement remained as the foundation of cooperation for Trident C4 and, second, that the United Kingdom would pay a contribution to the research and development costs for Trident C4 (set at a 5 per cent premium on the net cost). These conditions were accepted and in the following weeks the necessary agreements were reached between the two sides.[146]

Though the Carter administration had approved the sale of Trident C4, Washington looked to exploit this agreement to advance its other security interests with London. Thus, when discussions over Trident C4 took place, US officials pressed the case that the British government had to agree also to purchase the Rapier missile system from the United States. Harold Brown argued that this was essential if possible congressional opposition to the sale of Trident was to be overcome. London, unwillingly to complicate the Trident agreement at this point, reluctantly accepted that they would have to purchase the Rapier system too. Furthermore, the United States utilised the Trident C4 sale as additional leverage in ensuring that the British government approved the extension of US base rights on the British sovereign territory of Diego Garcia. Projecting greater American military power throughout the Persian Gulf and Indian Ocean was central to the Carter Doctrine so bases such as Diego Garcia had assumed greater importance in US strategic thinking. Obtaining British agreement to extend US base rights upon Diego Garcia had assumed higher priority in US circles than it otherwise might have. Thatcher would deny that the two agreements had any connection, writing that 'it made sense on its own merits and had nothing to do with the Trident decision'.[147] Yet it was hardly a coincidence that when Brown and Pym discussed the sale of Trident C4 the US defense secretary also broached the subject of Diego Garcia. Whilst there may have been no explicit quid pro quo and, indeed, Thatcher supported the extension of US base rights on Diego Garcia for broader security and strategic reasons, it hardly seems feasible that the British government could have rejected this American request over Diego Garcia whilst at the same time finalising the agreement on the sale of Trident. Thatcher's account within her memoir therefore obfuscates this important point.[148]

This episode suggests that the Anglo-American nuclear relationship was not something which could completely transcend the broader strategic and political relationship. The Carter administration sought, successfully as it would turn out, to promote its other interests with the United Kingdom.[149] However, it never undertook the type of coercive diplomacy that had been practised by the Nixon–Ford administrations against the British government in the nuclear realm in order to achieve its other political ambitions with London.[150] At a time when the British government was looking to Washington for additional support whilst concurrently pursuing policies that were irritating to Washington in relation to the implementation of economic or political sanctions against both the Soviet Union and Iran, it is at least worth pondering why Washington never pursued a more robust approach with London. First, the Carter administration had a very different world view than that possessed by the administrations of Nixon and Ford. Coercion, linkage and leverage were the very essence of US foreign policy during 1969–77 and applying pressure against foes and allies was the leitmotif of US grand strategy during this period. In contrast, Carter was not prepared to be as forceful in dealing with America's allies as his immediate predecessors had been.

Second, the extent of the disagreement between London and Washington during this period was really not all that serious. Thatcher had carefully ensured throughout the years that she remained resolutely in support of the president in her public speeches and carefully orchestrated the impression that she only differed with Washington on the tactics to employ against the Soviet Union and Iran. Thatcher also approved Carter's NATO improvement policies, which would include the stationing of ground-launched nuclear capable cruise missiles on British soil, even though it was likely to create enormous domestic political difficulties for the prime minister.[151] Under Thatcher's leadership the British government carefully maintained the impression that Britain was 'generally seen to be pulling her weight in the alliance'.[152] As such, the

The End of Détente

nuclear relationship was never seen by Washington as a viable tool to persuade London to pursue alternative policies in relation to the Soviet Union or Iran. There were clearly limits to American power but these were as much imposed by Carter's unwillingness to exploit the Anglo-American relationship to obtain leverage in pursuing his other ambitions with London. When Nixon, Ford and Kissinger had ruthlessly exploited Britain's nuclear and intelligence relationship with London, they had been able to extract political concessions from the British government. In some ways, Carter was not as politically shrewd as his two Republican predecessors. Yet, Margaret Thatcher was also far more astute than her Conservative predecessor in Edward Heath. Her strong rhetorical support for Washington allowed her to credibly claim that she was in fundamental alignment with the Carter administration and merely differed on the tactical approach to common problems. Carter was no Nixon, but Thatcher was no Heath.

Conclusion

When analysing the Anglo-American relationship during the presidency of Jimmy Carter, it is evident that disagreement between the two countries on a number of international topics of mutual interest was a prominent aspect of the relationship. Many of these differences can be explained by virtue of the fact that the United States was a global power and the United Kingdom was simply not. As one author has suggested, 'Small powers have a whole set of different priorities in their foreign policies than great powers.'[1] Such logic helps to explain why Anglo-American differences during the period under examination here were so considerable. Taking the example of the SALT II treaty, for instance, the Carter administration's decision to pursue discussions with Moscow bilaterally was the only reasonable way in which to bring about an agreement in the timeframe afforded to the president. Yet by operating bilaterally and raising difficult questions about arms limitations it created considerable apprehension in London. The conduct of foreign policy often involves balancing competing interests, and in this regard the promotion of US interests was perceived in London as potentially damaging to British interests.

Though Carter had come to office declaring that he wanted to improve America's alliance relations, the SALT II negotiations remained the exclusive superpower domain that they had originally been during the presidencies of Nixon and Ford. In the Middle East peace negotiations, Carter charted his own course independently of London. The creation of the Camp David Accords that established a formal Israeli–Egyptian peace agreement was exclusively negotiated between Egypt, Israel and the United States. The British role was largely restricted to providing a neutral location

Conclusion

for the discussions at Leeds Castle in July 1978.[2] As one British official noted, 'throughout the history of Arab–Israeli negotiation, [the United States] have always found their position to be more flexible and pressure to be more effective when they are working on their own'.[3] Carter did not alter this position throughout his time in office. The diminished international influence and power of the United Kingdom had an impact on the Anglo-American relationship in that London could not foster the levels of cooperation with Washington that it once had been able to simply because Britain was not as important, or powerful, as it once was.

Differences in power also help to explain why London largely ceded to Washington's wishes in regards to settling the question of majority rule in Rhodesia; why the British government engaged in the discourse of international human rights promotion; and why it supported American proposals for overhauling the NATO alliance, even though American plans were seen in all three cases as either naïvely optimistic or as an expensive waste of resources. The Callaghan government, however, realised that America's predominant position within the Western alliance afforded the president the opportunity to chart the course that he largely wanted in spite of any opposition encountered from London. But whilst appreciating the dynamics of power within the Anglo-American relationship, the Callaghan government believed that personal diplomacy could allow the British government to exercise a profound level of influence over the course of US foreign policy.

By and large this approach did not lead to the level of influence which Callaghan hoped for. Yet it did have a number of notable and more subtle successes. To be sure, in the majority of instances where London advised Washington to alter course, such as with SALT II or in pushing a human rights agenda with Moscow, Carter had already decided to change trajectory anyhow. London's greatest influence, therefore, was in helping to cement changes in Carter's policy direction after he had already decided to change course. But in other fields, Callaghan certainly exerted a level of influence over the president. This is most clearly seen with regards to the discussions relating to international monetary reform and trade policy. Throughout the negotiations of 1977–9, Callaghan had consistently argued for less protectionist policies to be pursued and for constant dialogue to be conducted between the members of the G7. Callaghan's influence may have not been decisive in convincing the president to refrain from implementing new protectionist policies but again the British prime minister's weight was added to the advice proffered in Washington against protectionism. Careful and professional diplomacy could therefore lead to beneficial results for the British government. Power political explanations are only so useful in better understanding the dynamics of the Anglo-American strategic, diplomatic and political relationship in this period.

Carter's decision to approve the sale of Trident C4 to the British government ensured the continuation of the Anglo-American nuclear relationship for the foreseeable future. Given that the nuclear relationship between London and Washington was well established, Carter's decision to sell Trident C4 to the British government could be considered inevitable. Perhaps so, but this was certainly not how British policy makers viewed things at the time.[4] Securing Carter's agreement to sell Trident C4 ensured that Callaghan or any successor to him would be able to purchase a replacement system for Polaris on preferential terms. Thatcher's decision to take up Carter on his private offer guaranteed the continuation of the Anglo-American nuclear relationship. Whilst the Carter administration had initially decided to re-examine whether the British government deserved continued access to the most sensitive intelligence material, the relationship endured. Anglo-American institutional cooperation was so well entrenched that it could overcome transitional political differences. When coupled to the continued cooperation in the realm of nuclear weapons, the most intimate and 'special' aspects of the Anglo-American relationship remained relevant during the Carter presidency.[5]

The Carter–Thatcher relationship has often been overshadowed by the more intimate one which followed it during the presidency of Ronald Reagan. This has not been helped by Thatcher's criticism of Carter in her memoirs, which historians have taken as indicative of a relationship beset by disagreement.[6] Certainly, London and Washington disagreed over how to react to the Soviet invasion of Afghanistan. Anglo-American cooperation was decidedly absent and strained as it pertained to implementing economic sanctions against Moscow, partaking in a boycott of the Moscow Olympic Games and in dealing with the rise of Islamic fundamentalism in Iran. Disagreement may have existed but in other areas of mutual interest between the two countries, remarkable cooperation existed. Thus, London agreed to support Carter's plans for overhauling the NATO alliance and signed up to the Dual Track decision of September 1979. Thatcher ensured that she provided political legitimacy to the president in her public speeches and supported Carter's efforts to rescue the American hostages held in Iran. Finally, the sale of Trident C4 was agreed under Carter and Thatcher. The Carter–Thatcher relationship, however brief, had significant longer-term strategic and political consequences for both countries.

Once out of office, Carter wrote that 'as president, I hoped and believed that the expansion of human rights might be the wave of the future throughout the world, and I wanted the United States to be on the crest of this movement'.[7] Carter's ambition was never achieved to the extent that he may have wished for but, as recently demonstrated by James Cronin, the adoption by American and British policy makers of the discourse of promoting international human rights (even if the actual practice of American and British foreign policy fell short on this front) meant that legitimate governments had to be 'democratic' and publicly adhere to certain standards of human rights (if not actually practise them) over the course of the next forty years of international relations. It was this rhetoric of human rights promotion which therefore encouraged major international institutions to place the promotion of human rights at the heart of their global missions following the end of the Cold War. Likewise, Carter's legacy was an enduring one in the domestic sphere given that 'the US executive branch has not found it easy to ignore norms and laws that had been put in place' under Carter's administration.[8] When this is coupled to the nuclear agreements between London and Washington, the Carter presidency, though short in duration, had profound and long-lasting consequences for both the Anglo-American relationship and international relations more broadly.

What also becomes apparent on reading the previously classified government documentation is that Thatcher was far more practical in her dealings with the United States than she has tended to suggest in her public writings and speeches. Cementing the impression of being the closest ally to the United States has been a consistent and clear message throughout Thatcher's writings which her adherents have keenly promoted.[9] As Carrington suggested, Margaret Thatcher's personality has led to her often being caricatured and this equally applies to her handling of the Anglo-American relationship.[10] Thatcher's engagement with the Carter administration demonstrates that she was cold blooded in the pursuit of British interests. Moreover, she appears far less of a Cold Warrior than she has presented herself as being in her memoirs and post-premiership speeches. In regards to the Soviet Union, Thatcher's rhetoric was damning yet her actions were often reticent and cautious. For all of her bombast, Thatcher in the first years of her premiership appeared to be little different from her predecessors when it came to handling the Soviet Union. Caution and restraint was thus the essence of Thatcher's advice to Washington as the Carter administration struggled to formulate a coherent response to the breakdown of superpower détente and establish policies for fighting the Second Cold War.[11]

The entire period of détente was difficult for the Anglo-American relationship as Washington sought to galvanise its international position following its extrication from Vietnam and as it confronted enormous economic and energy-related challenges. For the United Kingdom, successive British governments tried to cope with the dual problems of international decline and economic stagnation. Given these external factors, it should come as little surprise that London and Washington were often in disagreement. As Henry Kissinger, who was no stranger to experiencing difficulties with London, wryly noted, 'Nobody ever said that the special relationship precluded disagreements.'[12] Indeed, the Carter presidency experienced its share of difficulties with London but it was also marked by considerable cooperation between the two sides. No better example can be found than the diplomacy which surrounded the implementation of a majority rule

Conclusion

settlement in Rhodesia. Of course, Anglo-American cooperation was not harmonious and critical differences of opinion existed between Washington and London. But the level of consultation and the joint Anglo-American plan is revealing of an intimate and cooperative relationship which can shape international relations decisively. As the Second Cold War began, the Anglo-American relationship would again become more important to both countries and to international affairs more broadly. Yet the hardening of US national security and foreign policy and the galvanising of the Anglo-American relationship had begun under the Carter presidency.

Notes

Introduction

1. Margaret Thatcher, *Statecraft: Strategies for a Changing World* (London: HarperCollins, 2002), p. 19.
2. Visit of Prime Minister Margaret Thatcher, 17 December 1979, in *Public Papers of the Presidents of the United States: Jimmy Carter, 1979, Book Two* (Washington DC: United States Government Printing Office, 1980) (hereafter *PPP: Jimmy Carter, 1979, Book Two*), p. 2257.
3. Winston S. Churchill, 'The Sinews of Peace', 5 March 1946, in *Winston S. Churchill: His Complete Speeches, 1897–1963*, ed. Robert Rhodes James (London: Chelsea House Publishers, 1974), Vol. VII, p. 7289.
4. For a good survey of the Anglo-American relationship see Alex Danchev, 'On Specialness', *International Affairs*, 72:4 (1996), pp. 727–50.
5. On these two aspects of the 'Special Relationship' see John Dumbrell, *A Special Relationship: Anglo-American Relations in the Cold War and After* (Basingstoke: Palgrave Macmillan, 2001), pp. 124–46; David Reynolds, 'A "Special Relationship"? America, Britain and the International Order since the Second World War', *International Affairs*, 62:1 (1986), p. 11; Richard J. Aldrich, 'British Intelligence and the Anglo-American "Special Relationship"', *Review of International Studies*, 24:1 (1998), p. 337; Richard J. Aldrich, *GCHQ: The Uncensored Story of Britain's Most Secret Intelligence Agency* (London: HarperPress, 2010), pp. 89–106; Keith Jeffery, *MI6: The History of the Secret Intelligence Service, 1909–1949* (London: Bloomsbury, 2010), p. 721. Peter Hennessy contrasts military cooperation with economic differences in the post-war period to highlight that the special relationship existed in spite of considerable

economic competition between London and Washington. See Peter Hennessy, *Never Again: Britain 1945–51* (London: Vintage, 1993), p. 345. The classic text on Anglo-American security matters remains John Baylis, *Anglo-American Defence Relations, 1939–1984: The Special Relationship* (London: Macmillan, 1984).
6. H. C. Allen, *Great Britain and the United States: A History of Anglo-American Relations 1783–1952* (London: Odhams, 1954), pp. 17–18.
7. David Reynolds, 'Roosevelt, Churchill, and the Wartime Anglo-American Alliance, 1939–1945: Towards a New Synthesis', in William Roger Louis and Hedley Bull (eds), *The 'Special Relationship': Anglo-American Relations since 1945* (Oxford: Clarendon Press, 1986), p. 39. See also David Reynolds, *The Creation of the Anglo-American Alliance 1937–41: A Study in Competitive Co-operation* (London: Europa, 1981), pp. 284–5; David Reynolds, *In Command of History: Churchill Fighting and Writing the Second World War* (London: Allen Lane, 2004), pp. 43–4.
8. Alec Cairncross and Barry Eichengreen, *Sterling in Decline: The Devaluations of 1931, 1949 and 1967* (Basingstoke: Palgrave Macmillan, 2003), p. xvii; Paul Kennedy, *The Realities Behind Diplomacy: Background Influences on British External Policy, 1865–1980* (London: Fontana, 1981), p. 317. For the 25 per cent figure see Kathleen Burk, *Old World, New World: The Story of Britain and America* (London: Little, Brown, 2007), p. 561. For contemporary comparisons see Robert W. Kolb (ed.), *Sovereign Debt: From Safety to Default* (Hoboken, NJ: Wiley, 2011), p. xv.
9. David Sanders, *Losing an Empire, Finding a Role: British Foreign Policy since 1945* (Basingstoke: Palgrave Macmillan, 1990), p. 48; David Reynolds, *Britannia Overruled: British Policy and World Power in the 20th Century* (London: Longman, 1991), pp. 178–9.
10. Peter Clarke, *The Last Thousand Days of the British Empire: Churchill, Roosevelt, and the Birth of the Pax Americana* (London: Bloomsbury, 2009), pp. 378–9; Robert Skidelsky, *John Maynard Keynes. Vol. 3: Fighting for Freedom, 1937–1946* (London: Macmillan, 2000), pp. 403–58. See also Corelli Barnett, *Collapse of British Power*, reprinted edn (London: Faber & Faber, 2011), p. 592.
11. Ritchie Ovendale, *Anglo-American Relations in the Twentieth Century* (Basingstoke: Palgrave Macmillan, 1998), p. 66.
12. Christopher Hitchens, *Blood, Class and Nostalgia: Anglo-American Ironies* (London: Farrar, Straus & Giroux, 1990), p. 23. On the

broader ambition of British policy makers seeking to influence American policy for their own ends see Klaus Larres, *Churchill's Cold War: The Politics of Personal Diplomacy* (New Haven, CT: Yale University Press, 2002), pp. xiv–xv.
13. Hennessy, *Never Again*, p. 365.
14. 'UK Intelligence Work Defends Freedom, Say Spy Chiefs', BBC News, 7 November 2013, available at <http://www.bbc.com/news/uk-politics-24847399> (last accessed 13 May 2016).
15. Henry A. Kissinger, *The Troubled Partnership: A Reappraisal of the Atlantic Alliance* (New York: McGraw-Hill for the Council on Foreign Relations, 1965), p. 78.
16. This decline of Britain's international position is emphasised throughout Kennedy, *The Realities Behind Diplomacy*, pp. 315–44.
17. RG 218, Geographic File 1942–5, JIC 340/1 'Estimate of British Post-War Capabilities and Intentions', 13 February 1946, Folder 'CCS 000.1 Great Britain', Box 82, National Archives II, College Park, Maryland, United States of America (hereafter NAII).
18. The National Archives (hereafter TNA), FO 371/126666 Harold Caccia to Selwyn Lloyd, Annual Review for 1956, 1 January 1957. For the Anglo-American discord during the Suez crisis see Keith Kyle, *Suez: Britain's End of Empire in the Middle East*, revised edn (London: I. B. Tauris, 2003), pp. 500–14.
19. This phased withdrawal was announced in mid-1967; in January 1968 withdrawal was accelerated for full implementation by 1971. See Saki Dockrill, *Britain's Retreat from East of Suez: The Choice between Europe and the World?* (Basingstoke: Palgrave Macmillan, 2002), pp. 178–90. Britain retained intelligence stations in Cyprus and Hong Kong as well as a number of other global outposts. The most notable of these was the Indian Ocean island of Diego Garcia, which was leased to the United States Air Force. See David M. McCourt, 'What Was Britain's "East of Suez" Role? Reassessing the Withdrawal, 1964–1968', *Diplomacy and Statecraft*, 20:3 (2009), pp. 454–5.
20. On America's multiple 'special relationships' see John Dumbrell and Axel Schäfer (eds), *America's 'Special Relationships': Foreign and Domestic Aspects of the Politics of Alliance* (London: Routledge, 2009).
21. On Wilson's influence in relation to nuclear diplomacy see David James Gill, *Britain and the Bomb: Nuclear Diplomacy, 1964–1970* (Stanford, CA: Stanford University Press, 2014), pp. 141–70. On Wilson's efforts at influencing Washington see for example Jonathan

Colman, *A Special Relationship? Harold Wilson, Lyndon Johnson and Anglo-American Relations at the Summit, 1964–1968* (Manchester: Manchester University Press, 2004); Geraint Hughes, *Harold Wilson's Cold War: The Labour Government and East–West Politics, 1964–1970* (Rochester, NY: Boydell Press, 2009).

22. Thomas Robb, *A Strained Partnership? U.S.–UK Relations in the Era of Détente, 1969–77* (Manchester: Manchester University Press, 2013), pp. 175–209. For the quotes see William Simon, *A Time for Reflection: An Autobiography* (New York: Regnery, 2003), pp. 152–3; Memorandum of Conversation, 8 January 1975, File: January 8, 1975 Ford–Kissinger, National Security Adviser Memoranda of Conversations, Box 8, Gerald R. Ford Library, Ann Arbor, Michigan, United States of America (hereafter GFL); RG 59 Entry 5403 Records of Henry Kissinger, 1973–1977, Folder 4, Box 2, 'The Problem of Britain', undated [circa November 1973], NAII.

23. Callaghan was informed of this development but had been reassured by Stansfield Turner, the Director of the CIA, that access to this high-level material would soon be made available. Tellingly, the prime minister was advised not to raise the subject with President Carter personally. See TNA: PREM 16/1912 John Hunt to Mr Cartledge, 16 March 1978. For further discussion see Christopher Andrew, *For the President's Eyes Only: Secret Intelligence and the American Presidency from Washington to Bush* (London: HarperCollins, 1996), pp. 426–9.

24. David Watt, 'Introduction', in Louis and Bull, *The 'Special Relationship'*, p. 13. For similar accounts see Robert M. Hathaway, *Great Britain and the United States: Special Relations since World War II* (Boston: Twayne, 1990), pp. 111–17. For works that have also given short shrift to the Carter presidency see David Dimbleby and David Reynolds, *An Ocean Apart: The Relationship between Britain and America in the Twentieth Century* (New York: Random House, 1988); C. J. Bartlett, *'The Special Relationship': Anglo-American Relations since 1945* (London: Longman, 1992), pp. 88–101; John Dickie, *'Special' No More: Anglo-American Relations: Rhetoric and Reality* (London: Weidenfeld & Nicolson, 1994); Robin Renwick, *Fighting with Allies: America and Britain in Peace and War* (Basingstoke: Macmillan, 1996), pp. 206–11; Ovendale, *Anglo-American Relations*, pp. 120–31; Sean Greenwood, *Britain and the Cold War 1945–91* (Basingstoke: Macmillan, 2000), pp. 177–8. One recent account of the Anglo-American relationship has omitted the Carter presidency altogether! See Burk, *Old World*.

25. On the Second Cold War see Campbell Craig and Fredrick Logevall, *America's Cold War: The Politics of Insecurity* (Cambridge, MA: Harvard University Press, 2009), pp. 289–322.
26. James Cronin argues that the Anglo-American relationship remained a central feature of international affairs from the 1970s to the contemporary day, especially in relation to the agendas that global institutions have pursued. See James E. Cronin, *Global Rules: America, Britain and a Disordered World* (New Haven, CT: Yale University Press, 2014), pp. 4–21.
27. Brian J. Auten, *Carter's Conversion: The Hardening of American Defense Policy* (Columbia: University of Missouri Press, 2009). For other accounts which had sought to reappraise the Carter presidency see John Dumbrell, *The Carter Presidency: A Reevaluation* (Manchester: Manchester University Press, 1995); Douglas Brinkley, 'The Rising Stock of Jimmy Carter: The "Hands on" Legacy of Our Thirty-ninth President', *Diplomatic History*, 20:4 (1996), pp. 505–30; Peter Bourne, *Jimmy Carter: A Comprehensive Biography from Plains to Postpresidency* (New York: Scribner, 1997); Burton I. Kaufman, *The Presidency of James Earl Carter* (Lawrence: University Press of Kansas, 1997); Robert Strong, *Working in the World: Jimmy Carter and the Making of American Foreign Policy* (Baton Rouge, LA: Louisiana State University Press, 2000); Burton I. Kaufman and Scott Kaufman, *The Presidency of James Earl Carter* (Lawrence: University of Kansas Press, 2006); Mary E. Stuckey, *Jimmy Carter, Human Rights, and the National Agenda* (College Station: Texas A&M University Press, 2009); Betty Glad, *An Outsider in the White House: Jimmy Carter, His Advisors, and the Making of American Foreign Policy* (Ithaca: Cornell University Press, 2010); Barbara J. Keys, *Reclaiming American Virtue: The Human Rights Revolution of the 1970s* (Cambridge, MA: Harvard University Press, 2014); Daniel J. Sargent, *A Superpower Transformed: The Remaking of American Foreign Relations in the 1970s* (Oxford: Oxford University Press, 2015).
28. 'How the Americans See Us', Peter Jay to David Owen, 11 February 1979, in File: 2/33, The Papers of Peter Jay, Churchill Archives Centre, Cambridge University, United Kingdom (hereafter Jay Papers).
29. David Reynolds, *From World War to Cold War: Churchill, Roosevelt, and the International History of the 1940s* (Oxford: Oxford University Press, 2006), pp. 4–5. 'Soft Power' was coined by the American political scientist Joseph Nye Jr. The concept explains how states

Notes

attempt to co-opt rather than coerce cooperation from other states. See Joseph S. Nye Jr, *Soft Power: The Means to Success in World Politics* (New York: Public Affairs, 2004)

Chapter 1

1. Henry Kissinger, *Years of Upheaval* (Boston: Little Brown, 1982). On the 1976 election and the need for an 'outsider' see Edward Berkowitz, *Something Happened: A Political and Cultural Overview of the Seventies* (New York: Columbia University Press, 2006), pp. 1–3; Betty Glad, *An Outsider in the White House: Jimmy Carter, His Advisors, and the Making of American Foreign Policy* (Ithaca: Cornell University Press, 2010), pp. 2–12; Julian E. Zelizer, *Jimmy Carter* (New York: Time Books, 2010), pp. 31–52.
2. Mancur Olson, *The Rise and Decline of Nations: Economic Growth, Stagflation and Social Rigidities* (Cambridge, MA: Harvard University Press, 1982), p. 6.
3. Kathleen Burk, *Old World, New World: The Story of Britain and America* (London: Little, Brown, 2007), p. 629. Good overviews on Britain in the 1970s are provided by Alwyn W. Turner, *Crisis? What Crisis?: Britain in the 1970s* (London: Aurum, 2008); Dominic Sandbrook, *State of Emergency: The Way We Were: Britain, 1970–1974* (London: Penguin, 2011). For a broader overview see Gerard DeGroot, *The Seventies Unplugged: A Kaleidoscopic Look at a Violent Decade* (Basingstoke: Macmillan, 2010). On British global withdrawal see W. David McIntyre, *Winding Up the British Empire in the Pacific Islands* (Oxford: Oxford University Press, 2014); Tore T. Peterson, *Richard Nixon, Great Britain and the Anglo-American Alignment in the Persian Gulf and Arabian Peninsula: Making Allies out of Clients* (Brighton: Sussex Academic Press, 2009), pp. 116–34; W. Taylor Fein, *American Ascendance and British Retreat in the Persian Gulf Region* (Basingstoke: Palgrave Macmillan, 2008). On the IMF Crisis see Kathleen Burk and Alec Cairncross, *Goodbye Great Britain: The 1976 IMF Crisis* (New Haven, CT: Yale University Press, 1992). The following paper from Peter Jay to David Owen captures this sense of 'decline' in British policy making circles during this period: 'Britain's Decline: Its Causes and Consequences', Peter Jay to David Owen, 31 March 1979, in File: 2/31, Jay Papers.
4. Thomas Robb, 'Henry Kissinger, Great Britain and the "Year of Europe": The "Tangled Skein"', *Contemporary British History*,

24:3 (2010), pp. 297–318; Thomas Robb, 'The "Limit of What is Tolerable": British Defence Cuts and the "Special Relationship," 1974–1976', *Diplomacy and Statecraft*, 22:2 (2011), pp. 321–37.
5. For works emphasising a similar line of argument see Luke A. Nichter, *Richard Nixon and Europe: The Reshaping of the Postwar Atlantic World* (New York: Cambridge University Press, 2015); Andrew Scott, *Allies Apart: Heath, Nixon and the Anglo-American Relationship* (Basingstoke: Palgrave Macmillan, 2011); Catherine Hynes, *The Year that Never Was: Heath, the Nixon Administration and the Year of Europe* (Dublin: University College Dublin Press, 2009); Niklas Rossbach, *Heath, Nixon and the Rebirth of the Special Relationship: Britain, the US and the EC, 1969–74* (Basingstoke: Palgrave Macmillan, 2009).
6. On the lack of influence Callaghan was able to exercise over the Ford administration during the IMF Crisis see Thomas Robb, *A Strained Partnership? U.S.–UK Relations in the Era of Détente, 1969–77* (Manchester: Manchester University Press, 2013), pp. 199–200. On Nixon's 1974 decision to continue to assist the British government with its Polaris improvement programme see Thomas Robb, 'Antelope, Poseidon or a Hybrid: The Upgrading of the British Strategic Nuclear Deterrent, 1970–1974', *Journal of Strategic Studies*, 33:6 (2010), pp. 797–817.
7. TNA: FCO 82/687 G. N. Smith to Mr Edmonds, 16 February 1977.
8. Memorandum to David Aaron from Gregory Treverton, 11 April 1977, File: Meeting PRC 12 4-14-77, Zbigniew Brzezinski Collection, Box 24, Jimmy Carter Presidential Library, Atlanta, Georgia, United States of America (hereafter JCL); Four Year Policy Objectives, attached to Memorandum for the President from Zbigniew Brzezinski, 18 April 1977, File: Four Year Goals 4/77, Zbigniew Brzezinski Collection, Box 23, JCL; Policy Review Committee Meeting, 14 May 1979, File: Meetings PRC 106: 5/14/79, Zbigniew Brzezinski Collection, Box 25, JCL; Policy Review Committee Meeting, 8 July 1977, File: Meetings PRC 22 7-8-77, Zbigniew Brzezinski Collection, Box 24, JCL; Jimmy Carter, *White House Diary* (New York: Farrar, Straus and Giroux, 2010), p. 10.
9. From the Ambassador in the Embassy in London to the Secretary of State, 24 February 1977, Document Number: 1977LONDON03166, File Number: D770064-0882, State Department Electronic Telegrams, available at <http://aad.archives.gov/aad/createpdf?rid=42845&dt=2532&dl=1629> (last accessed 13 May 2016). The January 1977 appraisal of the United Kingdom was

equally as pessimistic in its assessment: From the Ambassador in the Embassy in London to the Secretary of State, 4 February 1977, Document Number: 1977LONDON02014, File Number: D770040-1106, State Department Electronic Telegrams, available at <http://aad.archives.gov/aad/createpdf?rid=43585&dt=2532&dl=1629> (last accessed 13 May 2016).

10. 'Overview of Foreign Policy Issues and Positions', by Cyrus Vance, undated, in MS 1664, Series II, Folder 12, Box 9, Cyrus R. Vance and Grace Sloane Vance Papers, Sterling Library, Yale University, United States of America (hereafter Vance Papers).
11. TNA: PREM 16/2290 Peter Jay to David Owen, 13 February 1979.
12. Nigel Ashton, 'Harold Macmillan and the "Golden Days" of Anglo-American Relations', *Diplomatic History*, 29:4 (2005), pp. 691–723.
13. Peter Rodman, *Presidential Command: Power, Leadership and the Making of Foreign Policy from Richard Nixon to George W. Bush* (New York: Alfred Knopf, 2009), p. 117.
14. John Lewis Gaddis, *The Cold War* (London: Allen Lane, 2005), p. 198.
15. Nancy Mitchell, 'The Cold War and Jimmy Carter', in Melvyn Leffler and Odd Arne Westad (eds), *The Cambridge History of the Cold War: Endings* (Cambridge: Cambridge University Press, 2010), Vol. III, p. 71. William McKinley (US president 1897–1901) and Theodore Roosevelt (US president 1901–9) embodied the realist tilt in US foreign policy at the turn of the nineteenth century. Woodrow Wilson's presidency (1913–21) personifies the idealistic turn in US foreign policy. Of course, Roosevelt's and Wilson's foreign policy was rather more complicated than labels such as 'realist' or 'idealistic' would suggest. For a good overview see George C. Herring, *From Colony to Superpower: U.S. Foreign Relations since 1776* (Oxford: Oxford University Press, 2008), pp. 337–44, 379–83; Henry Kissinger, *Diplomacy* (New York: Simon & Schuster, 1994), pp. 29–55; Barbara J. Keys, *Reclaiming American Virtue: The Human Rights Revolution of the 1970s* (Cambridge, MA: Harvard University Press, 2014), pp. 3–11. On the long history of human rights in international relations see R. J. Vincent, *Human Rights in International Relations* (Cambridge: Cambridge University Press, 1986).
16. As noted by one historian, Carter had hardly mentioned international human rights promotion in any of his public speeches prior to the subject becoming politically fortuitous in the summer of 1976. See Keys, *Reclaiming American Virtue*, p. 232.

17. Andrew Preston, *Sword of the Spirit, Shield of Faith: Religion in American War and Diplomacy* (New York: Harper, 2012), pp. 7–11, at p. 8. On Carter see Francis L. Lowenheim, 'From Helsinki to Afghanistan: American Diplomats and Diplomacy, 1975–1979', in Gordon A. Craig and Francis L. Lowenheim (eds), *The Diplomats 1939–1979* (Princeton, NJ: Princeton University Press, 1994), pp. 640–5; James E. Cronin, *Global Rules: America, Britain and a Disordered World* (New Haven, CT: Yale University Press, 2014), pp. 64–9. On how moral considerations and Carter's Christianity influenced his presidency see Leo P. Ribuffo, 'God and Jimmy Carter', in M. L. Bradbury and James B. Gilbert (eds), *Transforming Faith: The Sacred and Secular in Modern American History* (Westport, CT: Greenwood, 1989), pp. 141–59; Kenneth E. Morris, *Jimmy Carter: American Moralist* (Athens, GA: University of Georgia Press, 1996); Burton I. Kaufman, *The Presidency of James Earl Carter* (Lawrence: University Press of Kansas, 1997), pp. 37–50; Randall H. Balmer, *Redeemer: The Life of Jimmy Carter* (London: Basic Civitas, 2013).
18. Darren. J. McDonald, 'Blessed Are the Policy Makers: Jimmy Carter's Faith-based Approach to the Arab–Israeli Conflict', *Diplomatic History*, 39:3 (2015), p. 452. See also Richard Hutcheson, *God in the White House: How Religion Has Changed the Modern Presidency* (New York: Macmillan, 1988), pp. 133–6.
19. For one work that emphasises how Carter's morality affected his position towards majority rule in Rhodesia see Andrew J. DeRoche, 'Standing Firm for Principles: Jimmy Carter and Zimbabwe', *Diplomatic History*, 23:4 (1999), pp. 657–85.
20. Jody Powell, who served as the president's press secretary, is the official cited. See Blake W. Jones, '"How Does a Born-Again Christian Deal with a Born-Again Moslem?" The Religious Dimension of the Iranian Hostage Crisis', *Diplomatic History*, 39:3 (2015), pp. 423–51, at p. 457.
21. Preston, *Sword of the Spirit*, pp. 575–6.
22. The organisation is still in existence. See <http://www.trilateral.org/> (last accessed 13 May 2016).
23. John Dumbrell, *The Carter Presidency: A Re-evaluation* (Manchester: Manchester University Press, 1995), p. 111; Daniel J. Sargent, 'The United States and Globalization in the 1970s', in Niall Ferguson, Charles S. Maier, Erez Manela and Daniel J. Sargent (eds), *The Shock of the Global: The 1970s in Perspective* (Cambridge, MA: Harvard University Press, 2010), p. 61. See also Barbara Zanchetta,

The Transformation of American International Power in the 1970s (Cambridge: Cambridge University Press, 2014), p. 197; Daniel J. Sargent, *A Superpower Transformed: The Remaking of American Foreign Relations in the 1970s* (Oxford: Oxford University Press, 2015), pp. 231–50.

24. Zelizer's work on the interplay between domestic politics and foreign policy making within the US political system is perhaps the strongest of its kind. See Julian E. Zelizer, *Arsenal of Democracy: The Politics of National Security – From World War II to the War on Terrorism* (New York: Basic Books, 2010). In his memoir, Carter titled an entire section 'An Outsider in Washington'. It is in this section that Carter explains why he decided to run for the presidency. See Jimmy Carter, *Keeping Faith: Memoirs of a President* (London: Collins, 1982), pp. 63–138.

25. Glad, *An Outsider in the White House*, pp. 2–15. For specific examples of how Carter and his key advisers sought to utilise his outsider status to his advantage see Address by Jimmy Carter, 28 May 1975, in *Foreign Relations of the United States: Foundations of Foreign Policy, 1977–1980* (Washington DC: United States Government Printing Office, 2014), Vol. I, Doc. 2, pp. 3–8 (hereafter *FRUS: Foundations of Foreign Policy, 1977–1980*); 'A Suggested Carter Administration Agenda', by Cyrus Vance, undated [circa December 1976], in MS 1664, Series II, Folder 4, Box 8, Vance Papers. In 1976 Carter published a book titled *Why Not the Best?* It was in this book that he outlined his political, moral and religious beliefs to the American public. See Jimmy Carter, *Why Not the Best?* (New York: Bantam Books, 1976). On Carter's early life see his illuminating reflections in Jimmy Carter, *A Full Life: Reflections at Ninety* (New York: Simon & Schuster, 2015); Jimmy Carter, *An Hour before Daylight: Memories of My Rural Boyhood* (New York: Simon & Schuster, 2001).

26. Burton I. Kaufman and Scott Kaufman, *The Presidency of James Earl Carter* (Lawrence: University of Kansas Press, 2006), pp. 5–18; Odd Arne Westad, *The Global Cold War: Third World Interventions and the Making of Our Times* (Cambridge: Cambridge University Press, 2006), pp. 247–9. For contemporary criticism of Ford's nuclear weapons policies see Paul H. Nitze, 'Assuring Strategic Stability in the Era of Détente', *Foreign Affairs*, 54:2 (1976), p. 207; Richard Pipes, 'Why the Soviet Union Thinks It Could Fight and Win a Nuclear War', *Commentary*, 64:1 (1977), p. 34. The debates between Carter and Ford are transcribed and printed in full

in Lloyd Bitzer and Theodore Rueter, *Carter vs Ford: The Counterfeit Debates of 1976* (Madison: University of Wisconsin Press, 1980), pp. 253–394.
27. Remarks by Jimmy Carter, 15 March 1976, in *FRUS: Foundations of Foreign Policy, 1977–1980*, Vol. I, Doc. 4, p. 15.
28. Raymond Garthoff, *Détente and Confrontation: American–Soviet Relations from Nixon to Reagan* (Washington DC: The Brookings Institution, 1994), p. 564.
29. Remarks by Jimmy Carter, 15 March 1976, in *FRUS: Foundations of Foreign Policy, 1977–1980*, Vol. I, Doc. 4, p. 18; Carter, *Keeping Faith*, p. 142.
30. The role of the vice president is one that has been long derided for its insignificance. Harry Truman, US president 1945–53, and vice president under Franklin Roosevelt, 1944–5, described the position as 'about as useful as a fifth teat on a cow'. See Richard Nixon, *RN: The Memoirs of Richard Nixon* (London: Book Club Associates, 1978), p. 85. Hubert Humphrey, vice president under Lyndon Johnson, 1964–8, joked that a 'mother had two sons . . . one went to sea, and the other became vice president, and neither was heard of again'. See Randall B. Woods, *LBJ: Architect of American Ambition* (New York: Free Press, 2006), p. 377. Under Jimmy Carter such epithets did not, however, apply. Walter Mondale was to have a significant role in the formation of domestic and foreign policy and his opinion was actively sought by Carter throughout his presidency. Indeed, Mondale would write to Carter: 'I want to make it very clear at the outset that I am completely satisfied with the role that you have allowed me to play in your administration. I feel that you have treated me as a full working partner and that we have established a solid foundation for a fruitful personal and political relationship in the years ahead.' See Memorandum for the President from the Vice President, 6 September 1977, in Office of the Chief of Staff Files, Hamilton Jordan's Confidential Files, Vice President, Box 37, JCL. For Mondale's role within the administration see Zbigniew Brzezinski, *Power and Principle: Memoirs of the National Security Adviser 1977–1981* (London: Weidenfeld & Nicolson, 1983), pp. 33–5; Walter F. Mondale, *The Good Fight: A Life in Liberal Politics* (New York: Simon & Schuster, 2010), pp. 199–228.
31. Statement by Senator Walter F. Mondale, 2 June 1975, in *FRUS: Foundations of Foreign Policy, 1977–1980*, Vol. I, Doc. 2, p. 10.

32. Mondale, *The Good Fight*, pp. 199–226, at p. 225.
33. Dumbrell, *The Carter Presidency*, p. 113.
34. William Odom Interview, 18 February 1982, p. 35, The Miller Center, available at <http://web1.millercenter.org/poh/transcripts/ohp_1982_0218_brzezinski.pdf> (last accessed 13 May 2016).
35. Transcript of Interview with President Ford, 1 March 1976, in *Foreign Relations of the United States: Soviet Union, 1974–76* (Washington DC: United States Government Printing Office, 2012), Vol. XVI, Doc. 268, p. 1014; Aldo Beckman, '"Détente" a Dirty Word, Ford Decides to Shun It', *Chicago Tribune*, 2 March 1976, p. 3; Zanchetta, *The Transformation of American International Power*, p. 185.
36. Stephen E. Ambrose and Douglas Brinkley, *Rise to Globalism: American Foreign Policy since 1938* (London: Penguin, 1997), p. 281. See also Joshua Muravchik, *The Uncertain Crusade: Jimmy Carter and the Dilemmas of Human Rights Policy* (Lanham, MD: Hamilton Press, 1986).
37. Address by Jimmy Carter, 8 September 1976, in *FRUS: Foundations of Foreign Policy, 1977–1980*, Vol. I, Doc. 9, p. 46.
38. John Dumbrell, *American Foreign Policy: Carter to Clinton* (Basingstoke: Palgrave, 1996), p. 19.
39. See for example Minutes of a Policy Review Committee Meeting, 24 March 1977, in *FRUS: Foundations of Foreign Policy, 1974–1980*, Vol. I, Doc. 30, pp. 117–23.
40. Briefing Memorandum from the Director of the Policy Planning Staff (Lake) to Secretary of State Vance, undated, attached to Action Memorandum from the Director of the Policy Planning Staff (Lake) to Secretary of State Vance, 20 January 1978, in *Foreign Relations of the United States 1977–1980: Human Rights* (Washington DC: United States Government Printing Office, 2013), Vol. II, Doc. 105, p. 357 (hereafter *FRUS 1977–1980: Human Rights*).
41. David F. Schmitz and Vanessa Walker, 'Jimmy Carter and the Foreign Policy of Human Rights: The Development of a Post-Cold War Foreign Policy', *Diplomatic History*, 28:1 (2004), p. 117. For works that have similarly emphasised Carter's efforts to transcend the Cold War paradigm see Jerel A. Rosati, *The Carter Administration's Quest for Global Community: Beliefs and Their Impact on Behavior* (Columbia: The University of South Carolina Press, 1991), p. 2; David Schmitz, *The United States and Right Wing Dictatorships, 1965–1989* (Cambridge: Cambridge University Press, 2006), pp. 143–5. See also Dumbrell, *The Carter Presidency*, pp. 63–85;

John Dumbrell, 'Jimmy Carter and Moral Purpose', in Michael Cox, Timothy Lynch and Nicholas Bouchet (eds), *US Foreign Policy and Democracy Promotion: From Theodore Roosevelt to Barack Obama* (New York: Routledge, 2012), pp. 121–38; Herring, *From Colony to Superpower*, pp. 833–4; Sargent, *A Superpower Transformed*, pp. 250–5.
42. Mondale, *The Good Fight*, p. 223.
43. Memorandum from the President's Assistant for National Security Affairs (Brzezinski) to President Carter, 1 April 1977, in *FRUS: Foundations of Foreign Policy, 1974–1980*, Vol. I, Doc. 32, pp. 129–30.
44. Memorandum from the President's Assistant for National Security Affairs (Brzezinski) to President Carter, 16 April 1977, in *FRUS: Foundations of Foreign Policy, 1974–1980*, Vol. I, Doc. 34, p. 142.
45. Westad, *The Global Cold War*, pp. 207–87. Brzezinski set out this type of thinking neatly in a long 'Four Year Policy Objectives' paper for the president. See 'Four Year Policy Objectives', attached to Memorandum for the President from Zbigniew Brzezinski, 18 April 1977, File: Four Year Goals 4/77, Zbigniew Brzezinski Collection, Box 23, JCL. See also 'A Human Rights Strategy for the United States', undated [circa April 1977], File: Human Rights 2/4/77, National Security Affairs Collection 7 Brzezinski Material, Box 28, JCL.
46. Anatoly Dobrynin, *In Confidence: Moscow's Ambassador to America's Six Cold War Presidents* (New York: Times Books, 1995), p. 195.
47. Jimmy Carter to Cabinet Officers, 27 April 1977, in MS 1664, Series II, Folder 21, Box 9, Vance Papers.
48. James Schlesinger interview, 19–20 July 1984, The Miller Center, p. 3, available at <http://web1.millercenter.org/poh/transcripts/ohp_1984_0719_schlesinger.pdf> (last accessed 13 May 2016).
49. Quoted in Hal Brands, *What Good Is Grand Strategy?: Power and Purpose in American Statecraft from Harry S. Truman to George W. Bush* (Ithaca: Cornell University Press, 2014), p. 14. See also Rodman, *Presidential Command*, pp. 68–9; Mark Atwood Lawrence, 'Containing Globalism: The United States and the Developing World in the 1970s', in Ferguson et al., *The Shock of the Global*, p. 216.
50. Address by Jimmy Carter, 23 June 1976, in *FRUS: Foundations of Foreign Policy, 1974–1980*, Vol. I, Doc. 6, pp. 28–38. On US–European relations during the Nixon–Ford years see Matthias

Schulz and Thomas A. Schwartz (eds), *The Strained Alliance: US–European Relations from Nixon to Carter* (Cambridge: Cambridge University Press, 2009).
51. Zbigniew Brzezinski, 'America and Europe', *Foreign Affairs*, 49:1 (1970), pp. 11–30.
52. Wolf Mendl, *Western Europe and Japan between the Superpowers* (London: St Martin's Press, 1984), pp. 64–6; Dumbrell, *American Foreign Policy*, p. 25.
53. Inaugural Address of President Jimmy Carter, 20 January 1977, *Public Papers of the Presidents of the United States: Jimmy Carter, 1977, Book One* (Washington DC: United States Government Printing Office, 1977) (hereafter *PPP: Jimmy Carter, 1977, Book One*), pp. 1–4; Hayes Johnson, 'Carter Is Sworn in as President, Asks "Fresh Faith in Old Dream"', *The Washington Post*, 21 January 1977.
54. 'Four Year Policy Objectives', attached to Memorandum for the President from Zbigniew Brzezinski, 18 April 1977, File: Four Year Goals 4/77, Zbigniew Brzezinski Collection, Box 23, JCL. See also Kenneth Weisbrode, *The Atlantic Century: Four Generations of Extraordinary Diplomats Who Forged America's Vital Alliance with Europe* (Cambridge, MA: Da Capo Press, 2009), p. 276.
55. John Young, *The Labour Governments 1964–70: International Policy* (Manchester: Manchester University Press, 2003), pp. 142–65; David Reynolds, *Britannia Overruled: British Policy and World Power in the 20th Century* (London: Longman, 1991), p. 248; Bernard Donoughue, *Prime Minister: The Conduct of Policy under Harold Wilson and James Callaghan* (London: Jonathan Cape, 1987), p. 86; Dennis Kavanagh and Anthony Seldon, *The Powers behind the Prime Minister: The Hidden Influence of Number Ten* (London: HarperCollins, 1999), pp. 103–5.
56. David Owen, *Time to Declare* (London: Michael Joseph, 1991), p. 266. On interviewing Lord (David) Owen, the author was informed that even today the United Kingdom had to foster as close a relationship with Washington as possible in order to better promote Britain's international interests. Author interview with Lord Owen, London, 22 January 2008.
57. Peter Hennessy, *The Prime Minister: The Office and Its Holders since 1945* (London: Penguin, 2001), pp. 337–45; Edward Pearce, *Denis Healey: A Life in Our Times* (Boston: Little, Brown, 2002), pp. 428–50; Kenneth O. Morgan, *Callaghan: A Life* (Oxford: Oxford University Press, 1997), pp. 588–60.

58. James Callaghan, *Time & Chance* (London: Collins, 1987), pp. 482–3.
59. Cyrus Vance, *Hard Choices: Critical Years in America's Foreign Policy* (New York: Simon & Schuster, 1983), p. 262.
60. Owen, *Time to Declare*, p. 283.
61. Brzezinski, *Power and Principle*, p. 291.
62. For such assessments see Robin Renwick, *A Journey with Margaret Thatcher: Foreign Policy under the Iron Lady* (London: Biteback, 2013); Gillian Shephard, *The Real Iron Lady: Working with Margaret Thatcher* (London: Biteback, 2013); Robin Harris, *Not for Turning: The Life of Margaret Thatcher* (London: Bantam Press, 2013), pp. 252–3; Charles Moore, *Margaret Thatcher: The Authorized Biography, Volume One: Not for Turning* (London: Allen Lane, 2013), pp. 371–2.
63. Jonathan Aitken, *Margaret Thatcher* (London: Bloomsbury, 2013), p. 298.
64. Moore, *Margaret Thatcher*, p. 495.
65. Raymond Seitz, *Over Here* (London: Weidenfeld & Nicolson, 1998), p. 324.
66. James Cooper, *Margaret Thatcher and Ronald Reagan: A Very Political Special Relationship* (Basingstoke: Palgrave Macmillan, 2012), pp. 90–3; Richard Aldous, *Reagan and Thatcher: The Difficult Relationship* (London: Hutchinson, 2012), pp. 118–23.
67. John Dumbrell, *A Special Relationship: Anglo-American Relations in the Cold War and After* (Basingstoke: Palgrave Macmillan, 2001), p. 101.
68. David Gill, 'Peter Carrington', in Jennifer Mackby and Paul Cornish (eds), *US–UK Nuclear Cooperation after Fifty Years* (Washington DC: CSIS Press, 2008), p. 267.

Chapter 2

1. On Northern Ireland see TNA: CJ 4/1835 'President Carter and Northern Ireland', P. G. Wallis to M. R. Melhuish, 8 February 1977.
2. TNA: PREM 16/1909 Michael Palliser to Private Secretary, 8 November 1976.
3. On Ramsbotham's tenure as Ambassador to Washington see Raj Roy, 'Peter Ramsbotham', in Michael Hopkins, Saul Kelly and John Young (eds), *The Washington Embassy: British Ambassadors to the*

Notes

United States, 1939–77 (Basingstoke: Palgrave Macmillan, 2009), pp. 209–28.
4. TNA: PREM 16/1485 Ramsbotham to the FCO, Tel. 946, 3 March 1977.
5. TNA: PREM 16/1488 Ramsbotham to FCO, Tel. 1343, 25 March 1977; TNA: PREM 16/1909 Ramsbotham to FCO, Tel. 4131, 3 December 1976; TNA: PREM 16/1909 Bridges to FCO, Tel. 4356, 23 December 1976.
6. TNA: PREM 16/1485 'Record of a Telephone Conversation between the Prime Minister and President-elect Carter', 13 January 1977; TNA: FCO 82/662 Fred Mulley to Dr Harold Brown, 23 December 1976; TNA: FCO 82/662 Fred Mulley to Cyrus Vance, 23 December 1976; TNA: PREM 16/1485 Anthony Crosland to the Prime Minister, 9 December 1976.
7. TNA: PREM 16/1909 Jimmy Carter to James Callaghan, undated [circa February 1977]; TNA: PREM 16/1909 Ramsbotham to FCO, Tel. 337, 26 January 1976; Peter Ramsbotham, British Diplomatic Oral History Project (hereafter *BDOHP*), p. 41.
8. TNA: FCO 82/687 G. N. Smith to Mr Edmonds, 16 February 1977; TNA: PREM 16/1485 Ramsbotham to the FCO, Tel. 946, 3 March 1977.
9. TNA: FCO 82/764 Sue Darling to Davidson, 18 May 1977; TNA: FCO 82/687 G. N. Smith to Mr Edmonds, 16 February 1977; TNA: PREM 16/1488 E. A. J. Fergusson to Patrick Wright, 31 March 1977; TNA: PREM 16/1488 Smith to FCO, Tel. 239, 31 March 1977; TNA: FCO 58/1169 Ramsbotham to FCO, Tel. 1324, 25 March 1977; TNA: FCO 82/761 Ramsbotham to FCO, Tel. 294, 24 January 1977. For Callaghan's stance see James Callaghan, *Time & Chance* (London: Collins, 1987), p. 430.
10. Kenneth O. Morgan, *Callaghan: A Life* (Oxford: Oxford University Press, 1997), pp. 437–9. Mondale was provided with an appraisal of the Callaghan cabinet whom he would meet in London. Generally speaking the British cabinet was seen in a positive light as Callaghan, Crosland, Healey and Mulley were all described as being favourably disposed to the United States. One amusing highlight, however, suggested that Denis Healey was a 'political thug' though it was not indicated whether this was a negative characteristic or not! See From the Ambassador in the Embassy in London to the US Mission in Berlin, 25 January 1977, Document Number: 1977LONDON01307, File Number: D770026-0867, State Department Electronic Telegrams,

available at <http://aad.archives.gov/aad/createpdf?rid=18055&dt=2532&dl=1629> (last accessed 13 May 2016).
11. On the Vladivostok agreements see Barbara Zanchetta, *The Transformation of American International Power in the 1970s* (Cambridge: Cambridge University Press, 2014), pp. 165–6, 179–80.
12. TNA: PREM 16/1910 Extract from PMs meeting with US vice president Mondale, 29 January 1977.
13. The *Daily Mail* newspaper reported that the American administration had been unhappy with the hospitality that they had received at Downing Street. This incident appears to have caused Mondale quite a lot of embarrassment and he therefore wrote and telephoned Callaghan to deny the reports and to offer an apology. Callaghan appears to have taken the report rather magnanimously and instructed Mondale to forget the incident. See TNA: PREM 16/1487 Walter Mondale to the Prime Minister, attached in Ann Armstrong to the Prime Minister, 31 January 1977; TNA: PREM 16/1487 Telephone conversation between the Prime Minister and Mr Mondale, 4 February 1977. In contrast to the negative report provided in the *Daily Mail*, Bernard Donoughue recorded in his diary that the dinner with Mondale had been 'very jolly', so much so that Mondale had sung 'Glasgow Belongs to Me' and Callaghan responded with 'Jerusalem'. Bernard Donoughue, *Downing Street Diary: Volume 2 – With James Callaghan in No. 10* (London: Jonathan Cape, 2008), 27 January 1977, p. 139.
14. Letter from President Carter to the Soviet General Secretary Brezhnev, 26 January 1977, in *FRUS: Foundations of Foreign Policy, 1974–1980*, Vol. I, Doc. 17, p. 74. Further speeches which pushed the Human Rights agenda can be found in Address by Secretary of State Vance, 30 April 1977, in *FRUS: Foundations of Foreign Policy, 1974–1980*, Vol. I, Doc. 37, pp. 154–60; Address by President Carter, 22 May 1977, in *FRUS: Foundations of Foreign Policy, 1974–1980*, Vol. I, Doc. 40, pp. 169–75.
15. Owen provides the misleading impression in his memoirs that he was fully supportive of promoting international human rights and believed in the necessity of pushing this agenda in bilateral diplomacy with the Soviet Union. See David Owen, *Time to Declare* (London: Michael Joseph, 1991), pp. 337–41. On the points made in the text see James E. Cronin, *Global Rules: America, Britain and a Disordered World* (New Haven, CT: Yale University Press, 2014), pp. 68–71; Ritchie Ovendale, *Anglo-American Relations in the Twentieth Century* (Basingstoke: Palgrave Macmillan, 1998),

Notes

p. 137; John Dickie, *'Special' No More: Anglo-American Relations: Rhetoric and Reality* (London: Weidenfeld & Nicolson, 1994), p. 160.

16. Address at Commencement Exercises at the University, 22 May 1977, in *PPP: Jimmy Carter, 1977, Book One*, pp. 954–62.
17. TNA: PREM 16/1485 Record of a Telephone Conversation between the Prime Minister and President-elect Carter, 13 January 1977.
18. TNA: PREM 16/1486 Carter Talks: UK–US Defence Nuclear and Intelligence Co-operation, undated [March 1977]; TNA: PREM 16/1485 Michael Palliser to John Hunt, 14 February 1977; TNA: PREM 16/1486 Carter Talks, undated [March 1977]; TNA: PREM 16/1485 K. R. S. (Stowe) to the Prime Minister, 16 February 1977.
19. TNA: PREM 16/1486 Note of a Meeting between the Prime Minister and Dr Zbigniew Brzezinski at Blair House, 10 March 1977.
20. TNA: PREM 16/1486 Note of a Meeting between the Prime Minister and the United States Secretary of Defence at Blair House, 10 March 1977.
21. TNA: PREM 16/1486 Note of a Meeting between the Prime Minister and the United States Secretary of Defence at Blair House, 10 March 1977. On the evolution of Carter's SALT policy during the early days of the administration see Brian J. Auten, *Carter's Conversion: The Hardening of American Defense Policy* (Columbia: University of Missouri Press, 2009), pp. 117–73.
22. TNA: PREM 16/1486 Record of a Meeting held at the White House, 11 March 1977; Exchange of Remarks between the President and James Callaghan, 10 March 1977, File: 3/10–11/77 (United Kingdom) Visit, 2-3-77, National Security Affairs Collection 13 Brzezinski Material, Box 11, JCL.
23. Dickie, *'Special' No More*, p. 161.
24. TNA: PREM 16/1486 Peter Ramsbotham to David Owen, 18 March 1977.
25. TNA: PREM 16/1909 John Moreton to Michael Palliser, 22 June 1977.
26. TNA: PREM 16/1486 Record of a Meeting held at the White House, 11 March 1977. Washington suspected that these problems would likely be raised again very soon, which indeed they would be during Vance's visit to London at the end of March 1977. See From the Ambassador in London to the Secretary of State, 30 March 1977, Document Number: 1977LONDON05230, File Number: D770109-0235, State Department Electronic Telegrams,

available at <http://aad.archives.gov/aad/createpdf?rid=52335&dt=2532&dl=1629> (last accessed 13 May 2016); TNA: FCO 82/766 'Visit of Mr Vance', From the FCO to UKRep Brussels, Tel. 689, 6 April 1977.
27. Exchange of Remarks between the President and James Callaghan, 10 March 1977, File: 3/10–11/77 (United Kingdom) Visit, 2-3-77, National Security Affairs Collection 13 Brzezinski Material, Box 11, JCL; TNA: PREM 16/1486 Record of a Meeting held at the White House, 11 March 1977.
28. On the broader point about the nuclear relationship being exploited by Washington see R. Gerald Hughes and Thomas Robb, 'Kissinger and the Diplomacy of Coercive Linkage in the "Special Relationship" between the United States and Great Britain, 1969–77', *Diplomatic History*, 37:4 (2013), pp. 861–906. Brown's reflections on the nature of the Anglo-American nuclear relationship are recorded in Cassandra Smith, 'Harold Brown', in Jennifer Mackby and Paul Cornish (eds), *US–UK Nuclear Cooperation after Fifty Years* (Washington DC: CSIS Press, 2008), pp. 271–2.
29. TNA: PREM 16/1909 Ramsbotham to FCO, Tel. 4131, 3 December 1976.
30. PRM-NSC 10, Military Strategy and Force Posture Review Final Report, undated [circa March 1977], File: Presidential Review Memorandum 1-10, Vertical File, Box 105, JCL.
31. 'Four Year Policy Objectives', attached to Memorandum for the President from Zbigniew Brzezinski, 18 April 1977, File: Four Year Goals 4/77, Zbigniew Brzezinski Collection, Box 23, JCL.
32. Douglas Brinkley, 'The Rising Stock of Jimmy Carter: The "Hands on" Legacy of our Thirty-ninth President', *Diplomatic History*, 20:4 (1996), pp. 522–3; *PPP: Jimmy Carter, 1977, Book One*, pp. 957–62; Remarks by Secretary of Defense Brown, 29 July 1977, in *FRUS: Foundations of Foreign Policy, 1974–1980*, Vol. I, Doc. 53, pp. 237–44.
33. Policy Review Committee Meeting, 8 July 1977, File: Meetings PRC 22 7-8-77, Zbigniew Brzezinski Collection, Box 24, JCL; Memorandum for the President from Harold Brown, 10 December 1977, File: NATO, 12/77–5/78, National Security Affairs Collection 8 Brzezinski Material, Box 12, JCL; Presidential Directive-NSC 18, 24 August 1977, File: Presidential Directives 1–20, Vertical File, Box 100, JCL.
34. Jimmy Carter, *White House Diary* (New York: Farrar, Straus and Giroux, 2010), 9 May 1977, p. 51. See also Policy Review Committee

Meeting, 8 July 1977, File: Meetings PRC 22 7-8-77, Zbigniew Brzezinski Collection, Box 24, JCL.
35. TNA: PREM 16/1486 Record of a Meeting held at the White House, 11 March 1977.
36. TNA: T 381/31 Seminar on the External Balance Sheet: Brief A attached to D. A. Walker to Mrs Gedley-Miller, 30 June 1977; TNA: T 381/141 'General Government Transfers and the Balance of Payments', K. E. Couzens to Mr Middleton, 31 May 1978; TNA: PREM 16/1486 Ramsbotham to Owen, 18 March 1977.
37. Donoughue, *With James Callaghan*, 10 March 1977, p. 161.
38. Memorandum for the President from Harold Brown, 10 December 1977, File: NATO, 12/77–5/78, National Security Affairs Collection 8 Brzezinski Material, Box 12, JCL; Jonathan Haslam, *The Soviet Union and the Politics of Nuclear Weapons in Europe, 1969–87: The Problem of the SS-20* (Basingstoke: Macmillan, 1989), pp. 89–90.
39. Memorandum for the President from Bert Lance and Zbigniew Brzezinski, 21 June 1977, File: Enhanced Radiation Weapons and Radiological Warfare, 6-8-77, National Security Affairs Collection 7, Box 16, JCL.
40. Carter was informed about the perceived capabilities of the SS-20. For the American analysis of SS-20 see Memorandum for the President from Zbigniew Brzezinski, undated [circa 10 December 1978], File: Enhanced Radiation Weapons and Radiological Warfare 9/77–1/78, National Security Affairs Collection 7 Brzezinski Material, Box 17, JCL.
41. Gordon S. Barrass, *Great Cold War: A Journey through the Hall of Mirrors* (Stanford, CA: Stanford University Press, 2009), p. 216.
42. An excellent British survey on nuclear weapons strategy is contained in TNA: PREM 19/127 'Nuclear Strategy: Background', attached to Frank Cooper to Robert Armstrong, 12 December 1979. One paper provided to Fred Mulley by Dan Smith of the Richardson Institute observed that 'Distinctions between tactical and strategic weapons are always confusing and often merely academic. NATO's 7000 tactical nuclear weapons in Europe could kill millions of people, rendering vast areas uninhabitable – a "strategic" effect if ever there were one.' See TNA: DEFE 24/1065 'Arms Control and Long Range Cruise Missiles: A Proposal', by Dan Smith, December 1976. On long-term British and European problems with the concept of nuclear war fighting see Marc Trachtenberg, *A Constructed Peace:*

The Making of a European Settlement, 1945–63 (Princeton, NJ: Princeton University Press, 1999), pp. 283–351.
43. As one observer has noted, whilst the president and Congress are separate institutions, they share power for the implementation of both domestic and foreign policies. See Richard E. Neustadt, *Presidential Power and the Modern Presidents: The Politics of Leadership from Roosevelt to Reagan* (New York: Free Press, 1990), p. 29. See also Carter's notes on a discussion he had with Senator Henry 'Scoop' Jackson (D-Washington). In this meeting, the president was left in no doubt as to how difficult it would be to attain the necessary congressional support for the successful ratification of SALT II. Carter, *White House Diary*, 15 December 1977, p. 149. See also Joe Renouard and D. Nathan Vigil, 'The Quest for Leadership in a Time of Peace: Jimmy Carter and Western Europe, 1977–1981', in Matthias Schulz and Thomas A. Schwartz (eds), *The Strained Alliance: US–European Relations from Nixon to Carter* (Cambridge: Cambridge University Press, 2009), pp. 314–15; Jimmy Carter to Mel Price, 21 July 1977, File: 7/1/77–7/31/77, White House Central Files, Box ND-49, JCL. Carter was warned very early into his administration about the importance of retaining congressional support if he was to achieve his foreign policy ambitions. Carter emphasised that he wanted key Democratic and Republican congressmen briefed on foreign policy matters as a 'matter of routine'. Both Cyrus Vance and Hamilton Jordan drew up lengthy assessments on the possible positions of senators in relation to Carter's foreign policy goals. For Carter's instruction to brief Republicans and Democrats see Jimmy Carter to Cyrus Vance and Zbigniew Brzezinski, 1 April 1977, in MS 1664, Series II, Folder 4, Box 8, Vance Papers. For Vance and Jordan's advice see Paper prepared by the President's Assistant (Jordan), June 1977, in *FRUS: Foundations of Foreign Policy, 1974–1980*, Vol. I, Doc. 42, pp. 179–80; Memorandum, 'Work Plan for the Middle East', 25 June 1977, in File: Foreign Policy Issues – Work Plans, 6/77, Office of the Chief of Staff Files, Hamilton Jordan's Confidential Files, Box 34a, JCL; 'An Agenda for the First Six Months', by Cyrus Vance, undated [circa January 1977], MS 1664, Series II, Folder 4, Box 8, Vance Papers.
44. Raymond Garthoff, *Détente and Confrontation: American–Soviet Relations from Nixon to Reagan* (Washington DC: The Brookings Institution, 1994), p. 937.
45. Memorandum for the President from Bert Lance and Zbigniew Brzezinski, 21 June 1977, File: Enhanced Radiation Weapons and

Radiological Warfare, 6-8-77, National Security Affairs Collection 7, Box 16, JCL; Carter, *White House Diary*, 7 July 1977, p. 68.
46. Herbet P. Kitschelt, 'Political Opportunity and Political Protest: Anti-nuclear Movements in Four Democracies', *British Journal of Political Science*, 16:1 (1986), pp. 56–85.
47. Memorandum for the President from Cyrus Vance, 25 July 1977, File: Enhanced Radiation Weapons and Radiological Warfare, 6-8-77, National Security Affairs Collection 7 Brzezinski Material, Box 16, JCL; Memorandum for Zbigniew Brzezinski from Jim Thomson and Victor Utgoff, 8 September 1977, File: Enhanced Radiation Weapons and Radiological Warfare 9/77–1/78, National Security Affairs Collection 7 Brzezinski Material, Box 17, JCL.
48. Memorandum for the President from Cyrus Vance, 25 July 1977, File: Enhanced Radiation Weapons and Radiological Warfare, 6-8-77, National Security Affairs Collection 7 Brzezinski Material, Box 16, JCL.
49. TNA: PREM 16/1911 Jay to FCO, Tel. 4173, 24 September 1977; TNA: PREM 16/1911 Dr Brzezinski's Call on the Prime Minister, 27 September 1977.
50. The British were right to be concerned given that Brzezinski told Jay that ERWs would allow the United States to develop limited nuclear war fighting options. See TNA: PREM 16/1911 Jay to FCO, Tel. 4173, 24 September 1977.
51. On the interplay between Labour Party politics and foreign policy see Paul Corthorn and Jonathan Davies (eds), *The British Labour Party and the Wider World: Domestic Politics, Internationalism and Foreign Policy* (London: I. B. Tauris, 2007). This debate about the merits of nuclear weapons would come to a head in 1983 when the Labour Party entered the general election promising unilateral nuclear disarmament. As the 1983 manifesto read, 'We are the only party that offers a non-nuclear defence policy.' See 'The New Hope for Britain', Labour Party manifesto, 1983, available at <http://www.politicsresources.net/area/uk/man/lab83.htm#Young> (last accessed 13 May 2016).
52. Peter Hennessy, *The Prime Minister: The Office and Its Holders since 1945* (London: Penguin, 2001), pp. 390–2. For an interesting insider account of Callaghan's troubles within the Labour Party see Donoughue, *With James Callaghan*, pp. 176–300.
53. TNA: PREM 16/1911 Prime Minister's Meeting with Dr Brzezinski, Brief No. 2, 27 September 1977.
54. From AmEmbassy Bonn to SecState Washington DC, Tel. Bonn 14834, September 1977, File: Enhanced Radiation Weapons and

Radiological Warfare 9/77–1/78, National Security Affairs Collection 7 Brzezinski Material, Box 17, JCL; TNA: PREM 16/1911 Dr Brzezinski's Call on the Prime Minister, 27 September 1977.
55. Within the Carter administration discussion continued as to what the president should do in relation to the ERW. See for example Special Coordination Committee Meeting, 16 November 1977, File: Meetings SCC 41 11/16/77, Zbigniew Brzezinski Collection, Box 27, JCL.
56. TNA: FCO 58/1162 Record of a Call by Sir Michael Palliser and the Honourable Sir Peter Ramsbotham on Dr Zbigniew Brzezinski, 26 May 1977.
57. Thomas Robb, 'The "Limit of What is Tolerable": British Defence Cuts and the "Special Relationship," 1974–1976', *Diplomacy and Statecraft*, 22:2 (2011), pp. 321–37; TNA: DEFE 24/1658 'NATO Long Term Defence Programme', attached to G. C. Safford to Chief of Defence Staff, 13 April 1977; TNA: DEFE 24/1302 Harold [Brown] to Fred [Mulley], 13 May 1977; TNA: DEFE 24/1302 Fred [Mulley] to Harold [Brown], 24 May 1977.
58. TNA: PREM 16/1489 David Owen to James Callaghan, 1 October 1977.
59. For British fears see TNA: PREM 16/1489 Note of a Meeting called by the Prime Minister on 27 September 1977 to discuss President Carter's letter of 19 September to discuss nuclear deterrence, 27 September 1977.
60. On the problems confronting Carter see Julian E. Zelizer, *Arsenal of Democracy: The Politics of National Security – From World War II to the War on Terrorism* (New York: Basic Books, 2010), pp. 278–80; Warren Christopher, *Chances of a Lifetime: A Memoir* (New York: Scribner, 2001), pp. 81–8; Robert Siner, 'Brown Denies Shift in Policy Conceding Big German Loss', *International Herald Tribune*, 4 August 1977; Betty Glad, *An Outsider in the White House: Jimmy Carter, His Advisors, and the Making of American Foreign Policy* (Ithaca: Cornell University Press, 2010), pp. 43–76.
61. Presidential Directive-NSC 18, 24 August 1977, File: Presidential Directives 1–20, Vertical File, Box 100, JCL.
62. Policy Review Committee Meeting, 8 July 1977, File: Meetings PRC 22 7-8-77, Zbigniew Brzezinski Collection, Box 24, JCL; Presidential Directive-NSC 18, 24 August 1977, File: Presidential Directives 1–20, Vertical File, Box 100, JCL.
63. Memorandum for the President from Harold Brown, 10 December 1977, File: NATO, 12/77–5/78, National Security Affairs Collection

8 Brzezinski Material, Box 12, JCL; C. J. Bartlett, *'The Special Relationship': Anglo-American Relations since 1945* (London: Longman, 1992), p. 141.
64. John Lewis Gaddis, *The Cold War* (London: Allen Lane, 2005), p. 201; Inaugural Address of President Jimmy Carter, 20 January 1977, in *PPP: Jimmy Carter, 1977, Book One*, pp. 1–4; Matthias Schulz, 'The Reluctant European: Helmut Schmidt, the European Community, and Transatlantic Relations', in Schulz and Schwartz, *The Strained Alliance*, p. 299. Carter publicly announced his commitment to drastically reduce existing nuclear stockpiles in Jimmy Carter address to United Nations General Assembly, 17 March 1977, *PPP: Jimmy Carter, 1977, Book One*, pp. 444–51.
65. Memorandum of Conversation, 1 February 1977, File: Memcons: President, 2/77, National Security Affairs Collection 7 Brzezinski Material, Box 34, JCL.
66. See Gerald Segal, *The Simon & Schuster Guide to the World Today* (New York: Simon & Schuster, 1987), p. 82.
67. John Prados, *Keepers of the Keys: A History of the National Security Council from Truman to Bush* (New York: William Morrow, 1991), pp. 389–91; Olav Njølstad, 'Key of Keys? SALT II and the Breakdown of Détente', in Odd Arne Westad (ed.), *The Fall of Détente: Soviet–American Relations during the Carter Years* (Oslo: Scandinavian Press, 1997), p. 37; Presidential Directive-NSC 7, 23 March 1977 File: Presidential Directives 1–20, Vertical File, Box 100, JCL.
68. A non-circumvention clause would prevent either Moscow or Washington providing third parties with nuclear weapons in order to gain a strategic advantage and thus circumvent the SALT II agreement. For British concerns and the American thinking about the need to accept a non-circumvention agreement see David Owen, *Nuclear Papers* (Liverpool: Liverpool University Press, 2010), pp. 150–78; TNA: FCO 58/1169 Ramsbotham to FCO, Tel. 1324, 25 March 1977; TNA: PREM 16/1488 Note of a Discussion between the Prime Minister and the United States Secretary of State at 10 Downing Street, 31 March 1977; TNA: PREM 16/1184 John Hunt to the Prime Minister, 22 July 1977; Memorandum of Conversation, 23 July 1977, Memcons: President 7/77, National Security Affairs Collection 7 Brzezinski Material, Box 35, JCL; Glad, *An Outsider in the White House*, pp. 53–4.
69. For private concerns see TNA: FCO 82/760 Secretary of State's Visit to the United States: Brief 13, Meeting with the US Secretary of

State, 20 September 1977; TNA: PREM 16/1489 Jay to FCO, Tel. 4324, 5 October 1977. For bilateral reassurances see TNA: PREM 16/1911 Dr Brzezinski's Call on the Prime Minister, 27 September 1977; TNA: PREM 16/1489 B. G. Cartledge to W. K. Prendergast, 4 October 1977; TNA: PREM 16/1489 W. K. Prendergast to Bryan Cartledge, 4 October 1977. Such was the success of British diplomacy that the president noted privately that it appeared as if the British were in full support of his overall foreign policy objectives. See Carter, *White House Diary*, 29 September 1977, pp. 11–12.
70. TNA: PREM 16/1184 John Hunt to the Prime Minister, 22 July 1977.
71. Memorandum of Conversation, 27 September 1977, Memcons: Brzezinski 1/9/77, National Security Affairs Collection 7 Brzezinski Material, Box 33, JCL.
72. Cyrus Vance, *Hard Choices: Critical Years in America's Foreign Policy* (New York: Simon & Schuster, 1983), p. 97.
73. TNA: PREM 16/1489 Note of a Meeting called by the Prime Minister on 27 September 1977 to discuss President Carter's letter of 19 September to discuss nuclear deterrence, 27 September 1977; TNA: FCO 58/1162 Michael Palliser to Private Secretary, 23 July 1977. Extensive Anglo-American discussion did take place over SALT II, nuclear weapons policy and technological developments. See for example TNA: DEFE 24/1343 Record of Anglo-US Consultations on Cruise Missiles, 29 July 1977; TNA: DEFE 24/1065 Discussions with the New American Administration, 24 March 1977.
74. Jay was appointed as the British Ambassador to the United States in 1977 amid a storm of controversy. Jay happened to be married to the prime minister's daughter and his appointment was seen by many as an act of nepotism on Callaghan's part. Moreover, the dismissal of Sir Peter Ramsbotham was seen as unfair both within the diplomatic service and by the wider public. Jay's appointment was hardly helped by the fact that his wife, Susan Jay, was having indiscreet affairs with several American servicemen. See Callaghan, *Time & Chance*, pp. 448–9; Owen, *Time to Declare*, pp. 323–4; Peter Ramsbotham, *BDOHP*, pp. 42–3; Peter Jay, *BDOHP*, pp. 29–34. The US Embassy in London informed Washington about the mounting controversy that Jay's appointment had created and concluded that the episode had 'certainly damaged [Callaghan's] reputation, probably more seriously than we originally anticipated'. See From the Ambassador in the Embassy in London to the Secretary of State, 16 May 1977, Document Number: 1977LONDON08030,

File Number: D770173-0434, State Department Electronic Telegrams, available at <http://aad.archives.gov/aad/createpdf?rid=11 1131&dt=2532&dl=1629> (last accessed 13 May 2016). Indeed, Bernard Donoughue noted that Callaghan's decision to appoint Jay had undermined the 'Mr Clean' image which he had cultivated. See Donoughue, *With James Callaghan*, 11 May 1977, p. 187. Officials within the British Foreign Office were certainly unimpressed with Ramsbotham's dismissal. See for example Curtis Keeble, *BDOHP*, p. 33.

75. TNA: PREM 16/1184 Jay to FCO, Tel. 4560, 20 October [1977].
76. TNA: FCO 82/687 G. N. Smith to Mr Edmonds, 16 February 1977.
77. Donoughue, *With James Callaghan*, 7 March 1977, p. 157. Following his first meeting with Carter, Donoughue again recorded Callaghan's concern with the president's religious beliefs. See ibid., 10 March 1977, p. 161.
78. TNA: PREM 16/1485 'Annex A: Prime Minister's Visit to Washington', attached to John Hunt to Mr Stowe, 18 February 1977; TNA: FCO 58/1162 Note of an Interdepartmental Meeting with Mr W. S. Ryrie at the ODM, 24 November 1977. On 'The Troubles' see Paul Bew, *Ireland: The Politics of Enmity 1789–2006* (Oxford: Oxford University Press, 2007), pp. 486–555.
79. British concerns would prove to be misplaced as US arms embargoes were undertaken unilaterally. The United Kingdom, along with other European states, quickly filled the void left in arms contracts and, in an ironic turn, the United Kingdom actually benefited economically from Carter's decision to enforce arms embargoes against certain regimes for human rights violations. For British concerns see TNA: FCO 58/1162 Note of an Interdepartmental Meeting with Mr W. S. Ryrie at the ODM, 24 November 1977; TNA: FCO 58/1162 Richard to FCO, Tel. 226, 23 December 1977; TNA: FCO 58/1160 Richard to FCO, Tel. 278, 13 March 1977. On the broader point that British arms manufacturers benefited from Carter's decision to implement arms embargoes against certain countries see Hugh Bicheno, *Razor's Edge: The Unofficial History of the Falklands War* (London: Weidenfeld & Nicolson, 2006), pp. 64–7.
80. TNA: PREM 16/1488 E. A. J. Fergusson to Patrick Wright, 31 March 1977; TNA: PREM 16/1488 Smith to FCO, Tel. 239, 31 March 1977; TNA: FCO 58/1169 Ramsbotham to FCO, Tel. 1324, 25 March 1977.
81. TNA: PREM 16/1911 'Dr Brzezinski's Call on the Prime Minister', 27 September 1977

82. TNA: FCO 58/1160 Peter Ramsbotham to R. A. Hibbert, 10 February 1977; TNA: PREM 16/1485 'Annex A: Prime Minister's Visit to Washington', attached to John Hunt to Mr Stowe, 18 February 1977; TNA: FCO 58/1160 Ramsbotham to FCO, Tel. 396, 31 January 1977; TNA: FCO 58/1161 M. E. Pike to B. G. Cartledge, 2 July 1977.
83. Burton I. Kaufman, *The Presidency of James Earl Carter* (Lawrence: University Press of Kansas, 1997), pp. 39–42; Glad, *An Outsider in the White House*, pp. 46–54; Thomas M. Nichols, 'Carter and the Soviets: The Origins of the US Return to a Strategy of Confrontation', *Diplomacy and Statecraft*, 13:2 (2002), pp. 21–42, esp. p. 22.
84. TNA: PREM 16/1488 Smith to FCO, Tel. 227, 29 March 1977; TNA: PREM 16/1488 E. A. J. Fergusson to Patrick Wright, 31 March 1977. Vance had proposed deep cuts to the existing strategic stockpiles in opposition to what had been previously agreed at the Vladivostok summit, which would have only limited the growth of the respective stockpiles of nuclear weapons. For Vance's denial that Carter's human rights agenda had contributed to the failure of the SALT talks see TNA: FCO 82/767 'Secretary Vance's Trip to Moscow', 6 April 1977.
85. Olav Njølstad, 'The Collapse of Superpower Détente, 1975–1980', in Melvyn Leffler and Odd Arne Westad (eds), *The Cambridge History of the Cold War: Endings* (Cambridge: Cambridge University Press, 2010), Vol. III, p. 145.
86. Memorandum of Conversation, 23 September 1977, Memcons: President 9/19–30/77, National Security Affairs Collection 7 Brzezinski Material, Box 35, JCL; Jonathan Haslam, *Russia's Cold War: From the October Revolution to the Fall of the Wall* (New Haven, CT: Yale University Press, 2011), p. 305.
87. Vance denied in discussion with David Owen that the Carter administration's promotion of human rights concerns with the Soviet leadership explained why the Moscow talks had failed to produce a SALT II agreement. See TNA: FCO 82/766 'Secretary Vance's Visit to Moscow', A. Carter to C. J. Rawlinson, 6 April 1977. See also Memorandum prepared in the Department of State, 26 June 1977, in *FRUS: Foundations of Foreign Policy, 1974–1980*, Vol. I, Doc. 46, pp. 195–8. For reference to the 'linkages' required in US foreign policy see Memorandum from the President's Assistant for National Security Affairs to President Carter, 21 October 1977, in *FRUS: Foundations of Foreign Policy, 1974–1980*, Vol. I, Doc. 57, p. 264. For the quote see Memorandum from the President's

Assistant for National Security Affairs to President Carter, 7 April 1978, in *FRUS: Foundations of Foreign Policy, 1974–1980*, Vol. I, Doc. 73, p. 355.
88. Memorandum from the Executive Secretary of the Department of State to the President's Assistant for National Security Affairs, 28 June 1977, in *FRUS: Foundations of Foreign Policy, 1974–1980*, Vol. I, Doc. 47, pp. 202–6; Address by President Carter before the United Nations General Assembly, 4 October 1977, in *FRUS: Foundations of Foreign Policy, 1974–1980*, Vol. I, Doc. 56, pp. 255–64.
89. Glad, *An Outsider in the White House*, pp. 30–75. Certainly, the public rhetoric of the Carter administration began to emphasise the need for maintaining a strong defence posture and less attention was given to the promotion of human rights. Yet, simultaneously, efforts were made to remind the American people that the Carter administration was committed to the cause of international human rights. This juxtaposition in Carter's foreign policy was never satisfactorily rectified and contradictory messages continued to emanate throughout the Carter presidency. Little wonder then that Soviet policy makers would protest about the mixed messages they received from Washington. See for example Address by Secretary of State Vance: Foreign Policy Decision for 1978, 13 January 1978, in *FRUS: Foundations of Foreign Policy, 1974–1980*, Vol. I, Doc. 63, pp. 296–305; Address by the Deputy Secretary of State, Human Rights: The Diplomacy of the First Year, 13 February 1978, in *FRUS: Foundations of Foreign Policy, 1974–1980*, Vol. I, Doc. 69, pp. 328–36; Memorandum of Conversation, 23 September 1977, Memcons: President 9/19–30/77, National Security Affairs Collection 7 Brzezinski Material, Box 35, JCL.
90. George C. Herring, *From Colony to Superpower: U.S. Foreign Relations since 1776* (Oxford: Oxford University Press, 2008), p. 836.
91. TNA: PREM 16/1909 Ramsbotham to FCO, Tel. 2311, 25 May 1977; Carter, *White House Diary*, 7 May 1977, p. 49; TNA: PREM 16/1911 Dr Brzezinski's Call on the Prime Minister, 27 September 1977; TNA: 16/1488 Note of a Conversation between the Prime Minister and the US Secretary of State at 10 Downing Street, Thursday 31 March 1977 at 1845, 31 March 1977; TNA: FCO 58/1162 Record of a Meeting held between the Secretary of State for Foreign and Commonwealth Affairs and Mrs Patricia Derian at the Foreign and Commonwealth Office, 9 December 1977; TNA: FCO 58/1162 Peter Ramsbotham to Zbigniew Brzezinski, 13 June 1977; TNA: PREM 16/1488 Record of a Conversation between the Foreign and

Commonwealth Secretary and Mr Cyrus Vance in the Foreign and Commonwealth Office, 1 April 1977.
92. Memorandum from the President's Assistant for National Security Affairs to President Carter, undated [circa July 1977], in *FRUS: Foundations of Foreign Policy, 1974–1980*, Vol. I, Doc. 49, pp. 209–10.
93. Graeme Mount, *895 Days that Changed the World: The Presidency of Gerald R. Ford* (London: Black Rose Books, 2006), pp. 8–11.
94. John Dumbrell, *The Carter Presidency: A Re-evaluation* (Manchester: Manchester University Press, 1995), pp. 132–3.
95. TNA: CJ 4/1835 'President-elect Carter and Northern Ireland', November 1976; Roy Mason, *Paying the Price* (London: Robert Hale, 1999), p. 206; TNA: CJ 4/1835 'Governor Carter and Northern Ireland', E. J. Hughes to Miss Darling, 3 December 1976. Carter denied that he had ever stated that he would support a unified Ireland. Commentary in the *Irish Times* suggested that Carter's southern accent (he was from Georgia) meant that he sometimes slurred his words which made fully comprehending his statements somewhat difficult. See 'What Carter Said that Day in Pittsburgh', *Irish Times*, 10 November 1976.
96. This they were legally obligated to provide as the State Department had to provide an assessment of the Human Rights situation within every country with which the United States shared a security relationship. The British section of the report was provided to the FCO. See TNA: FCO 58/1169 'UK Section of Human Rights report transmitted to Congress', attached to S. Darling to Mr Willson, 16 March 1977. For British irritation see TNA: FCO 58/1169 P. L. V. Mallet to Mr Mathers, 22 March 1977; Mason, *Paying the Price*, p. 206.
97. Dumbrell, *The Carter Presidency*, p. 134.
98. Mason, *Paying the Price*, p. 206.
99. From the Secretary of State to USDEL Secretary, 1 October 1977, Document Number: 1977STATE235933, File Number: D770357-0954, Department of State Electronic Telegrams, available at <http://aad.archives.gov/aad/createpdf?rid=252456&dt=2532&dl=1629> (last accessed 13 May 2016).
100. See From the Embassy in London to the Secretary of State, 30 September 1977, Document Number: 1977LONDON16372, File Number: D770357-0318, State Department Electronic Telegrams, available at <http://aad.archives.gov/aad/createpdf?rid=217945&dt=2532&dl=1629> (last accessed 13 May 2016); From the

Ambassador in the Embassy in Dublin to the Secretary of State, 23 December 1977, Document Number: 1977DUBLIN02919, File Number: D770480-0547, State Department Electronic Telegrams, available at <http://aad.archives.gov/aad/createpdf?rid=301231&dt=2532&dl=1629> (last accessed 13 May 2016); From the Ambassador in the Embassy in Dublin to the Secretary of State, 20 April 1978, Document Number: 1978DUBLIN01309, File Number: D780171-0900, Department of State Electronic Telegrams, available at <http://aad.archives.gov/aad/createpdf?rid=101677&dt=2694&dl=2009> (last accessed 13 May 2016).

101. 'Carter and Northern Ireland', Airey Neave to Margaret Thatcher, 1 September 1977, in File: 2/1/1/46, Margaret Thatcher Papers, Churchill Archives Centre, Cambridge University, United Kingdom (hereafter Thatcher Papers).
102. TNA: CJ 4/1835 'President Carter and Northern Ireland', P. G. Wallis to M. R. Melhuish, 8 February 1977; TNA: CJ 4/1835 'Carter and Northern Ireland', I. M. Burns to P. L. V. Mallet, 13 January 1977.
103. Luke Devoy, 'The British Response to American Interest in Northern Ireland, 1976–79', *Irish Studies in International Affairs*, 25 (2014), pp. 221–38.
104. Carl Peter Watts, *Rhodesia's Unilateral Declaration of Independence: An International History* (Basingstoke: Palgrave Macmillan, 2012), pp. 155–82.
105. On Kissinger's efforts at this point see Andrew DeRoche, *Black, White and Chrome: The United States and Zimbabwe, 1953 to 1998* (Trenton, NJ: Africa World Press, 2001), pp. 194–242. On Smith's efforts to resist the rising tide of black African nationalism see Graham Boynton, *Last Days in Cloud Cuckooland: Dispatches from White Africa* (New York: Random House, 1997), pp. 185–7.
106. Memorandum of Conversation, Ford, Kissinger, Scowcroft, 7 January 1977, in Box 21, Memoranda of Conversations – Ford Administration, GFL; Memorandum of Conversation, Ford, Kissinger, Scowcroft, 16 December 1977, in Box 21, Memoranda of Conversations – Ford Administration, GFL. Kissinger's talks with the various leaders are covered in Ian Smith, *Bitter Harvest: The Great Betrayal*, 2nd revised edn (London: Blake, 2001), pp. 183–210; Henry Kissinger, *Years of Renewal* (New York: Simon & Schuster, 1999), pp. 958–1018.
107. On efforts by the Ford administration to resolve the question of majority rule in Rhodesia see Sue Onslow, '"We Must Gain Time":

South Africa, Rhodesia and the Kissinger Initiative of 1976', *South African Historical Journal*, 56:1 (2006), pp. 123–53.
108. Carter told one historian that he 'spent more effort and worry on Rhodesia than I did on the Middle East'. Carter interview with Nancy Mitchell cited in H-Diplo Roundtable on The Transformation of American International Power in the 1970s, available at <https://networks.h-net.org/node/28443/discussions/53660/h-diplo-roundtable-transformation-american-international-power> (last accessed 13 May 2016). Carter overstates the point and it is telling that Rhodesia is barely mentioned within his memoir, *Keeping Faith* (twice) and features comparatively little in his published diaries (*White House Diaries*). Carter's other international policies such as implementing arms control with the Soviet Union and establishing a Middle East peace settlement between Egypt and Israel take precedence in these publications. On Carter's Rhodesian motivations see Nancy Mitchell, 'Tropes of the Cold War: Jimmy Carter and Rhodesia', *Cold War History*, 7:2 (2007), pp. 263–83; Andrew J. DeRoche, 'Standing Firm for Principles: Jimmy Carter and Zimbabwe', *Diplomatic History*, 23:4 (1999), pp. 657–85.
109. On Nkomo see Joshua Nkomo, *Nkomo: The Story of My Life* (London: Methuen, 1984). On Mugabe see Martin Meredith, *Mugabe: Power, Plunder, and the Struggle for Zimbabwe's Future* (London: PublicAffairs, 2007), pp. 19–50.
110. Zaki Laidi, *The Superpowers and Africa: The Constraints of Rivalry, 1960–1990* (Chicago: Chicago University Press, 1990), p. 161.
111. DeRoche, 'Standing Firm for Principles', pp. 657–8; John Hope Franklin and Alfred A. Moss, *From Slavery to Freedom: A History of African Americans* (New York: Knopf, 1994), pp. 555–7; Herschellle Challenor, 'The Influence of Black Americans on U.S. Foreign Policy towards Africa', in Abdul Aziz Said (ed.), *Ethnicity and U.S. Foreign Policy* (New York: Greenwood, 1981), pp. 143–81. Recent efforts concerning race and US foreign policy include Paul Gordon Lauren, *Power and Prejudice: The Politics and Diplomacy of Racial Discrimination* (Boulder, CO: Westview Press, 1996); Brenda Gayle Plummer, *Rising Wind: Black Americans and U.S. Foreign Policy* (Chapel Hill: North Carolina University Press, 1996); Penny Von Eschen, *Race against Empire: Black Americans and Anticolonialism, 1937–1957* (Ithaca, NY: Cornell University Press, 1997); Alexander DeConde, *Ethnicity, Race and American Foreign Policy: A History* (Chicago: Northeastern University Press, 1993); Thomas Borstelmann, *The Cold War and the Color Line: American Race Relations*

in the Global Arena (Cambridge, MA: Harvard University Press, 2001); Philip E. Muehlenbeck (ed.), *Race, Ethnicity, Religion and the Cold War: A Global Perspective* (Nashville: Vanderbilt University Press, 2012).
112. DeRoche, 'Standing Firm for Principles', p. 666.
113. Charles Diggs was the leader of the Black Caucus within Congress. Diggs liaised with British diplomats and lobbied them to take a more assertive position in relation to implementing majority rule in Rhodesia. For reference to these subtle domestic political influences see TNA: PREM 16/1916 From the Minister of the Ministry of Overseas Development to the Prime Minister, 23 June 1978. On Carter's approach to the persisting system of apartheid in South Africa see Alex Thomson, 'The Diplomacy of Impasse: The Carter Administration and Apartheid South Africa', *Diplomacy & Statecraft*, 21:1 (2010), pp. 107–24.
114. Mitchell, 'Tropes of the Cold War', p. 282.
115. Vance, *Hard Choices*, p. 257.
116. As pointed out by Sue Onslow, it is incorrect to assume that South Africa and Rhodesia's alliance was somehow harmonious for 'there were enduring political tensions between the politicians in Salisbury and Pretoria behind the facade of apparent racial and ideological affinity'. However, the shared assumption that both Salisbury and Pretoria were confronting common security threats ensured cooperation. See Sue Onslow, 'South Africa and the Owen/Vance Plan of 1977', *South African Historical Journal*, 51:1 (2004), p. 131.
117. Carter, *White House Diary*, 13 February 1977, p. 20.
118. Young had served as an assistant to Martin Luther King, the most famous Civil Rights leader, in the 1960s and had obtained a seat in Congress in the 1972 elections. On Young see Andrew J. DeRoche, *Andrew Young: Civil Rights Ambassador* (Wilmington, DE: Scholarly Resources, 2003); Bartlett C. Jones, *Flawed Triumphs: Andy Young at the United Nations* (Lanham, MD: University Press of America, 1996).
119. Stephen Low, 'The Zimbabwe Settlement, 1976–1979', in Saadia Touval and I. William Zartman (eds), *International Mediation in Theory and Practice* (Boulder, CO: Westview Press, 1985), pp. 91–109.
120. Carter, *White House Diary*, 3 March 1977, p. 30.
121. Carter, *White House Diary*, 23 March 1977, p. 36; ibid., 23 July 1977, p. 72.

122. On the Byrd Amendment see 'Statement on Rhodesia', by Cyrus Vance, undated, in MS 1664, Series II, Folder 21, Box 9, Vance Papers. For the Kissinger quote see Donoughue, *With James Callaghan*, 26 June 1977, p. 206.
123. From the Secretary of State in Washington to the Ambassador in Lagos, 20 August 1977, Document Number: 1977STATE199120, File Number: D770302-0486, State Department Electronic Telegrams, available at <http://aad.archives.gov/aad/createpdf?rid=190 218&dt=2532&dl=1629> (last accessed 13 May 2016).
124. Donoughue, *With James Callaghan*, 18 July 1977, pp. 222–3.
125. Vance, *Hard Choices*, pp. 264–5.
126. Memorandum for the President from Cyrus Vance, 8 June 1977, File: Evening Reports (State) 6/77, National Security Affairs Collection 7 Brzezinski Material, Box 18, JCL.
127. TNA: FCO 82/766 'Visit of Mr Vance', FCO to UKRep Brussels, Tel. 689, 6 April 1977; From the Ambassador in the Embassy in London to the Secretary of State, 28 July 1977, Document Number: 1977LONDON12445, File Number: D770270-0660, Department of State Electronic Telegrams, available at <http://aad.archives.gov/aad/createpdf?rid=158141&dt=2532&dl=1629> (last accessed 13 May 2016).
128. Carter, *White House Diary*, 14 August 1977, p. 83; Vance, *Hard Choices*, pp. 264–5; Low, 'The Zimbabwe Settlement', pp. 101–2; Memorandum for the President from Cyrus Vance, 8 June 1977, File: Evening Reports (State) 6/77, National Security Affairs Collection 7 Brzezinski Material, Box 18, JCL.
129. From the Secretary of State to the Ambassador in London, 16 August 1977, Document Number: 1977STATE193715, File Number: P840081-2537, Department of State Electronic Telegrams, available at <http://aad.archives.gov/aad/createpdf?rid=197830&dt=2532&dl=1629> (last accessed 13 May 2016). See also the Vance–Owen talks of 12 August 1977 where obvious Anglo-American differences existed: TNA: FCO 82/769 Record of a Meeting between the Foreign and Commonwealth Secretary, the US Secretary of State and the South African Foreign Minister, 12 August 1977.
130. A useful chronology of Owen's diplomacy is provided in Michael Kandiah and Sue Onslow, *Britain and Rhodesia: The Route to Settlement* (London: Institute of Contemporary British History, 2008), pp. 21–45.
131. British proposals were laid out to Washington in From the Ambassador in the Embassy in Lusaka to the Secretary of State, 18 August

1977, Document Number: 1977LUSAKA02452, File Number: D770297-1246, State Department Electronic Telegrams, available at <http://aad.archives.gov/aad/createpdf?rid=187991&dt=2532&dl=1629> (last accessed 13 May 2016); From the Ambassador in the Embassy in Gaborone to the Secretary of State, 19 August 1977, Document Number: 1977GABORO01930, File Number: D770301-0578, State Department Electronic Telegrams, available at <http://aad.archives.gov/aad/createpdf?rid=188926&dt=2532&dl=1629> (last accessed 13 May 2016).
132. Vance, *Hard Choices*, p. 268.
133. Callaghan informed Washington that he was writing to the leaders of the Front Line States to help win their support for further economic sanctions against Rhodesia. See From the Ambassador in London to the Secretary of State, 13 September 1977, Document Number: 1977LONDON15269, File Number: D770331-1031, State Department Electronic Telegrams, available at <http://aad.archives.gov/aad/createpdf?rid=209586&dt=2532&dl=1629> (last accessed 13 May 2016).
134. Address before the General Assembly, 4 October 1977, in *Public Papers of the Presidents of the United States: Jimmy Carter, 1977, Book Two* (Washington DC: United States Government Printing Office, 1978), p. 1720.
135. Vance, *Hard Choices*, p. 271.
136. On the sale of armaments see Mark Phythian, *The Politics of British Arms Sales since 1964* (Manchester: Manchester University Press, 2000), pp. 8–12.
137. TNA: FCO 36/2131 'Minutes of the Fifth Constitutional Settlement Talks', 15 December 1977; TNA: FCO 36/2131 'Minutes of the Sixth Constitutional Settlement Talks', 20 December 1977; 'Contains Codeword', 3 December 1977, File: 12/1/77–12/7/77, National Security Affairs Brzezinski Material, President's Daily Briefing, Box 4, JCL.

Chapter 3

1. Jimmy Carter, *White House Diary* (New York: Farrar, Straus and Giroux, 2010), 25 September 1977, p. 108.
2. Memorandum from the President's Assistant for National Security Affairs to President Carter, 12 January 1978, in *FRUS: Foundations*

of *Foreign Policy, 1974–1980*, Vol. I, Doc. 62, pp. 284–96. It is clear from the Brzezinski papers that he constantly measured his own foreign policy record against that of Kissinger. His staff provided constant analogies to Kissinger's actions in office and illustrated how Carter's approach differed and was evidently superior. See for example Memorandum from William Odom of the National Security Council Staff to the President's Assistant for National Security Affairs (Brzezinski), 24 January 1978, in *FRUS: Foundations of Foreign Policy, 1974–1980*, Vol. I, Doc. 66, pp. 313–17; Memorandum for the President from Zbigniew Brzezinski, 26 January 1978, File: Weekly Reports to the President 82–90: 12/78–3/79, Zbigniew Brzezinski Collection, Box 42, JCL.
3. Carter, *White House Diary*, 25 September 1977, p. 108.
4. Memorandum for the Vice President et al. from Richard Moe, 10 April 1978, in File: SALT, 1978, Office of the Chief of Staff Files, Hamilton Jordan's Confidential Files, Box 37, JCL.
5. Memorandum for the President from Zbigniew Brzezinski, 3 December 1977, in File: Human Rights Policy, 1977, Office of the Chief of Staff Files, Hamilton Jordan's Confidential Files, Box 34b, JCL; Hamilton Jordan to the President, 3 December 1977, in ibid.
6. Callaghan had long been sceptical of the benefits of European Economic Community Membership. See for example James Callaghan on the Common Market, MS Callaghan, Box 139, James Callaghan Papers, Bodleian Library, Oxford University, United Kingdom. For the tension that Callaghan's pursuit of strong relations with Washington created in European circles see for example Roy Jenkins, *European Diary, 1977–1981* (London: Collins, 1989), p. 22.
7. TNA: PREM 16/1909 Peter Jay to David Owen, 5 January 1978; TNA: PREM 16/1909 Peter Jay to David Owen, 28 June 1978. Jay's end-of-year review was even more damning about Carter's performance. See TNA: FCO 82/975 'United States: Annual Review for 1978', by Peter Jay, 9 January 1979. A similarly gloomy appraisal of Carter's presidency was provided by Jay prior to his departure as ambassador following Thatcher's election. See TNA: T 381/160 'The West: The Peril Within', From Her Majesty's Ambassador at Washington to the Secretary of State for Foreign and Commonwealth Affairs, 20 June 1979. Within the British foreign policy making bureaucracy there was a sense that Jay's damning assessments of the president were far too candid. As one official noted, Jay could write whatever he pleased as a journalist but as the British Ambassador to Washington he had to realise that committing such

thoughts to paper could embarrass or hurt British interests if they became public. See TNA: FCO 82/975 Ramsey Melhuish to Mr Middleton, 12 February 1979.
8. Memorandum from Vice President Mondale to President Carter, 19 April 1978, in *FRUS: Foundations of Foreign Policy, 1974–1980*, Vol. I, Doc. 75, p. 371.
9. Hamilton Jordan, *No Such Thing as a Bad Day: A Memoir* (New York: Pocket Books, 2001), p. 65; Foreign Policy and Domestic Politics, Paper prepared by Hamilton Jordan, Memorandum to the President, June 1977, in File: HJ Memo, 6/77, Office of the Chief of Staff Files, Hamilton Jordan's Confidential Files, Foreign Policy/Domestic Politics Memo, Box 34a, JCL.
10. Memorandum from the President's Assistant for National Security Affairs to President Carter, 9 February 1978, in *FRUS: Foundations of Foreign Policy, 1974–1980*, Vol. I, Doc. 68, pp. 325–6.
11. Paper prepared by the National Security Council Staff, undated [circa April 1978], in *Foreign Relations of the United States 1977–1980: Foreign Economic Policy* (Washington DC: United States Government Printing Office, 2013), Vol. III, Doc. 128, p. 387, (hereafter *FRUS 1977–1980: Foreign Economic Policy*).
12. Memorandum from the President's Assistant for National Security Affairs to President Carter, 21 April 1978, in *FRUS: Foundations of Foreign Policy, 1974–1980*, Vol. I, Doc. 76, pp. 373–6.
13. Memorandum from the President's Assistant for National Security Affairs to President Carter, 2 December 1978, in *FRUS: Foundations of Foreign Policy, 1974–1980*, Vol. I, Doc. 100, p. 488.
14. Comprehensive Net Assessment 1978, attached to Memorandum for the President from Zbigniew Brzezinski, 30 March 1979, File: Weekly Reports to the President 91–101: 3/79–6/79, Zbigniew Brzezinski Collection, Box 42, JCL.
15. Memorandum from the President's Assistant for National Security Affairs to President Carter, 2 December 1978, in *FRUS: Foundations of Foreign Policy, 1974–1980*, Vol. I, Doc. 100, p. 488.
16. TNA: DEFE 24/1659 Jay to the FCO, Tel. 2161, 24 May 1978.
17. Memorandum of Conversation, 23 March 1978, in *FRUS 1977–1980: Foreign Economic Policy*, Vol. III, Doc. 121, p. 359. British briefing material can be found in TNA: CAB 133/488 'Prime Minister's Visit to Washington 17 March 1978: The World Economic Situation', Briefing provided by the Treasury, 17 March 1978.
18. The G7 forum originated with a 1975 summit hosted by France that brought together representatives of six governments: France,

Italy, Japan, United Kingdom, United States and West Germany, thus leading to the name Group of Six (G6). The summit became known as the Group of Seven (G7) in 1976 with the addition of Canada. The G7 was comprised of the seven wealthiest developed countries measured by GDP. See Callaghan's previous argument to this effect during a discussion with the US Ambassador in August 1977: From the Ambassador in London to the Secretary of State, 1 August 1977, Document Number: 1977LONDON12610, File Number: N/A, State Department Electronic Telegrams, available at <http://aad.archives.gov/aad/createpdf?rid=198631&dt=2532&dl=1629> (last accessed 13 May 2016). See also TNA: PREM 16/1912 Note for the Record: Meeting with the President of the United States at the White House, 23 March 1978; TNA: PREM 16/1912 The Chancellor of the Exchequer to the Prime Minister, 3 March 1978; Harold Lever to the Prime Minister, 14 February 1978, in File: 2/27, Jay Papers; Memorandum of Conversation, 23 March 1978, in *FRUS 1977–1980: Foreign Economic Policy*, Vol. III, Doc. 121, p. 361.

19. Memorandum of Conversation, 23 March 1978, in *FRUS 1977–1980: Foreign Economic Policy*, Vol. III, Doc. 122, p. 365. See also TNA: PREM 16/1912 From the Prime Minister to the President of the United States, 16 March 1978.
20. From the Ambassador in London to the Secretary of State, 15 June 1978, Document Number: 1978LONDON09489, File Number: D780250-1052, Department of State Electronic Telegrams, available at <http://aad.archives.gov/aad/createpdf?rid=150323&dt=2694&dl=2009> (last accessed 13 May 2016).
21. See TNA: CAB 133/488 PMKV (78)2 'Multilateral Trade Negotiations', 17 March 1978.
22. TNA: PREM 16/1912 Note for the Record: Meeting with the President of the United States at the White House, 23 March 1978. Callaghan's ambitions are laid out in 'The Objectives', Memorandum for the Prime Minister, undated [circa March 1978], in File: 2/28, Jay Papers.
23. Memorandum of Conversation, 23 March 1978, in *FRUS 1977–1980: Foreign Economic Policy*, Vol. III, Doc. 122, pp. 369–70.
24. Letter from President Carter to West German Chancellor Schmidt, 27 March 1980, in *FRUS 1977–1980: Foreign Economic Policy*, Vol. III, Doc. 124, pp. 374–5.
25. Memorandum of Conversation, 17 April 1978, in *FRUS 1977–1980: Foreign Economic Policy*, Vol. III, Doc. 127, pp. 382–5; TNA:

PREM 16/1912 Note of a Meeting between the Prime Minister and Vice President Mondale at the White House, 28 March 1978; TNA: PREM 16/1618 Ryrie to the FCO, Tel. 2856, 12 July 1978; 'Draft instructions for Mr Jay to speak to the President', undated, File: 2/28, Jay Papers.

26. Discussion Paper prepared for the Economic Policy Group, undated [circa June 1978], in *FRUS 1977–1980: Foreign Economic Policy*, Vol. III, Doc. 136, pp. 415–16. The president had tried to win Callaghan's support for this prior to the summit in TNA: PREM 16/1916 The Prime Minister's Conversations with President Carter, 26 June 1978.

27. Memorandum from the Special Representative for Economic Summits (Owen) to President Carter, 23 June 1978, in *FRUS 1977–1980: Foreign Economic Policy*, Vol. III, Doc. 138, p. 423. See also the further breakdown of US objectives in Memorandum from the Special Representative for Economic Summits (Owen) to President Carter, 3 July 1978, in *FRUS 1977–1980: Foreign Economic Policy*, Vol. III, Doc. 140, pp. 426–31.

28. *The Guardian*, 21 June 1978; From the Ambassador in London to the Secretary of State in Washington, 21 June 1978, Document Number: 1978LONDON09838, File Number: D780259-0033, Department of State Electronic Telegrams, available at <http://aad.archives.gov/aad/createpdf?rid=155896&dt=2694&dl=2009> (last accessed 13 May 2016).

29. Minutes of the Bonn Economic Summit Meeting, 16 July 1978, in *FRUS 1977–1980: Foreign Economic Policy*, Vol. III, Doc. 145, pp. 443–4. British ambitions and intentions at the summit can be viewed in TNA: PREM 16/1618 'Steering Brief: Quadripartite Breakfast, Bonn', 17 July 1978; TNA: FCO 59/1549 Henderson to the FCO, Tel. 572, 13 July 1978; ibid., K. E. Couzens to John Hunt, 10 July 1978; ibid., Economic Summit, Bonn: Brief by the Foreign and Commonwealth Office, 12 July 1978. See also Denis Healey, *The Time of My Life* (London: Michael Joseph, 1989), pp. 452–3.

30. Minutes of the Bonn Economic Summit Meeting, 16 July 1978, in *FRUS 1977–1980: Foreign Economic Policy*, Vol. III, Doc. 145, pp. 451–3; Minutes of the Bonn Economic Summit Meeting, 16 July 1978, in *FRUS 1977–1980: Foreign Economic Policy*, Vol. III, Doc. 146, pp. 456–9; Minutes of the Bonn Economic Summit Meeting, 17 July 1978, in *FRUS 1977–1980: Foreign Economic Policy*, Vol. III, Doc. 147, pp. 464–6; Minutes of the Bonn Economic Summit

Meeting, 17 July 1978, in *FRUS 1977–1980: Foreign Economic Policy*, Vol. III, Doc. 148, pp. 466–8.
31. Bernard Donoughue, *Downing Street Diary: Volume 2 – With James Callaghan in No. 10* (London: Jonathan Cape, 2008), 18 July 1978, p. 348. A slightly more optimistic assessment of the results of the summit was provided by a number of Callaghan's other advisers, including Palliser, Stowe and Hunt. Yet they also agreed that outstanding difficulties with Japan about its commitment to growth levels and monetary policy would likely create considerable problems between Tokyo and Washington in the near future. Such fears would materialise in the New Year as the decision by the Japanese Central Bank to sell US dollars caused enormous swings in the foreign exchange markets throughout 1979 and considerable diplomatic tension within US–Japanese relations. See TNA: PREM 16/2017 John Hunt to Mr Stowe, 12 December 1978; TNA: T 381/160 The Schroder Group: US and International Money Markets, 2 April 1979; TNA: T 364/217 'Official Sterling Balances and the Demand for Sterling', K. E. Couzens to the Chancellor of the Exchequer, 20 July 1979. One recent overview of the summit highlights the positive results from it. See Daniel J. Sargent, *A Superpower Transformed: The Remaking of American Foreign Relations in the 1970s* (Oxford: Oxford University Press, 2015), pp. 248–50.
32. TNA: PREM 16/2017 Note for the Record: Tokyo Economic Summit, 16 January 1979; TNA: PREM 16/2017 Four Power Discussions in Guadeloupe, 5–6 January 1979.
33. The British made the Carter administration aware of this Brezhnev contact. See Memorandum for Mr George Vest et al. from Leslie Gelb, 22 November 1977, File: Enhanced Radiation Weapons and Radiological Warfare 9/77–1/78, National Security Affairs Collection 7 Brzezinski Material, Box 17, JCL; From the Ambassador in London to the Secretary of State, 11 November 1977, Document Number: 1977LONDON18614; File Number: D770417-0904 from State Department Electronic Telegrams 1977, available at <http://aad.archives.gov/aad/createpdf?rid=261342&dt=2532&dl=1629> (last accessed 13 May 2016). See also Memorandum for Zbigniew Brzezinski and David Aaron from Roberts Hunter, Jim Thomson and Gregory Treverton, 28 January 1978, File: Enhanced Radiation Weapons and Radiological Warfare 9/77–1/78, National Security Affairs Collection 7 Brzezinski Material, Box 17, JCL.
34. To Zbig and others from Jimmy [Carter], 8 February 1978, Zbigniew Brzezinski Collection, Box 22, JCL; Memorandum for the

President from Zbigniew Brzezinski, undated [circa 10 December 1978], File: Enhanced Radiation Weapons and Radiological Warfare 9/77–1/78, National Security Affairs Collection 7 Brzezinski Material, Box 17, JCL. Schmidt gave an address at the International Institute of Strategic Studies in London in December 1977 and publicly urged the NATO alliance to adopt the necessary weaponry to uphold the strategy of deterrence. See Helmut Schmidt, 'The 1977 Alistair Buchan Memorial Lecture', *Survival*, 20:1 (1978), pp. 2–10.

35. Given the limited range of ERWs, it was unlikely that they would be stationed on mainland Britain. However, missile warheads or spare parts for ERWs would be stationed in Britain.
36. TNA: CAB 133/488 PMKV (78) 5 Enhanced Radiation Warheads, Brief by the Ministry of Defence, 17 March 1978; Jimmy Carter, *Keeping Faith: Memoirs of a President* (London: Collins, 1982), p. 226; Interview with President Carter, 29 November 1982, Carter Presidency Project, The Miller Center, p. 33, available at <http://web1.millercenter.org/poh/transcripts/ohp_1982_1129_carter.pdf> (last accessed 13 May 2016).
37. John Killick, *BDOHP*, p. 34.
38. On Carter's thinking see for example Chronology of Events involving Enhanced Radiation Warheads, File: Defense Enhanced Radiation Warhead 3/78–8/78, Zbigniew Brzezinski Collection, Box 22, JCL; Zbigniew Brzezinski, *Power and Principle: Memoirs of the National Security Adviser 1977–1981* (London: Weidenfeld & Nicolson, 1983), p. 305; James Schlesinger interview, 19–20 July 1984, The Miller Center, p. 3, available at <http://web1.millercenter.org/poh/transcripts/ohp_1984_0719_schlesinger.pdf> (last accessed 13 May 2016).
39. Brzezinski, *Power and Principle*, p. 306. On the furore caused in US–West German relations by this decision see Kristina Spoher Readman, 'Germany and the Politics of the Neutron Bomb, 1975–1979', *Diplomacy and Statecraft*, 21:2 (2010), pp. 259–85.
40. Memorandum for Zbigniew Brzezinski from Reginald Bartholome, 20 March 1978, File: Defense Enhanced Radiation Warhead 3/78–8/78, Zbigniew Brzezinski Collection, Box 22, JCL.
41. Memorandum for Zbigniew Brzezinski from Robert Hunter, 3 April 1978, File: Enhanced Radiation Weapons and Radiological Warfare 2–4/78, National Security Affairs Collection 7 Brzezinski Material, Box 17, JCL.
42. From the Ambassador in London to the Secretary of State, 14 April 1978, Document Number: 1978LONDON05862, File Number:

D780163-0724, Department of State Electronic Telegrams, available at <http://aad.archives.gov/aad/createpdf?rid=95747&dt=2694&dl=2009> (last accessed 13 May 2016).
43. Thus, on 6 April 1978, Carter wrote to Callaghan of his decision. See From President Carter to Prime Minister Callaghan, 6 April 1978, File: Zbigniew Brzezinski Collection, Box 22, JCL. See also Memorandum for Zbigniew Brzezinski from Reginald Bartholome, 20 March 1978, File: Defense Enhanced Radiation Warhead 3/78–8/78, Zbigniew Brzezinski Collection, Box 22, JCL; Memorandum for the President from Harold Brown, 3 April 1978, Zbigniew Brzezinski Collection, Box 22, JCL.
44. Carter, *White House Diary*, 20 March 1978, p. 179.
45. From AmEmbassy London to SecState Washington DC, Tel. London 25214, April 1978, File: Defense Enhanced Radiation Warhead 3/78–8/78, Zbigniew Brzezinski Collection, Box 22, JCL; TNA: PREM 16/1912 Note of a Meeting between the Prime Minister and Vice President Mondale, 28 March 1978.
46. From the White House to Dr Brzezinski, Sitto 102, April 1978, File: Defense Enhanced Radiation Warhead 3/78–8/78, Zbigniew Brzezinski Collection, Box 22, JCL.
47. For example, the British proposed that a joint US–UK–West German tank should be built. See Letter from the President to the Prime Minister, 22 August 1978, in From the Secretary of State to the Ambassador in London, 22 August 1978, Document Number: 1978STATE199606, File Number: D780342-0244, Department of State Electronic Telegrams, available at <http://aad.archives.gov/aad/createpdf?rid=206999&dt=2694&dl=2009> (last accessed 13 May 2016). See also From the Ambassador in London to the Secretary of State, 2 May 1978, Document Number: 1978LONDON06855, available at <http://aad.archives.gov/aad/createpdf?rid=137483&dt=2694&dl=2009> (last accessed 13 May 2016).
48. Memorandum of Conversation, 11 April 1978, Memcons: Brzezinski 10/77–8/78, National Security Affairs Collection 7 Brzezinski Material, Box 33, JCL. Quote is from Donoughue, *With James Callaghan*, 4 April 1978, p. 308.
49. Muzorewa was the leader of the United African National Council. Sithole had founded ZANU but following his imprisonment and a number of rifts with Mugabe, he left the party to form ZANU-NDONGA which renounced violent struggle. Chirau was a notable figure within the Rhodesian tribal community and formed the Zimbabwe United

People's Party that largely comprised of Rhodesian chiefs and also renounced violent struggle. On Muzorewa see Abel Muzorewa, *Rise Up and Walk: An Autobiography* (London: Evans Bros, 1978). For Smith's account of the diplomacy that led to the settlement see Ian Smith, *Bitter Harvest: The Great Betrayal*, 2nd revised edn (London: Blake, 2001), pp. 223–48.

50. See Owen's glowing reference to Muzorewa in TNA: FCO 36/2134 Call on the Secretary of State by Mr Byron Hove, 8 May 1978, where he further encouraged Byron Hove, an associate of Muzorewa, to build up his own political identity so that he could run for the presidency in future Rhodesian elections. Overall, Muzorewa was viewed as the best hope for a peaceful transition to majority rule in Rhodesia.

51. TNA: FCO 36/2135 P. R. A. Mansfield to Mr Stephen, 4 July 1978. The discussion between Owen and Smith is recorded in TNA: FCO 36/2134 'Rhodesia', G. G. H. Walden to Mr Laver, 18 April 1978. On British policy see TNA: FCO 36/2134 Scott to the Foreign Office, Tel. 374, 24 May 1978; TNA: FCO 36/2134 Rhodesia Department Telegram to J. A. N. Graham, 1 June 1978; TNA: FCO 36/2135 Note for the Record: Meeting with Mr Sithole, Dr Gopo and Mr Kadzviti, 6 June 1978.

52. 'Salisbury Sell-Out', *Zambia Daily Mail*, 18 February 1978, in TNA: FCO 36/2132.

53. Cyrus Vance, *Hard Choices: Critical Years in America's Foreign Policy* (New York: Simon & Schuster, 1983), p. 285; Carter, *White House Diary*, 30 January 1978, p. 167; Andrew J. DeRoche, 'Standing Firm for Principles: Jimmy Carter and Zimbabwe', *Diplomatic History*, 23:4 (1999), pp. 657–85, at p. 672. Young and Low's analysis is reported in TNA: PREM 16/1912 'Report from London', for the Prime Minister, 28 March 1978. The British government privately accepted that these criticisms of the internal settlement were indeed valid but this did not mean it should not be supported by London. See TNA: FCO 36/2135 'Rhodesia: Defects of the Internal Agreement', undated [circa June 1978].

54. American mining companies were particularly interested in lifting economic sanctions so as to exploit Rhodesia's vast quantities of chrome. See Anthony Lake, *The Tar Baby Option: American Policy toward Southern Rhodesia* (New York: Columbia University Press, 1976), p. 201; William Minter, *King Solomon's Mines Revisited: Western Interests and the Burdened History of Southern Africa*

(New York: Basic Books, 1986), pp. 220–55. The British Embassy was monitoring congressional opinion closely and informed London in March 1978 that Senator Case's (R-New Jersey) public statements on the internal settlement were indicative of a shift in opinion in the US Senate towards supporting the internal settlement. Democrats such as Senator Byrd (D-West Virginia) also vocally supported the Salisbury Plan and urged the Carter administration to at least give it a chance to succeed. See TNA: FCO 36/2132 'Senator Case's Statement', 2 March 1978.

55. See for example the reports on discussions with Nyerere in From the Ambassador at Dar Es Salaam to the Secretary of State, 10 March 1978, Document Number: 1978DARES01053, File Number: D780108-0182, Department of State Electronic Telegrams, available at <http://aad.archives.gov/aad/createpdf?rid=56559&dt=2694&dl=2009> (last accessed 13 May 2016).

56. Washington was made aware of British criticism in From the Ambassador in London to the Secretary of State, 9 March 1978, Document Number: 1978DARES01033, File Number: D780106-0866, Department of State Electronic Telegrams, available at <http://aad.archives.gov/aad/createpdf?rid=55284&dt=2694&dl=2009> (last accessed 13 May 2016). British thinking is explained in TNA: CAB 133/488 PMKV (78) 8i 'Africa: Rhodesia', Brief by the Foreign and Commonwealth Office, 21 March 1978.

57. The British government was keen to press home to its American counterpart that it was indeed following the agreed plan. See for example From the Ambassador in Pretoria to the Secretary of State in Washington, 25 July 1978, Document Number: 1978PRETOR04236, File Number: D780304-0829, Department of State Electronic Telegrams, available at <http://aad.archives.gov/aad/createpdf?rid=186288&dt=2694&dl=2009> (last accessed 13 May 2016); From the Secretary of State to the Ambassador in Pretoria, 19 September 1978, Document Number: 1978STATE237005, File Number: D780380-0656, Department of State Electronic Telegrams, available at <http://aad.archives.gov/aad/createpdf?rid=231332&dt=2694&dl=2009> (last accessed 13 May 2016); Memorandum for the President from Warren Christopher, 6 September 1978, File: State Department Evening Reports, 9/78, Plains File, Box 39, JCL. For joint letters see for example President Carter and Prime Minister Callaghan to President Nyerere, 2 October 1978, in From the Secretary of State to the Ambassador in Dar Es Salaam, 2 October 1978, Document Number: 1978STATE249884,

File Number: P840157-2047, Department of State Electronic Telegrams, available at <http://aad.archives.gov/aad/createpdf?rid=268958&dt=2694&dl=2009> (last accessed 13 May 2016); President Carter and Prime Minister Callaghan to President Kauda, 2 October 1978, in From the Secretary of State to the Ambassador in Lusaka, 2 October 1978, Document Number: 1978STATE249885, File Number: P840157-2059, Department of State Electronic Telegrams, available at <http://aad.archives.gov/aad/createpdf?rid=268959&dt=2694&dl=2009> (last accessed 13 May 2016). For British efforts to convince Smith to make further concessions to the Patriotic Front see for example TNA: FCO 36/2135 Record of a Meeting held at Milton Buildings, Salisbury, 14 June 1978; TNA: FCO 36/2135 Record of a Meeting held at Milton Buildings, Salisbury, 9 June 1978; TNA: FCO 36/2135 Record of a Meeting held at Milton Buildings, Salisbury, 7 June 1978.

58. Owen and Vance held a meeting with Smith in April 1978 to persuade him to make additional concessions. Their efforts proved largely unsuccessful. See TNA: FCO 36/2134 Record of a Meeting between the Foreign and Commonwealth Secretary and the United States Secretary of State and the parties to the Salisbury Agreement, 17 April 1978.
59. TNA: FCO 36/2134 Rhodesia Department Telegram to J. A. N. Graham, 1 June 1978.
60. TNA: FCO 36/2135 From Salisbury to the FCO, Tel. 159, 8 June 1978.
61. Smith is quoted in TNA: FCO 36/2136 S. J. Gomersall to Miss Spencer, 7 September 1978. Smith had made this speech to the Rhodesian parliament on 6 September 1978. On the escalation of the violence see David Martin and Phyllis Johnson, *The Struggle for Zimbabwe* (London: Faber & Faber, 1981), p. 296; George Houser, *No One Can Stop the Rain: Glimpses of Africa's Liberation Struggle* (New York: Pilgrim Press, 1989), pp. 331–5; Robin Renwick, *Unconventional Diplomacy in Southern Africa* (Basingstoke: Palgrave Macmillan, 1997), pp. 17–19.
62. TNA: FCO 36/2136 Miss R. J. Spencer to Mr Laver, 28 September 1978; TNA: FCO 36/2136 K. D. Evetts to Rosemary Spencer, 20 September 1978.
63. Memorandum for the President from Warren Christopher, 19 September 1978, File: State Department Evening Reports, 9/78, Plains File, Box 39, JCL.

64. Memorandum for the President from Zbigniew Brzezinski, 6 October 1978, File: Weekly Reports to the President 71–81: 9/78–12/78, Zbigniew Brzezinski Collection, Box 42, JCL.
65. From the Ambassador in Lagos to the Secretary of State, 25 September 1978, Document Number: 1978LAGOS11948, File Number: D780392-1126, Department of State Electronic Telegrams, available at <http://aad.archives.gov/aad/createpdf?rid=237311&dt=2694&dl=2009> (last accessed 13 May 2016).
66. TNA: PREM 16/2290 Peter Jay to David Owen, 4 November 1978.
67. TNA: PREM 16/2290 Peter Jay to David Owen, 4 November 1978. On Brzezinski's growing interest in the affairs of Southern Africa see Alex Thomson, 'The Diplomacy of Impasse: The Carter Administration and Apartheid South Africa', *Diplomacy & Statecraft*, 21:1 (2010), pp. 107–24, at p. 120.
68. In contrast to the interpretation provided here, the extant literature gives the impression of Anglo-American unity on this subject. For example see DeRoche, 'Standing Firm for Principles', pp. 673–4.
69. TNA: FCO 36/2136 Richard to the FCO, Tel. 2104, 7 October 1978; TNA: FCO 36/2137 Minutes of a meeting between the United States, United Kingdom and Rhodesia, Secretary of State Vance's Conference Room, Washington DC, 20 October 1978.
70. Interview with the President, 13 October 1978, in *Public Papers of the Presidents of the United States: Jimmy Carter, 1978, Book Two* (Washington DC: United States Government Printing Office, 1979), p. 1777.
71. TNA: FCO 36/2137 Minutes of a meeting between the United States, United Kingdom and Rhodesia, Secretary of State Vance's Conference Room, Washington DC, 20 October 1978.
72. Owen informed the prime minister about Washington's encouragement to deploy peacekeepers in TNA: FCO 36/2136 The Secretary of State to the Prime Minister, 4 October 1978.
73. TNA: FCO 82/769 Record of the Meeting between the Foreign and Commonwealth Secretary, the US Secretary of State and the South African Foreign Minister, 12 August 1977.
74. These latest British efforts were all reported to Washington in From the Ambassador in Dar Es Salaam to the Secretary of State, 22 November 1978, Document Number: 1978DARES05103, File Number: P840166-1719, Department of State Electronic Telegrams, available at <http://aad.archives.gov/aad/createpdf?rid=290745&dt=2694&dl=2009> (last accessed 13 May 2016); From the Secretary of State to the Ambassador in Dar Es Salaam, 22 November 1978, Document

Number: 1978STATE295254, File Number: P840166-1712, Department of State Electronic Telegrams, available at <http://aad.archives.gov/aad/createpdf?rid=291448&dt=2694&dl=2009> (last accessed 13 May 2016).
75. TNA: FCO 36/2136 Owen to the Private Secretary (Prime Minister's Office), 26 September 1978. Reports on British talks with various African leaders can be found throughout TNA: FCO 36/2136 Allison to the FCO, Tel. 671, 29 September 1978; TNA: FCO 36/2136 R. J. Spencer to Mr Laver, 28 September 1978.
76. Memorandum for the President from Warren Christopher, 9 December 1978, File: State Department Evening Reports, 12/78, Plains File, Box 39, JCL; From the Ambassador in Lusaka to the Secretary of State, 22 November 1978, Document Number: 1978LUSAKA04080, File Number: P850101-2279, Department of State Electronic Telegrams, available at <http://aad.archives.gov/aad/createpdf?rid=290979&dt=2694&dl=2009> (last accessed 13 May 2016); From the State Department to the US Mission in New York, 28 November 1978, Document Number: 1978STATE300645, File Number: N780009-0694, Department of State Electronic Telegrams, available at <http://aad.archives.gov/aad/createpdf?rid=296794&dt=2694&dl=2009> (last accessed 13 May 2016); From the Ambassador in Lusaka to the Secretary of State, 3 December 1978, Document Number: 1978LUSAKA04227, File Number: D780497-0552, Department of State Electronic Telegrams, available at <http://aad.archives.gov/aad/createpdf?rid=302263&dt=2694&dl=2009> (last accessed 13 May 2016); Memorandum for the President from Cyrus Vance, 19 December 1978, File: State Department Evening Reports, 12/78, Plains File, Box 39, JCL. US reporting on the Hughes mission can be found in From the Ambassador in London to the Secretary of State, 19 December 1978, Document Number: 1978LONDON20777, File Number: P850103-1967, Department of State Electronic Telegrams, available at <http://aad.archives.gov/aad/createpdf?rid=317354&dt=2694&dl=2009> (last accessed 13 May 2016); From the Secretary of State to the US Mission at the UN, 20 December 1978, Document Number: 1978STATE319740, File Number: N780010-0357, Department of State Electronic Telegrams, available at <http://aad.archives.gov/aad/createpdf?rid=318801&dt=2694&dl=2009> (last accessed 13 May 2016).
77. From the Ambassador in Lusaka to the Secretary of State, 23 December 1978, Document Number: 1978LUSAKA04468, File Number: P850101-2333, Department of State Electronic Telegrams,

available at <http://aad.archives.gov/aad/createpdf?rid=321698&dt=2694&dl=2009> (last accessed 13 May 2016); From the Secretary of State to the US Mission at the UN, 26 December 1978, Document Number: 1978STATE324164, File Number: N780010-0452, Department of State Electronic Telegrams, available at <http://aad.archives.gov/aad/createpdf?rid=322871&dt=2694&dl=2009> (last accessed 13 May 2016).
78. British concerns can be followed throughout TNA: FCO 36/2411 P. J. Barlow to Mr Renwick, 12 January 1979; TNA: FCO 36/2411 S. Gomersall to Mr Renwick, 10 January 1979.
79. TNA: FCO 36/2411 Text of a Statement, From the FCO to Washington, Tel. 211, 29 January 1979.
80. TNA: PREM 16/1978 Cabinet: Nuclear Defence Policy, Note of a Meeting held in 10 Downing Street, 2 January 1979.
81. TNA: FCO 93/1818 Owen to Damascus, Tel. 20, 14 January 1979.
82. TNA: PREM 16/1978 'Polaris Replacement', Memorandum for the Prime Minister, 23 March 1979. Jay was instructed to deliver a personal letter to President Carter which informed him that the United Kingdom was now making an official record of the private Callaghan–Carter discussion at Guadeloupe but the matter was not to be discussed further until any new prime minister raised the subject of Polaris replacement with the United States. See TNA: PREM 16/1978 From the Prime Minister to the President, 27 March 1979 attached to B. G. Cartledge to Peter Jay, 27 March 1979.
83. James Callaghan, *Time & Chance* (London: Collins, 1987), pp. 554–7; TNA: PREM 16/1978 Prime Minister's Conversation with President Carter at Guadeloupe, 5 January 1979.
84. TNA: PREM 16/1978 Prime Minister's Conversation with President Carter at Guadeloupe, 5 January 1979. See also TNA: PREM 16/1978 John Hunt to the Prime Minister, 18 January 1979. Callaghan's record of his private discussion with Carter can be found in TNA: PREM 16/1978 The Prime Minister to the Chancellor of the Exchequer, 17 January 1979.
85. TNA: PREM 16/1978 The Prime Minister to the Chancellor of the Exchequer, 17 January 1979.
86. The prime minister himself went to great lengths to argue that no firm decision to replace Polaris with Trident C4 had been agreed to with the president. See for example TNA: PREM 16/1978 'Chevaline', B. G. Cartledge to Roger Facer, 6 February 1979.
87. The October 1974 Labour Party manifesto had stated: 'Starting from the basis of the multilateral disarmament negotiations, we will

seek the removal of American Polaris bases from Britain. We have renounced any intention of moving toward a new generation of strategic nuclear weapons.' See 'Britain Will Win with Labour', Labour Party manifesto, October 1974, available at <http://www.politicsresources.net/area/uk/man/lab74oct.htm> (last accessed 13 May 2016).

88. TNA: PREM 16/1978 The Prime Minister to the Chancellor of the Exchequer, 17 January 1979; TNA: PREM 16/1978 Prime Minister's Conversation with President Carter at Guadeloupe, 5 January 1979.

89. TNA: PREM 16/1978 'Chevaline', B. G. Cartledge to Roger Facer, 6 February 1979; TNA: PREM 16/1978 Sir John Hunt to the Prime Minister, 2 February 1979; TNA: PREM 16/1978 'Chevaline', David Owen to the Prime Minister, 1 February 1979; TNA: PREM 16/1978 FM [Mulley] to the Prime Minister, 18 January 1979; David Owen, *Time to Declare* (London: Michael Joseph, 1991), p. 381; David Owen, *Nuclear Papers* (Liverpool: Liverpool University Press, 2010), pp. 39, 104; Healey, *The Time of My Life*, pp. 313, 455–6; Edward Pearce, *Denis Healey: A Life in Our Times* (Boston: Little, Brown, 2002), pp. 428–50. For a broader discussion on Callaghan's nuclear decision making see Kristan Stoddart, *Facing Down the Soviet Union: Britain, the USA, NATO and Nuclear Weapons, 1976–1983* (Basingstoke: Palgrave Macmillan, 2014), pp. 12–75.

90. TNA: PREM 16/1978 'Your letter to President Carter about Trident', B. Cartledge to the Prime Minister, 26 March 1979; TNA: PREM 16/1978 John Hunt to Mr Cartledge, 12 February 1979.

91. TNA: PREM 16/1978 John Hunt to B. Cartledge, 27 March 1979.

92. For works that have emphasised the importance of personalities upon the course of the Anglo-American relationship and the Cold War more broadly see Warren Kimball, *Forged in War: Churchill, Roosevelt and the Second World War* (London: HarperCollins, 1997), pp. 1–24; Frank Costigliola, *Roosevelt's Lost Alliances: How Personal Politics Helped Start the Cold War* (Princeton, NJ: Princeton University Press, 2012); David Dimbleby and David Reynolds, *An Ocean Apart: The Relationship between Britain and America in the Twentieth Century* (New York: Random House, 1988), p. 264; Ritchie Ovendale, *Anglo-American Relations in the Twentieth Century* (Basingstoke: Palgrave Macmillan, 1998), pp. 120–31; C. J. Bartlett, *'The Special Relationship': Anglo-American Relations since 1945* (London: Longman, 1992), pp. 88–101. For a good overview on the importance of

personal diplomacy within the Anglo-American relationship see John Dumbrell, 'Personal Diplomacy: Relations between Prime Ministers and Presidents', in Alan P. Dobson and Steve Marsh, *Anglo-American Relations: Contemporary Perspectives* (London: Routledge, 2012), pp. 82–104. A number of former officials and policy makers have emphasised the importance of personalities upon the Anglo-American relationship. See for example Raymond Seitz, *Over Here* (London: Weidenfeld & Nicolson, 1998), p. 71; author interview with Lord [David] Owen, 22 January 2008; author interview with Sir Richard Mottram, 7 February 2008; author interview with Lord [Geoffrey] Robertson, 27 February 2008; Oliver Wright, *BDOHP*, pp. 9–10, 12.

Chapter 4

1. Jimmy Carter, *White House Diary* (New York: Farrar, Straus and Giroux, 2010), 13 September 1977, p. 97.
2. Quoted in Niall Ferguson, 'Crisis, What Crisis? The 1970s and the Shock of the Global', in Niall Ferguson, Charles S. Maier, Erez Manela and Daniel J. Sargent (eds), *The Shock of the Global: The 1970s in Perspective* (Cambridge, MA: Harvard University Press, 2010), p. 1.
3. Bernard Donoughue, *Downing Street Diary: Volume 2 – With James Callaghan in No. 10* (London: Jonathan Cape, 2008), 5 January 1979.
4. US assessments on the prospects for Callaghan and Thatcher are in Political Constraints on Economic Policy, undated [summer 1978], File: President Germany 7/13–17/79 Economic Summit, National Security Affairs Brzezinski Material, Box 13, JCL; Memorandum for Zbigniew Brzezinski from The Situation Room, 3 May 1979, File: 5/1/79–5/10/79 Brzezinski Material, President's Daily Briefing, Box 10, JCL. This clearly contrasted with the appraisal of Callaghan's political position in October 1977. See From the Ambassador in London to the Secretary of State, 21 October 1977, Document Number: 1977LONDON17538, File Number: D770388-0952, State Department Electronic Telegrams, available at <http://aad.archives.gov/aad/createpdf?rid=245923&dt=2532&dl=1629> (last accessed 13 May 2016); From the Ambassador in London to the Secretary of State, 22 December 1978, Document Number: 1978LONDON21048, File Number: D780531-1092, Department

of State Electronic Telegrams, available at <http://aad.archives.gov/aad/createpdf?rid=320881&dt=2694&dl=2009> (last accessed 13 May 2016). On the 1979 general election see Charles Moore, *Margaret Thatcher: The Authorized Biography, Volume One: Not for Turning* (London: Allen Lane, 2013), pp. 393–418; Richard Vinen, *Thatcher's Britain: The Politics and Social Upheaval of the 1980s* (New York: Simon & Schuster, 2009), pp. 95–9. Thatcher's own account is recounted in Margaret Thatcher, *The Path to Power* (London: HarperCollins, 1995), pp. 435–61.
5. Richard [unclear] to Mrs Thatcher, 20 April 1979, in File: 2/7/1/41, Thatcher Papers.
6. Moore, *Margaret Thatcher*, p. 449.
7. Margaret Thatcher speech to the Chelsea Conservative Association, 26 July 1975, available at <http://www.margaretthatcher.org/speeches/displaydocument.asp?docid=102750> (last accessed 13 May 2016).
8. Margaret Thatcher speech to the Conservative Party Conference, 13 October 1978, available at <http://www.margaretthatcher.org/document/103764> (last accessed 13 May 2016).
9. TNA: PREM 19/212 General Haig's Farewell Call on the Prime Minister at 10 Downing Street, 13 June 1979; TNA: PREM 19/212 Record of the Prime Minister's Discussion with the Federal German Chancellor, Herr Schmidt at 10 Downing Street, 11 May 1979.
10. Memorandum for the President from Zbigniew Brzezinski, 12 May 1979, File: Weekly Reports to the President 91–101: 3/79–6/79, Zbigniew Brzezinski Collection, Box 42, JCL.
11. Jay to the Secretary of State (Carrington), 8 May 1979, in File: 2/31, Jay Papers.
12. Hailsham diary entry, 29 March 1977, available at <http://www.margaretthatcher.org/archive/displaydocument.asp?docid=111182> (last accessed 13 May 2016). For Hailsham's own assessment of Thatcher see Lord Hailsham, *A Sparrow's Flight: The Memoirs of Lord Hailsham of St Marylebone* (London: Collins, 1990), pp. 407–9.
13. Peter Carrington, *Reflect on Things Past* (London: Collins, 1988), p. 285. On Thatcher's distrust of the Foreign Office as an institution see David Summerhayes, *BDOHP*, p. 13; Charles Powell, *BDOHP*, p. 17.
14. Hurd remembered that 'Four times during her premiership Margaret Thatcher was persuaded into crucially important decisions which ran counter to her original instincts: the Rhodesia Settlement (1980), the European Budget Settlement (1980), the Anglo-Irish Agreement

(1985) and the Single European Act (1986). In her memoirs and private conversations she shows that to some extent she came to regret all these decisions once she no longer carried the responsibility of office. All four were clearly in the national interest. The first two were brought to a successful close by Peter Carrington.' See Douglas Hurd, *Memoirs* (London: Abacus, 2004), p. 287.

15. Memorandum for the President from Zbigniew Brzezinski, 12 May 1979, File: Weekly Reports to the President 91–101: 3/79–6/79, Zbigniew Brzezinski Collection, Box 42, JCL. Such concerns were merited given the events of a meeting with the leader of one communist country. Thatcher began the meeting by stating, 'I hate Communists.' See Richard Johnson, 'Henry Kissinger Praises the Iron Lady', *New York Post*, 15 June 2015, available at <http://pagesix.com/2015/06/15/henry-kissinger-praises-the-iron-lady/> (last accessed 13 May 2016). Lord (Charles) Powell, Thatcher's principle private secretary for foreign affairs, recollected that Thatcher's approach in personal discussion with foreign leaders and colleagues could often be provocative and matter-of-fact. See Charles Powell, *BDOHP*, p. 23; Michael Palliser, *BDOHP*, p. 45. One recent work suggests that Thatcher's religious beliefs were crucially important in influencing her strident opposition to Godless communism. See Eliza Filby, *God and Mrs Thatcher: The Battle for Britain's Soul* (London: Biteback, 2015).

16. Memorandum for the President from Zbigniew Brzezinski, 12 May 1979, File: Weekly Reports to the President 91–101: 3/79–6/79, Zbigniew Brzezinski Collection, Box 42, JCL

17. Carrington's advice was accurate given that Carter told Brezhnev during the Vienna Summit of June 1979 that he would expand 'all elements of arms control, including a comprehensive test ban with or without Great Britain'. See Jimmy Carter, *Keeping Faith: Memoirs of a President* (London: Collins, 1982), p. 249. For the transcript of the Carter–Brezhnev talks in Vienna see Memorandum of Conversation, 18 June 1979, in *Foreign Relations of the United States 1977–1980: Soviet Union* (Washington DC: United States Government Printing Office, 2013), Vol. VI, Doc. 206, pp. 615–23 (hereafter *FRUS 1977–1980: Soviet Union*). For examples of Carrington's influence see TNA: PREM 19/212 Carrington to the Prime Minister, 11 May 1979; TNA: PREM 19/212 Strategic Arms Limitation Talks, attached to John Hunt to the Prime Minister, 4 May 1979; TNA: PREM 19/212 Comprehensive Test Ban, 11 May 1979; R. L. L. Facer to B. G. Cartledge, 11 May 1979;

TNA: PREM 19/212 SALT II: Non-Circumvention, John Hunt to the Prime Minister, 21 May 1979.
18. For concerns about Thatcher see Memorandum for Zbigniew Brzezinski from The Situation Room, 30 March 1979, File: 3/21/79–3/31/79, National Security Affairs Brzezinski Material, President's Daily Briefing, Box 10, JCL. For the telephone conversation between Carter and Thatcher see Telephone Conversation between the Prime Minister and the President of the United States, 4 May 1979, in File: 3/1/1, Part 1, Thatcher Papers.
19. TNA: PREM 19/383 Note of the Prime Minister's Discussion with the US Secretary of State, Mr Cyrus Vance, at 10 Downing Street, 23 May 1979. Briefing material for the talks can be found in TNA: PREM 19/383 Your discussions with Mr Vance on 23 May at 1000, 22 May 1979.
20. On the contents of SALT II and the diplomacy leading up to its conclusion see Barbara Zanchetta, *The Transformation of American International Power in the 1970s* (Cambridge: Cambridge University Press, 2014), pp. 236–42.
21. TNA: PREM 19/383 Note of the Prime Minister's Discussion with the US Secretary of State, Mr Cyrus Vance, at 10 Downing Street, 23 May 1979.
22. Ibid. On Carter's efforts to modernise US strategic nuclear systems see Brian J. Auten, *Carter's Conversion: The Hardening of American Defense Policy* (Columbia: University of Missouri Press, 2009), pp. 257–304. During a bilateral discussion between Carrington and Vance the previous day, the British foreign and Commonwealth secretary had made a point of confirming the British government's support for SALT II and had warned Vance that Thatcher's likely quizzing of US policy was a reflection of her interest in the subject and not her opposition to SALT II. See TNA: FCO 82/992 G. G. H. Walden to B. G. Cartledge, 22 May 1979.
23. For the quotes see TNA: FCO 82/995 J. A. Robinson to Sir Michael Palliser, 22 June 1979. For Carter's letter to Thatcher see Jimmy Carter to the Prime Minister, May 1979, in File: 3/1/1 Part 1, Thatcher Papers. Thatcher's letter to Carter assuring him of British support can be viewed in The Prime Minister to the President of the United States, 15 June 1979, in File: 3/1/1 Part 1, Thatcher Papers.
24. Memorandum for Frank Moore from Dan Tate, 18 November 1977, in File: SALT, 1977, Office of the Chief of Staff Files, Hamilton Jordan's Confidential Files, Box 37, JCL.

25. Carter was being encouraged to pursue this option in Memorandum for the President from Zbigniew Brzezinski, 17 May 1979, File: Alpha Channel Miscellaneous – 5/79–8/79, Zbigniew Brzezinski Collection, Box 20, JCL. For Brzezinski informing the President that the United Kingdom would support the 'dual track' approach to arms limitations see Memorandum for the President from Zbigniew Brzezinski, 26 October 1979, File: Weekly Reports to the President 102–120: 7/79–12/79, Zbigniew Brzezinski Collection, Box 42, JCL.
26. TNA: PREM 19/383 Note for the Record: Record of a Meeting between the Defence Secretary and the United States Secretary of State held in the Ministry of Defence, 22 May 1979. See also Geoffrey Howe, *Conflict of Loyalty* (London: Macmillan, 1994), pp. 126–36.
27. TNA: FCO 82/993 Note of a Meeting between the Chancellor of the Exchequer and Mr Secretary of State Vance, 23 May 1979; TNA: PREM 19/383 Note of a Meeting between the Chancellor of the Exchequer and Mr Secretary of State Vance held in the Chancellor of the Exchequer's Room at the Treasury, 23 May 1979. One Treasury paper noted that the 'World economic prospects are gloomy. Inflation and unemployment are rising. The prospects for growth are not good, especially if oil prices rise.' See TNA: FCO 82/992 Agenda for the Tokyo Economic Summit: Secretary of State's Meeting with Mr Vance, 18 May 1979.
28. On the budget see Nigel Lawson, *The View from No. 11: Memoirs of a Tory Radical* (London: Bantam Press, 1992), pp. 44–7, 52–3. On Thatcher's commitment to maintaining defence expenditure over achieving her economic goals in the first years of her premiership see Edward Hampshire, 'Margaret Thatcher's First U-Turn: Francis Pym and the Control of Defence Spending, 1979–81', *Contemporary British History*, 29:3 (2015), pp. 359–79.
29. TNA: FCO 82/992 G. G. H. Walden to B. G. Cartledge, 22 May 1979; TNA: FCO 82/993 Record of a Meeting between the Defence Secretary and the United States Secretary of State, 22 May 1979; Jimmy Carter to Prime Minister Thatcher, June 1979, File: Alpha Channel Miscellaneous – 5/79–8/79, Zbigniew Brzezinski Collection, Box 20, JCL.
30. TNA: FCO 82/995 Meeting with President Carter: Brief by the Foreign and Commonwealth Office, 21 June 1979. Thatcher was, however, rather more forthright than her predecessor had been. For instance, she told the assembled group that there was little point in creating a 'communique with pious platitudes' but instead 'we should

be realistic and not cloak measures in soft phrases. This would give the world greater confidence than by hiding what we mean.' See Minutes of the Tokyo Economic Summit Meeting, 28 June 1979, in *FRUS 1977–1980: Foreign Economic Policy*, Vol. III, Doc. 222, pp. 646–7.
31. Carter, *Keeping Faith*, p. 113.
32. TNA: FCO 82/995 J. A. Robinson to Sir Michael Palliser, 22 June 1979. For similar appraisals see TNA: PREM 16/2290 Mr Peter Jay's call on the Prime Minister, 5 March 1979.
33. Vance had informed Thatcher that this would be a subject of discussion in the upcoming talks in Washington. See TNA: PREM 19/383 Record of a Discussion between the Prime Minister and the United States Secretary of State Mr Cyrus Vance at 10 Downing Street, 10 December 1979. On British estimates about Carter's intentions see TNA: FCO 82/989 Henderson to the FCO, Tel. 3845, 21 November 1979.
34. TNA: PREM 19/383 Record of a Discussion between the Prime Minister and the United States Secretary of State Mr Cyrus Vance at 10 Downing Street, 10 December 1979.
35. Moore, *Margaret Thatcher*, pp. 455–81; TNA: T 364/217 'Exchange Control', G. H. to the Prime Minister, 11 October 1979.
36. TNA: PREM 19/383 Record of a Discussion between the Prime Minister and the United States Secretary of State Mr Cyrus Vance at 10 Downing Street, 10 December 1979; TNA: PREM 19/127 Henderson to London, Tel. 4218, 14 December 1979.
37. TNA: PREM 19/127 Record of a Meeting between the Prime Minister and Members of the US Congress at the US Senate, 17 December 1979.
38. Ibid.
39. Ibid.
40. Ibid.
41. O'Neill had visited the United Kingdom in April 1979 when the British Parliament was formally dissolved pending the forthcoming general election. O'Neill met with both Callaghan and Thatcher where he raised concerns about the situation in Northern Ireland. However, O'Neill would receive short shrift in both meetings. Nevertheless, the meetings demonstrated the increasing importance of the United States in Northern Irish affairs. On this episode see James Cooper, '"A Log-rolling, Irish-American Politician Out to Raise Votes in the United States": Tip O'Neill and the Irish Dimension of Anglo-American Relations, 1977–1986', *Congress and the Presidency*, 41:1 (2015), pp. 7–9. The minutes of the Callaghan–O'Neill

meeting can be found in TNA: PREM 16/2291 Speaker O'Neill's Call on the Prime Minister at 10 Downing Street, 12 April 1979. The O'Neill–Thatcher report on the conversation can be found in 'Report on the Fact-finding Mission to the United Kingdom, Belgium, Hungary, and Ireland, April 11–23 1979', submitted by Thomas P. O'Neill Jr. Speaker of the US House of Representatives in the Kirk O'Donnell Files, Belgium, Great Britain, Hungary, Ireland Visit, Report, April 1979, Box 15, Folder 15/16, Tip O'Neill Papers, John J. Burns Library, Boston College, Massachusetts, United States of America. O'Neill makes no mention of his role in Irish affairs in his memoir. See Tip O'Neill, *Man of the House: The Life and Political Memoirs of Speaker Tip O'Neill* (New York: Random House, 1988).

42. TNA: PREM 19/127 Record of a Meeting held at Blair House, 17 December 1979.
43. TNA: PREM 19/127 Record of a Meeting held at Blair House, 17 December 1979. On the transnational interchange of ideas see Patricia Clavin, '"Defining Transnationalism": Transnational Communities in European History', *Contemporary European History*, 14:4 (2005), pp. 421–39; Diane Stone, 'Transfer Agents and Global Networks in the "Transnationalization" of Policy', *Journal of European Public Policy*, 11:3 (2004), pp. 545–66; James Cooper, *Margaret Thatcher and Ronald Reagan: A Very Political Special Relationship* (Basingstoke: Palgrave Macmillan, 2012), pp. 19–21.
44. TNA: PREM 19/127 Record of a Meeting held at Blair House, 17 December 1979.
45. TNA: PREM 19/127 Record of a Meeting between the Prime Minister and the American Secretary of Defense, Dr Harold Brown, at the Pentagon, 17 December 1979.
46. Ibid.
47. Ibid.
48. TNA: PREM 19/127 Note of a Meeting held in the Oval Office, White House, 17 December 1979.
49. Betty Glad, *An Outsider in the White House: Jimmy Carter, His Advisors, and the Making of American Foreign Policy* (Ithaca: Cornell University Press, 2010), pp. 219–29; Zbigniew Brzezinski, *Power and Principle: Memoirs of the National Security Adviser 1977–1981* (London: Weidenfeld & Nicolson, 1983), pp. 426–69.
50. British approval was given on the proviso that 'public references' to the expansion were played down. See TNA: PREM 19/127 Note

of a Meeting held in the Oval Office, White House, 17 December 1979.
51. TNA: PREM 19/127 From Washington to the FCO, Tel. 12, 18 December 1979.
52. The FCO produced a special briefing on this topic for the prime minister because the subject would involve a 'difficult bilateral' between the president and prime minister. See TNA: FCO 82/989 K. R. Stowe to Sir Robert Armstrong, 26 November 1979. Stowe was quoting Sir Michael Palliser's opinion. The US Ambassador to London, Kingman Brewster, also pre-warned the British government that the subject of guns for the RUC was wrapped up in the Democratic primaries so there was likely to be no movement on the issue. Thatcher informed Brewster that she understood this but she would nonetheless raise the subject. See TNA: FCO 82/989 Call by the US Ambassador, 5 December 1979. For a broader discussion on the US State Department's position vis-à-vis the RUC see Andrew Sanders, 'The Role of Northern Ireland in Modern Anglo-American Relations: The US Department of State and the Royal Ulster Constabulary, 1979', *The Journal of Transatlantic Studies*, 12:2 (2014), pp. 163–81.
53. TNA: PREM 19/127 Record of a Conversation between the Prime Minister and the President of the United States at the White House, 17 December 1979; TNA: PREM 19/383 Brief Number 17: Northern Ireland, 20 February 1980.
54. TNA: PREM 19/127 From Washington to the FCO, Tel. 12, 18 December 1979.
55. Jonathan Aitken, *Margaret Thatcher* (London: Bloomsbury, 2013), p. 296.
56. Visit of Prime Minister Margaret Thatcher, 17 December 1979, in *PPP: Jimmy Carter, 1979, Book Two*, p. 2257.
57. TNA: PREM 19/127 From Washington to the FCO, Tel. 4301, 20 December 1979.
58. TNA: PREM 19/127 From Washington to the FCO, Tel. 4301, 20 December 1979. Henderson noted this in his diary. See Nicholas Henderson, *Mandarin: The Diaries of Nicholas Henderson* (London: Weidenfeld & Nicolson, 1994), pp. 325–30.
59. Lord Hailsham, 'Is Rhodesia Next on Jimmy Carter's Give Away List', *Daily Express*, 9 April 1978, in File: 4/4/55, Lord Hailsham Papers, Churchill Archives Centre, Cambridge University, United Kingdom.

60. As Carrington remembered, both Carter and Vance had 'anxieties' about Thatcher's likely policies in relation to Rhodesia. See Michael Kandiah and Sue Onslow, *Britain and Rhodesia: The Route to Settlement* (London: Institute of Contemporary British History, 2008), p. 60.
61. 'Conservative Manifesto, 1979', 11 April 1979, available at <http://www.margaretthatcher.org/document/110858> (last accessed 13 May 2016). Thatcher's meeting with the Carter administration in 1977 had left the impression in Washington that she would be more supportive of Smith's position than Callaghan currently was. See Moore, *Margaret Thatcher*, p. 371.
62. Carrington, *Reflect on Things Past*, p. 289.
63. Nancy Mitchell, 'Tropes of the Cold War: Jimmy Carter and Rhodesia', *Cold War History*, 7:2 (2007), pp. 263–83, pp. 263–5; Thomas Borstlemann, *The Cold War and the Color Line: American Race Relations in the Global Arena* (Cambridge, MA: Harvard University Press, 2003), pp. 256–8; Andrew DeRoche, *Black, White and Chrome: The United States and Zimbabwe, 1953 to 1998* (Trenton, NJ: Africa World Press, 2001), pp. 17–18; Ernest B. Furgurson, *Hard Right: The Rise of Jesse Helms* (New York: W. W. Norton, 1986), pp. 210–15.
64. Helm's intervention was being monitored closely in London. It was predicted that the president would probably veto Helm's efforts at repealing sanctions against Rhodesia even if it cost the president crucial Senate support for the ratification of the SALT II treaty. Helms, in turn, was providing London with information pertaining to how senators would vote on the ratification of SALT II. See TNA: 36/2423 'Visit to Washington by Miles Hudson', 11–14 July 1979; Memorandum: Vote Count, Senate Vote on SALT II, 4 July 1979, in File: 1/10/13, The Julian Amery Papers, Churchill Archives Centre, Cambridge University, United Kingdom.
65. TNA: PREM 19/383 Lord Carrington's Talks with Mr Vance, 22 May 1979; Paul Sharp, *Thatcher's Diplomacy: The Revival of British Foreign Policy* (Basingstoke: Palgrave Macmillan, 1997), pp. 36–8.
66. Mitchell, 'Tropes of the Cold War', p. 277.
67. TNA: PREM 19/383 Lord Carrington's Talks with Mr Vance, 22 May 1979; TNA: FCO 82/993 Record of a Meeting between the Foreign and Commonwealth Secretary and the US Secretary of State at the FCO, 23 May 1979. The British government privately recognised that the Rhodesia Zimbabwe constitution born out of

the recent elections contained a number of provisions within it that could be construed as privileging the position of white Rhodesians. Other elements to the new constitution, such as the right of the government to detain people without trial, were also a cause of concern. See TNA: 36/2423 Rhodesia: Objections to the New Constitution, P. J. Barlow to Sir A. Duff, 20 July 1979.
68. Briefing Memorandum from the Assistant Secretary of State for Human Rights and Humanitarian Affairs (Derian) to Acting Secretary of State Christopher, 13 June 1979, in *FRUS 1977–1980: Human Rights*, Vol. II, Doc. 187, pp. 585–6. See also Julian E. Zelizer, *Jimmy Carter* (New York: Time Books, 2010), p. 93; Andrew J. DeRoche, 'Standing Firm for Principles: Jimmy Carter and Zimbabwe', *Diplomatic History*, 23:4 (1999), pp. 657–85, at p. 678, fn. 100.
69. DeRoche, 'Standing Firm for Principles', p. 679.
70. Carrington, *Reflect on Things Past*, pp. 287–8.
71. Washington's decision not to recognise the legitimacy of the internal settlement was especially important in Carrington's decision to pursue the all parties conference. See Michael Charlton, *The Last Colony in Africa: Diplomacy and the Independence of Rhodesia* (Oxford: Oxford University Press, 1990), p. 47; John Willson, *BDOHP*, pp. 19–20; Carrington testimony within Kandiah and Onslow, *Britain and Rhodesia*, p. 78. The position of African states can be seen in Kenneth Kaunda to the Prime Minister, 8 June 1979, in File: 3/1/1 Part 1, Thatcher Papers; Kenneth Kaunda to Margaret Thatcher, 7 November 1979, in File: 3/1/4 Part 1, Thatcher Papers.
72. TNA: FCO 36/2435 A. T. Muzorewa to the Prime Minister, 22 August 1979; TNA: FCO 36/2436 Rhodesia: Constitutional Conference, Attitudes of the Parties: The Patriotic Front, undated [circa September 1979]; TNA: FCO 36/2435 From the FCO to Bucharest, Tel. 895, 13 August 1979. The draft constitution that the British devised can be read in TNA: FCO 36/2435 Outline Constitutional Proposals, undated [circa August 1979]. The minutes of the meetings and Carrington's analysis of the discussions can be followed in TNA: FCO 36/2436 From the Secretary of State to the Prime Minister, 12 September 1979. For further accounts of the talks see Carrington, *Reflect on Things Past*, pp. 298–302; Robin Renwick, *BDOHP*, pp. 7–11; Charles Powell, *BDOHP*, pp. 15–16; Roderic Lyne, *BDOHP*, pp. 23–9; Anthony Parsons, *BDOHP*, pp. 19–21; Ian Smith, *Bitter Harvest: The Great Betrayal*, 2nd revised edn (London: Blake, 2001), pp. 305–30.

73. The British were aware that Nkomo was receiving armaments from Moscow. Mention of this is made in TNA: FCO 36/2136 K. D. Evetts to Rosemary Spencer, 20 September 1978; TNA: FCO 36/2436 Rhodesia: Constitutional Conference, Attitudes of the Parties: ZAPU, undated [circa September 1979]. British assessments on Muzorewa can be read in TNA: FCO 36/2436 Rhodesia: Constitutional Conference, Attitudes of the Parties: Bishop Muzorewa, undated [circa September 1979].
74. TNA: PREM 19/383 Mr Vance's Visit, G. G. H. Walden to Mr Powell, 22 February 1980.
75. TNA: PREM 19/383 Brief Number 10: Rhodesia, Southern African Department, 19 February 1980. For further British complaints about American policy see TNA: FCO 82/1030 Essential Facts: Recent Examples of American Failures to Consult, 20 February 1980; TNA: FCO 45/2409 South Africa: Brief by the Foreign and Commonwealth Office, 16 March 1978.
76. Carrington, *Reflect on Things Past*, p. 305.
77. Margaret Thatcher, *The Downing Street Years* (London: Harper, 1993), p. 78.
78. White House Briefing for Civic and Community Leaders, 30 April 1980, in *Public Papers of the Presidents of the United States: Jimmy Carter, 1980–81, Book One* (Washington DC: United States Government Printing Office, 1981) (hereafter *PPP: Jimmy Carter, 1980–81, Book One*), p. 805.
79. Democratic Congressional Campaign Dinner, Remarks at the Dinner, 26 March 1980, in *PPP: Jimmy Carter, 1980–81, Book One*, p. 541.
80. Jay's oral history testimony is contained in Kandiah and Onslow, *Britain and Rhodesia*, p. 59.

Chapter 5

1. Zbigniew Brzezinski, *Power and Principle: Memoirs of the National Security Adviser 1977–1981* (London: Weidenfeld & Nicolson, 1983), p. 426.
2. See the Reagan presidential campaign video, available at <http://www.livingroomcandidate.org/commercials/1980> (last accessed 13 May 2016). On Reagan's campaign see Sean Wilentz, *The Age of Reagan* (New York: HarperCollins, 2008), pp. 120–2.

3. Memorandum for the President from W. Michael Blumenthal, 14 March 1979, in File: Economics, 1978–79, Office of the Chief of Staff Files, Hamilton Jordan's Confidential Files, Box 34a, JCL.
4. Ibid.
5. The title of Hamilton Jordan's memoir which focuses upon the final year of Carter's presidency is *Crisis: The Last Year of the Carter Presidency*. See Hamilton Jordan, *Crisis: The Last Year of the Carter Presidency* (New York: G. P. Putman, 1982). On the Kennedy challenge see Timothy Stanley, *Kennedy vs. Carter: The 1980 Battle for the Democratic Party's Soul* (Lawrence: University Press of Kansas, 2010). Reagan won 50.8 per cent of the popular vote in contrast to Carter's 41 per cent. The third party candidate, John Anderson, picked up 6.6 per cent of the popular vote. In the Electoral College, Reagan secured a sweeping victory as he collected 489 electoral votes to Carter's 49. For the statistics see Julian E. Zelizer, *Jimmy Carter* (New York: Time Books, 2010), p. 124.
6. For example see the works cited in Introduction, note 24.
7. Brzezinski, *Power and Principle*, p. 403.
8. Charles S. Maier, '"Malaise": The Crisis of Capitalism in the 1970s', in Niall Ferguson, Charles S. Maier, Erez Manela and Daniel J. Sargent (eds), *The Shock of the Global: The 1970s in Perspective* (Cambridge, MA: Harvard University Press, 2010), p. 40.
9. James E. Cronin, *Global Rules: America, Britain and a Disordered World* (New Haven, CT: Yale University Press, 2014), p. 87.
10. See for example William Safire, 'The Second Cold War', *New York Times*, 10 January 1980.
11. Gaddis Smith, *Morality, Reason and Power: American Diplomacy in the Carter Years* (New York: Hill and Wang, 1986), p. 9.
12. Barbara Zanchetta, *The Transformation of American International Power in the 1970s* (Cambridge: Cambridge University Press, 2014), p. 13; Daniel J. Sargent, *A Superpower Transformed: The Remaking of American Foreign Relations in the 1970s* (Oxford: Oxford University Press, 2015), pp. 291–3.
13. Report on the situation in Afghanistan by Gromyko, Andropov, Ustinov and Ponomarev to the CPSU, 27–28 December 1979, available at <http://digitalarchive.wilsoncenter.org/document/110029> (last accessed 13 May 2016).
14. Rodric Braithwaite, *Afgantsy: The Russians in Afghanistan, 1979–89* (Oxford: Oxford University Press, 2011), pp. 58–102. The following documents reveal Soviet thinking clearly: Record of a

Conversation between Brezhnev and Taraki, 20 March 1979, available at <http://digitalarchive.wilsoncenter.org/document/111282> (last accessed 13 May 2016); Excerpt from Minutes of No. 156 CC CPSU Politburo Meeting, 29 June 1979, available at <http://digitalarchive.wilsoncenter.org/document/112514> (last accessed 13 May 2016); Telegram from Chief Soviet Military Adviser, Report from Kabul, 2 December 1979, available at <http://digitalarchive.wilsoncenter.org/document/118651> (last accessed 13 May 2016); Summary of a CC CPSU Meeting, 26 December 1979, available at <http://digitalarchive.wilsoncenter.org/document/111786> (last accessed 13 May 2016).

15. Brzezinski briefed Thatcher personally on the Soviet military build-up during her visit to Washington in December 1979. Soviet actions in Afghanistan were also discussed between the British and Harold Brown. See TNA: PREM 19/11 Extract from Record of Meeting between the Prime Minister and the American Secretary of Defense, Dr Brown, Washington DC, 17 December 1979.

16. Memorandum from Marshall Brement of the National Security Council Staff to the President's Assistant for National Security Affairs (Brzezinski), 7 January 1980, in *FRUS 1977–1980: Soviet Union*, Vol. VI, Doc. 255, p. 734.

17. Remarks to Reporters: American Hostages in Iran and Soviet intervention in Afghanistan, 28 December 1979, in *PPP: Jimmy Carter, 1979, Book Two*, p. 2287.

18. Jimmy Carter, *White House Diary* (New York: Farrar, Straus and Giroux, 2010), 27 December 1979, p. 382.

19. Ibid., p. 382.

20. Carter, *White House Diary*, 2 January 1980, p. 387.

21. Nancy Mitchell, 'The Cold War and Jimmy Carter', in Melvyn Leffler and Odd Arne Westad (eds), *The Cambridge History of the Cold War: Endings* (Cambridge: Cambridge University Press, 2010), Vol. III, p. 85.

22. Jimmy Carter, *Keeping Faith: Memoirs of a President* (London: Collins, 1982), pp. 471–2.

23. Michael Alexander, *BDOHP*, p. 18.

24. Margaret Thatcher, *The Downing Street Years* (London: Harper, 1993), p. 87.

25. Editorial Note, in *FRUS: Foundations of Foreign Policy, 1974–1980*, Vol. I, Doc. 133, p. 678. On Soviet grand strategy under Brezhnev and the decision to invade Afghanistan see Matthew Ouimet, *The Rise and Fall of the Brezhnev Doctrine in Soviet*

Foreign Policy (Chapel Hill: University of North Carolina Press, 2003), pp. 88–97.
26. Summary of Conclusions of a Special Coordination Committee Meeting, 2 January 1980, in *FRUS 1977–1980: Soviet Union*, Vol. VI, Doc. 251, pp. 725–6; Carter, *White House Diary*, 4 January 1980, pp. 388–9. Following the events in Herat, the CIA had already begun supplying limited funds to the Afghan insurgents via Pakistan. However, it was only following the Soviet invasion of Afghanistan that significant support was provided by Washington. See Robert Gates, *From the Shadows: The Ultimate Insider's Story of Five Presidents and How They Won the Cold War* (New York: Simon & Schuster, 1996), pp. 143–7; Lloyd Gardner, *The Long Road to Baghdad: A History of US Foreign Policy from the 1970s to the Present* (New York: The New Press, 2008), pp. 56–8.
27. Opinion polls indicated a sharp turn against SALT II's ratification. In October 1979, 30 per cent of respondents were in favour of SALT II ratification and 35 per cent opposed. By January 1980 this had shifted to 22 per cent in favour and 42 per cent opposed. See Gabriella Grasselli, *British and American Responses to the Soviet Invasion of Afghanistan* (Aldershot: Ashgate, 1996), p. 126.
28. The President's News Conference, 9 October 1979, in *PPP: Jimmy Carter, 1979, Book Two*, p. 1837.
29. 'Strategic Arms Limitation Treaty', Letter to 19 Members of the Senate, 17 December 1979, in *PPP: Jimmy Carter, 1979, Book Two*, p. 2257.
30. Memorandum from the President's Assistant for National Security Affairs (Brzezinski) to Vice President Mondale, Secretary of State Vance, and Secretary of Defense Brown, 2 January 1980, in *FRUS 1977–1980: Soviet Union*, Vol. VI, Doc. 252, p. 727; Memorandum of Conversation, 20 March 1980, in ibid., Doc. 271, pp. 779–81; Memorandum of Conversation, 21 March 1980, in ibid., Doc. 272, p. 787.
31. Zanchetta, *The Transformation of American International Power*, pp. 291–2.
32. For the deterioration of US–Soviet relations see for example Letter From Secretary of State Vance to Soviet Foreign Minister Gromyko, 8 February 1980, in *FRUS 1977–1980: Soviet Union*, Vol. VI, Doc. 260, pp. 746–8; Letter From Soviet Foreign Minister Gromyko to Secretary of State Vance, 16 February 1980, in ibid., Doc. 260, pp. 749–52; Telegram From the Embassy in the Soviet Union to the Department of State, 11 March 1980, in ibid., Doc. 266, pp. 766–9.

33. Cyrus Vance, *Hard Choices: Critical Years in America's Foreign Policy* (New York: Simon & Schuster, 1983), p. 394.
34. Memorandum from the President's Assistant for National Security Affairs (Brzezinski) to President Carter, 9 January 1980, in *FRUS 1977–1980: Soviet Union*, Vol. VI, Doc. 256, p. 738.
35. Ibid., pp. 738–9.
36. Ibid., p. 739.
37. This was a point that Brzezinski had also made known to the president. See Memorandum from the President's Assistant for National Security Affairs (Brzezinski) to President Carter, 9 January 1980, in *FRUS 1977–1980: Soviet Union*, Vol. VI, Doc. 256, p. 739.
38. Richard Smith, Patrick Salmon and Stephen Twigge (eds), *Documents on British Policy Overseas, the Invasion of Afghanistan and UK–Soviet Relations, 1979–82* (London: Routledge, 2012), Series III, Vol. III, pp. 98–9.
39. TNA: PREM 19/134 Carrington to the Prime Minister, 2 January 1980.
40. TNA: CAB 130/1137 MISC 29 (80) 1st Meeting, Minutes of a Meeting held in Conference room A, Cabinet Office, 8 January 1980.
41. TNA: PREM 19/134 Record of a Meeting between the Prime Minister and the Soviet Ambassador, 3 January 1980; TNA: PREM 19/134 Message from the Prime Minister to President Brezhnev, from the FCO to Moscow, 29 December 1979.
42. House of Commons Speech, 28 January 1980, in *Hansard*, 977/933-45.
43. Grasselli, *Responses to the Soviet Invasion*, p. 6.
44. TNA: PREM 19/134 'Iran and Afghanistan', Alexander to Walden, 3 January 1980; TNA: PREM 19/134 From London to certain mission abroad, 1 January 1980.
45. The working group was to be established in order to overcome any problems likely to be created by the French government. As both Washington and London were aware, the French did not appear to believe that the Soviet invasion of Afghanistan should lead to any major response from NATO. As a sign of the French attitude, Paris had even suggested that the Soviet invasion of Afghanistan should not be brought before the UN Security Council. On this see TNA: PREM 19/134 Parsons to the FCO, Tel. 9, 3 January 1980; TNA: PREM 19/134 From the UK Delegation at NATO to the Foreign and Commonwealth Office, Tel. 004, 1 January 1980; TNA: PREM 19/134 Douglas Hurd to the Secretary of State, 31 December 1979; TNA: PREM 19/134 Record of

Discussions held in the India Office Council Chamber at the Foreign and Commonwealth Office, 31 December 1979.
46. TNA: PREM 19/134 Forster to the FCO, Tel. 003, 1 January 1980; Donald Maitland, *BDOHP*, pp. 36–7; Anthony Parsons, *BDOHP*, pp. 19–21. Throughout the Cold War the British had consistently been opposed to implementing economic sanctions against the communist powers. See R. Gerald Hughes, *The Postwar Legacy of Appeasement: British Foreign Policy since 1945* (London: Bloomsbury, 2014), p. 31.
47. TNA: PREM 19/374 Note of a Meeting held at 10 Downing Street, 16 January 1980. Thatcher made this point clear to Helmut Schmidt in a telephone conversation a day earlier. See TNA: PREM 19/135 Telephone Conversation between the Prime Minister and Chancellor Schmidt, 15 January 1980.
48. TNA: CAB 130/1137 MISC 29 (80) 1st Meeting, Minutes of a Meeting held in Conference room A, Cabinet Office, 8 January 1980.
49. Carter handwritten note on: Memorandum for the President from Zbigniew Brzezinski, 29 January 1980, in Plain Files, Box 2, JCL.
50. Jordan, *Crisis*, 4 January 1980, p. 100.
51. TNA: CAB 130/1137 MISC 29 (80) 2nd Meeting, Minutes of a Meeting held in Conference room B, Cabinet Office, 14 January 1980.
52. Ibid.
53. TNA: CAB 130/1137 MISC 29 (80) 1, Afghanistan: Potential Costs of Measures Against the Soviet Union, Note by the Secretaries, 14 January 1980; TNA: CAB 130/1137 MISC 29 (80) 2nd Meeting, Minutes of a Meeting held in Conference room B, Cabinet Office, 14 January 1980; TNA: PREM 19/136 Western Strategy in the Wake of the Soviet Invasion of Afghanistan, undated [circa January/February 1980].
54. TNA: CAB 130/1137 MISC 29 (80) 1, Afghanistan: Potential costs of measures against the Soviet Union, Note by the Secretaries, 14 January 1980; TNA: PREM 19/135 Afghanistan: Potential Costs of Measures against the Soviet Union, undated [January 1980], Addendum to Annex G.
55. TNA: PREM 19/135 Telephone Conversation between the Prime Minister and Chancellor Schmidt, 15 January 1980.
56. Curtis Keeble, *BDOHP*, p. 102.
57. For an example of the argument that economic factors predominantly determined the reaction of the Thatcher government see

Daniel James Lahey, 'The Thatcher Government's Response to the Soviet Invasion of Afghanistan, 1979–1980', *Cold War History*, 13:1 (2013), pp. 21–42.
58. TNA: PREM 19/136 Western Strategy in the Wake of the Soviet Invasion of Afghanistan, undated [circa January/February 1980].
59. This explains why the British government was so interested in learning about the possible actions of other countries including the likes of France, India and Pakistan. See for example TNA: PREM 19/134 From the UK Mission at the UN, New York, to the FCO, Tel. 1985, 31 December 1979. Thatcher's message to Washington is contained in TNA: PREM 19/134 From London to Washington, Tel. 17, 3 January 1980.
60. Carter, *White House Diary*, 8 January 1980, p. 390.
61. Edward Kennedy, *True Compass: A Memoir* (New York: Twelve, 2009), pp. 356–65; Julian E. Zelizer, *Arsenal of Democracy: The Politics of National Security – From World War II to the War on Terrorism* (New York: Basic Books, 2010), pp. 291–2.
62. TNA: PREM 19/135 Note for the Record by Sir Robert Armstrong, 18 January 1980.
63. TNA: PREM 19/383 Record of a Conversation between the Prime Minister and the United States Secretary of State Mr Cyrus Vance at 10 Downing Street, 21 February 1980.
64. Memorandum of Conversation of a Special Coordination Committee Meeting, 28 February 1980, in *FRUS 1977–1980: Soviet Union*, Vol. VI, Doc. 264, pp. 761–2; Memorandum of Conversation, 17 March 1980, in ibid., Doc. 268, pp. 772–4; Carter, *White House Diary*, 6 December 1979, p. 376.
65. See Thatcher's conversation with Schmidt where Carter's handling of the NATO alliance is discussed in critical terms: TNA: PREM 19/137 Extract of Record of Discussion PM/Schmidt at Chequers, 28 March 1980.
66. TNA: PREM 19/137 Jimmy Carter to Margaret Thatcher, 7 April 1980.
67. TNA: PREM 19/137 Henderson to FCO, Tel. 1386, 8 April 1980.
68. TNA: PREM 19/137 P. Lever to M. Alexander, 28 February 1980. On the Year of Europe see Matthew Jones, 'A Man in a Hurry: Henry Kissinger, Transatlantic Relations, and the British Origins of the Year of Europe Dispute', *Diplomacy and Statecraft*, 24:1 (2013), pp. 77–99; Thomas Robb, 'Henry Kissinger, Great Britain and the "Year of Europe": The "Tangled Skein"', *Contemporary British History*, 24:3 (2010), pp. 297–318.

Notes

69. TNA: PREM 19/137 Text of Message to President Carter, 2 April 1980. See also Thatcher's efforts with Schmidt: TNA: PREM 19/137 Extract of Record of Discussion PM/Schmidt at Chequers, 28 March 1980; TNA: PREM 19/137 From Washington to FCO, Tel. 927, 1 March 1980. TNA: PREM 19/137 Afghanistan Neutrality proposal, attached to R. Q. Braithwaite to PS/PUS et al., 24 March 1980; TNA: PREM 19/137 Donald Maitland to Nicholas Henderson, 24 March 1980; TNA: PREM 19/137 Robert Cooper to Private Secretary, 1 March 1980; TNA: PREM 19/137 From the Prime Minister to Mrs Ghandi, draft telegram, undated [circa 1 March 1980]; TNA: PREM 19/137 G. G. H. Walden to Michael Palliser, 28 February 1980; TNA: PREM 19/137 From FCO to Moscow, Tel. 162, 29 February 1980.
69. Memorandum from Vice President Mondale to President Carter, 3 January 1980, in *FRUS 1977–1980: Soviet Union*, Vol. VI, Doc. 253, p. 730. See also Marshall Brement to Zbigniew Brzezinski, 10 January 1980, in Brzezinski Material, Subject File: Olympic 6/79–2/80, Box 48, JCL; Stansfield Turner to the President, 9 January 1980, in ibid.
70. Margaret Thatcher to Masayoshi Ohira, 1 April 1980, in File: 3/1/8 Part 1, Thatcher Papers.
71. TNA: PREM 19/381 Harold Brown to Francis Pym, 10 July 1980; TNA: PREM 19/381 Record of Meeting between the Prime Minister and the United States Secretary of State for Defense at 10 Downing Street, 2 June 1980. TNA: PREM 19/381 P. Lever to J. D. S. Dawson, 14 August 1980; TNA: PREM 19/381 Harold Brown to Francis Pym, 10 July 1980; TNA: PREM 19/381 Francis Pym to Harold Brown, 14 August 1980.
72. Inaugural Address of President Jimmy Carter, 20 January 1977, in *PPP: Jimmy Carter, 1977, Book One*, pp. 1–4.
73. Memorandum from Vice President Mondale to President Carter, 3 January 1980, in *FRUS 1977–1980: Soviet Union*, Vol. VI, Doc. 253, p. 730. See also Marshall Brement to Zbigniew Brzezinski, 10 January 1980, in Brzezinski Material, Subject File: Olympic 6/79–2/80, Box 48, JCL; Stansfield Turner to the President, 9 January 1980, in ibid.
74. Carter, *White House Diary*, 2 January 1980, p. 387.
75. Telegram from the Department of State to All Diplomatic Posts, the Embassy in Pakistan, and the Embassy in Libya, 20 January 1980, in *FRUS 1977–1980: Soviet Union*, Vol. VI, Doc. 259, p. 744. The president's State of the Union on 23 January 1980 provided additional

rhetorical flourishes of anger towards the Soviet Union. See State of the Union: Address Delivered Before a Joint Session of the Congress, 23 January 1980, in *PPP: Jimmy Carter, 1980–81, Book One*, pp. 194–200.
76. This point was something that the British government quickly informed Washington of. See TNA: PREM 19/134 From London to Washington, Tel. 17, 3 January 1980; TNA: PREM 19/374 From the FCO to the UKMis New York, Tel. 32, 10 January 1980.
77. TNA: PREM 19/134 From London to Washington, Tel. 17, 3 January 1980. See also TNA: PREM 19/374 Michael Alexander to Rodric Lyne, 8 January 1980.
78. On the information provided see TNA: PREM 19/374 Afghanistan: The Olympics, J. A. L. Morgan to the PUS, 14 January 1980. On the Schmidt discussions see TNA: PREM 19/374 The Prime Minister's Telephone conversation with Chancellor Schmidt, 15 January 1980. On Thatcher's deliberations to find an alternative venue see Olympic Games, Memorandum, undated, in BOA/ADM/3/3, Moscow 1980, British Olympic Association Archive, University of East London, United Kingdom (hereafter BOA).
79. TNA: PREM 19/374 Jimmy Carter to the Prime Minister, 20 January 1980.
80. See Neil Allen, 'Hand off the Olympics', *Evening Standard*, 2 January 1980; Article for Daily Express, Sir Denis Follows, January 1980, in File: BOA/Pub 2/3 Sir Denis Follows, Box BOA/PUB/1-4, BOA.
81. TNA: PREM 19/374 Margaret Thatcher to Sir Denis Follows, 22 January 1980.
82. The minutes of the BOC's deliberations can be followed in Minutes of a meeting of Olympic Team Managers held at the International Students House, 16 January 1980, in File: Team Managers and Administrators Minutes, April 1979–June 1980, Box BOA/M/3/1,3, BOA.
83. TNA: PREM 19/374 Sir Denis Follows to Margaret Thatcher, 23 January 1980; TNA: PREM 19/374 Geoff Needham to Michael Alexander, 28 January 1980; TNA: PREM 19/374 Sir Denis Follows to Margaret Thatcher, 1 February 1980.
84. TNA: PREM 19/374 Visit of Mr Fraser: Olympic Games, 4 February 1980; Record of a Conversation between the Prime Minister and the Australian Prime Minister, Mr Malcolm Fraser, 4 March 1980, in File: 3/1/7, Thatcher Papers.
85. TNA: PREM 19/383 Brief Number 2: Olympics, 20 February 1980; TNA: PREM 19/383 Record of a Conversation between the Prime

Minister and the United States Secretary of State Mr Cyrus Vance at 10 Downing Street, 21 February 1980; John Hamshire, 'Yes There Is a War On', *Daily Mail*, 16 April 1980.
86. Summary of Conclusions of a Special Coordination Committee Meeting, 28 February 1980, in *FRUS 1977–1980: Soviet Union*, Vol. VI, Doc. 263, pp. 754, 757.
87. TNA: PREM 19/374 P. Lever to Michael Alexander, 11 February 1980; TNA: PREM 19/374 Record of a Meeting held at the State Department, 12 February 1980; TNA: PREM 19/374 Henderson to the FCO, Tel. 691, 12 February 1980.
88. TNA: PREM 19/374 Carrington to Rome, Tel. 103, 19 February 1980; Nicholas Evan Sarantakes, *Dropping the Torch: Jimmy Carter, the Olympic Boycott, and the Cold War* (Cambridge: Cambridge University Press, 2010), p. 175.
89. Thatcher, *Downing Street Years*, p. 88.
90. Minutes of a Meeting of Olympic Team Managers held at the International Students House, 7 May 1980, in File: Team Managers and Administrators Minutes, April 1979–June 1980, Box BOA/M/3/1,3, BOA.
91. TNA: PREM 19/375 Jonathan Hudson to Nick Sanders, 15 April 1980. Sebastian Coe would join the House of Lords as a Tory peer in May 2000. In 1980 Coe was personally lobbied by Douglas Hurd not to attend the Games. Coe rejected the government's request and would go on to win Olympic gold. This incident would be revealed in 2006. See Rob Evans and Paul Kelso, 'How Thatcher Tried to Stop Olympic Hero Coe from Winning Gold in Moscow', *The Guardian*, 24 February 2006. At the time, Coe publicly hinted that he had come under 'unspeakable pressure' not to attend the Games. See Owen Smith, 'Seb Takes on Maggie', *The Sun*, 3 July 1980.
92. TNA: PREM 19/376 Margaret Thatcher to Sir Denis Follows, 20 May 1980.
93. David Leitch, 'The Demon Bowler Outplayed Mrs Thatcher', *The Sunday Times*, 30 March 1980.
94. Douglas Hurd, *Memoirs* (London: Abacus, 2004), p. 291.
95. Sarantakes, *Dropping the Torch*, pp. 226, 235–7.
96. Good overviews of the crisis are provided in Mark Bowden, *Guests of the Ayatollah, The Iran Hostage Crisis: The First Battle in America's War with Militant Islam* (New York: Grove Press, 2006); David Harris, *The Crisis: The President, the Prophet, and the Shah – 1979 and the Coming of Militant Islam* (Boston: Little, Brown, 2006). The US Ambassador to Iran at this time, Henry

Precht, has provided an illuminating oral history interview on his experience. See 'The Iranian Revolution: An Oral History with Henry Precht, then State Department Desk Officer', *Middle East Journal*, 58:1 (2004), pp. 9–31.

97. Carter, *White House Diary*, 3 December 1979, p. 375; Vance, *Hard Choices*, pp. 344–5; Jody Powell, *The Other Side of the Story* (New York: William Morrow, 1984), p. 204; Jordan, *Crisis*, 7 April 1980, p. 248.
98. Hamilton Jordan to President Carter, 8 November 1979, in File: Iran, 11/79, Office of the Chief of Staff Files, Hamilton Jordan's Confidential Files, Box 34b, JCL.
99. Blake W. Jones, '"How Does a Born-Again Christian Deal with a Born-Again Moslem?" The Religious Dimension of the Iranian Hostage Crisis', *Diplomatic History*, 39:3 (2015), pp. 423–51, pp. 423–5; Jimmy Carter, *Living Faith* (New York: Random House, 1996), p. 102.
100. Carter, *White House Diary*, 4 January 1980, p. 389.
101. Hamilton Jordan to the President, 15 January 1980, in File: Iran, 1/80, Office of the Chief of Staff Files, Hamilton Jordan's Confidential Files, Box 34b, JCL.
102. Thatcher interview with the BBC, 18 December 1979, available at <http://www.margaretthatcher.org/document/103914> (last accessed 13 May 2016); The Prime Minister to the President of the United States, 21 November 1979, in File: 3/1/4 Part 1, Thatcher Papers; Telephone Conversation between the Prime Minister and the President of the United States, 19 November 1979, in File: 3/1/4 Part 1, Thatcher Papers.
103. Carter, *Keeping Faith*, p. 465.
104. Jones, '"How Does a Born-Again Christian"', p. 423–51.
105. TNA: PREM 19/135 Telephone Conversation between the Prime Minister and Chancellor Schmidt, 15 January 1980.
106. TNA: PREM 19/134 Iran and Afghanistan, Alexander to Walden, 3 January 1980.
107. Zanchetta, *The Transformation of American International Power*, p. 286.
108. TNA: PREM 19/134 H. A. H. Cortezzi to the Private Secretary, 29 December 1979.
109. TNA: PREM 19/134 From the UK Delegation at NATO to the Foreign and Commonwealth Office, 1 January 1980. Later in the year, however, American analysts including Brzezinski did start to

think more positively about British ideas but at this point rejected them. See Memorandum for the President from Hamilton Jordan, 14 February 1980, in Hamilton Jordan Confidential File: Office of the Chief of Staff, Folder: Iran 2-80, Box 34B, JCL.
110. TNA: PREM 19/374 Call by Mr Warren Christopher, 14 January 1980.
111. TNA: PREM 19/374 The Prime Minister's Telephone conversation with Chancellor Schmidt, 15 January 1980.
112. TNA: PREM 19/383 Partial Record of a Discussion between the Prime Minister and the US Secretary of State, 21 February 1980.
113. TNA: PREM 19/383 Partial Record of a Discussion between the Prime Minister and the US Secretary of State, 21 February 1980.
114. Powell, *The Other Side*, p. 205.
115. Carter, *White House Diary*, 18 October 1979, p. 363. The mounting tensions within the administration had reached the level whereby Hamilton Jordan, the president's chief of staff, was now writing personal letters to Cyrus Vance to reassure him that he remained a central figure within the administration. See for example Hamilton Jordan to the Secretary [Vance], undated, in File: Vance, Cyrus, 1980, Office of the Chief of Staff Files, Hamilton Jordan's Confidential Files, Box 37, JCL.
116. Madeleine Albright, *Madam Secretary: A Memoir* (London: HarperCollins, 2003), p. 88. A good recent overview on Brzezinski's statecraft is provided in Robert A. Pastor, 'The Caricature and the Man', in Charles Gati (ed.), *Zbig: The Strategy and Statecraft of Zbigniew Brzezinski* (Baltimore: The Johns Hopkins University Press, 2013), pp. 104–11.
117. Carter, *White House Diary*, 21–23 March 1980, p. 411; ibid., 16 April 1980, p. 419; Powell, *The Other Side*, pp. 228–31. Brown quoted in Jordan, *Crisis*, 10 April 1980, p. 249.
118. Smith, *American Diplomacy in the Carter Years*, pp. 198–9; TNA: PREM 19/383 Record of a Discussion between the Prime Minister and the United States Secretary of State Mr Cyrus Vance at 10 Downing Street, 10 December 1979.
119. Warren Christopher, *Chances of a Lifetime: A Memoir* (New York: Scribner, 2001), p. 98.
120. Carter, *Keeping Faith*, p. 506.
121. Carter, *Keeping Faith*, pp. 506–22; Walter F. Mondale, *The Good Fight: A Life in Liberal Politics* (New York: Simon & Schuster, 2010), pp. 252–9; Vance, *Hard Choices*, pp. 407–9; Jordan,

Crisis, 3 April 1980, p. 246; Brzezinski, *Power and Principle*, pp. 395–8; Stansfield Turner, *Burn before Reading: Presidents, CIA Directors, and Secret Intelligence* (New York: Hyperion, 2006), pp. 176–9.
122. Mondale, *The Good Fight*, p. 257.
123. Stansfield Turner, Director of the CIA (1977–81), claimed in 2005 that the mission should have proceeded even though the helicopters had encountered technical difficulties because all eight helicopters remained in a 'flyable condition'. The commander on the scene evidently disagreed. See Turner, *Burn before Reading*, p. 179.
124. Carter, *White House Diary*, 24 April 1980, p. 422.
125. Christopher Andrew, *For the President's Eyes Only: Secret Intelligence and the American Presidency from Washington to Bush* (London: HarperCollins, 1996), p. 452.
126. Thatcher, *Downing Street Years*, pp. 88–9.
127. Hurd, *Memoirs*, p. 290.
128. Jody Powell announced the Carter administration's appreciation for London and the wider European Economic Community agreeing to the imposition of sanctions in Statement by the White House Press Secretary: Sanctions against Iran, 23 April 1980, in *PPP: Jimmy Carter, 1980–81, Book One*, p. 760.
129. Christopher, *Chances of a Lifetime*, pp. 101–2; Telephone Conversation between the Prime Minister and President Carter, 19 April 1980, in File: 3/1/8 Part 1, Thatcher Papers.
130. This was not always the case as demonstrated by US actions in Cambodia in 1969. However, Nixon and Kissinger made a point of informing the British government about American moves during the Easter bombing offensive of North Vietnam in 1972 and during the fourth Arab–Israeli War of October 1973. See Alexander J. Banks, 'Britain and the Cambodia Crisis of Spring 1970', *Cold War History*, 5:1 (2005), pp. 87–105.
131. Memorandum to the President from Brzezinski, 3 October 1980, in Brzezinski Material, File: NSC Weekly Reports 151–61, Box 42, JCL.
132. Mondale, *The Good Fight*, pp. 243–4.
133. Christopher, *Chances of a Lifetime*, p. 105.
134. MISC 7 is referred to in TNA: PREM 19/417 Polaris Successor: Memorandum from the Ministry of Defence to the Prime Minister, 10 June 1980.
135. TNA: PREM 19/417 Draft: Britain's Strategic Nuclear Force: the Choice of a System, to Succeed Polaris attached to: Polaris Successor:

Memorandum from the Ministry of Defence to the Prime Minister, 10 June 1980.
136. Ibid.
137. Ibid.
138. Ibid.
139. The Thatcher government's decision to pursue a successor system to Polaris is covered in Kristan Stoddart, *Facing Down the Soviet Union: Britain, the USA, NATO and Nuclear Weapons, 1976–1983* (Basingstoke: Palgrave Macmillan, 2014), pp. 112–53.
140. Anglo-French nuclear cooperation was sporadically discussed but was never viewed as a viable avenue for succeeding Polaris. See TNA: PREM 16/1564 President Giscard's Visit: Nuclear Matters, 22 December 1977; TNA: PREM 19/417 Polaris Successor: Memorandum from the Ministry of Defence to the Prime Minister 10 June 1980; TNA: PREM 19/417 UK–French Nuclear Cooperation, attached to G. G. H. Walden to M. Alexander, 5 September 1979; TNA: PREM 19/417 Lord Carrington to the Prime Minister, 12 June 1980.
141. Jimmy Carter to Margaret Thatcher, 15 October 1979, File: Great Britain 6/77–12/80, Plains File, Box 2, JCL.
142. This is recorded in TNA: PREM 19/417 Prime Minister's Meeting with President Carter: Brief by the Cabinet Office, 20 June 1980. Talks over the summer had taken placed between American and British officials. See for example Zbigniew Brzezinski to John Hunt, June 1979, File: Alpha Channel Miscellaneous – 5/79–8/79, Zbigniew Brzezinski Collection, Box 20, JCL.
143. TNA: PREM 19/417 Anglo-American Negotiations on Polaris Replacement, R. L. Wade-Grey to the Prime Minister, 13 June 1980; Thatcher, *Downing Street Years*, p. 245.
144. British assessments and reports on their discussions with the United States can be followed in TNA: DEFE 24/2125 D. C. Fakley to Head of DS 17, 27 August 1980; TNA: DEFE 24/2125 PS/US of S (RN) to PS/DUS (N) 22 August 1980.
145. Vance, *Hard Choices*, p. 98.
146. TNA: PREM 19/417 Harold Brown to Francis Pym, 14 June 1980. See also TNA: PREM 19/417 The Prime Minister to President Carter, 10 June 1980; TNA: PREM 19/417 Jimmy Carter to the Prime Minister, 14 July 1980. Ostensibly this was the end of the episode but Reagan's election complicated matters as Trident C4 was now abandoned by the United States in favour of Trident D5. After a period of negotiating, the sale of Trident D5 was approved

but Trident's cancellation was tabled by Geoffrey Howe in 1983 as a means of saving public expenditure. This proposal was rejected outright and Trident D5 was purchased. See Thatcher, *Downing Street Years*, pp. 246–8.
147. Thatcher, *Downing Street Years*, p. 246.
148. Discussion on Trident and Diego Garcia and the linkage between the deals is evident throughout TNA: PREM 19/417 Anglo-American Negotiations on Polaris Replacement, R. L. Wade-Grey to the Prime Minister, 13 June 1980; TNA: PREM 19/381 Record of a Meeting between the Prime Minister and the United States Secretary of Defense at 10 Downing Street, 2 June 1980; TNA: PREM 19/381 Visit of US Defense Secretary: Diego Garcia, 30 May 1980.
149. This is something generally omitted in existing accounts of the Trident C4 decision. See for example Stoddart, *Facing Down the Soviet Union*, pp. 112–53.
150. R. Gerald Hughes and Thomas Robb, 'Kissinger and the Diplomacy of Coercive Linkage in the "Special Relationship" between the United States and Great Britain, 1969–77', *Diplomatic History*, 37:4 (2013), pp. 861–906, pp. 864–6.
151. See the discussion Thatcher had with Harold Brown here about stationing GLCMs in Britain and the negative political consequences this would cause for the prime minister. See TNA: PREM 19/381 Record of Meeting between the Prime Minister and the United States Secretary of State for Defense at 10 Downing Street, 2 June 1980.
152. TNA: PREM 19/381 Prime Minister's Meeting with Harold Brown: Brief E: US Defence Stance: The Public Mood, North American Department, 30 May 1980.

Conclusion

1. Robert L. Rothstein, *Alliances and Small Powers* (New York: Columbia University Press, 1968), p. 1.
2. Robert M. Hathaway, *Great Britain and the United States: Special Relations since World War II* (Boston: Twayne, 1990), p. 114. For good overviews of Carter's policy towards the Middle East see William Quandt, *Peace Process: American Diplomacy and the Arab–Israeli Conflict since 1967* (Washington DC: The Brookings

Institution, 2001), pp. 177–204; Patrick Tyler, *A World of Trouble: The White House and the Middle East, from the Cold War to the War on Terror* (New York: Farrar, Straus and Giroux, 2009), pp. 176–209.
3. TNA: FCO 93/1818 J. Cornish to Mr Powell, 15 December 1978.
4. TNA: PREM 16/1978 Cabinet: Nuclear Defence Policy, Note of a Meeting held at 10 Downing Street, 21 December 1978.
5. Richard J. Aldrich, *GCHQ: The Uncensored Story of Britain's Most Secret Intelligence Agency* (London: HarperPress, 2010), pp. 89–106; Richard Aldrich, *The Hidden Hand: Britain, America and Cold War Secret Intelligence* (London: John Murray, 2001), pp. 83–8.
6. Margaret Thatcher, *The Downing Street Years* (London: Harper, 1993), pp. 68–9. Thatcher's criticism was balanced by her statement: 'I repeat that I liked Jimmy Carter; he was a good friend to me and to Britain; and if he had come to power in the different circumstances of the post-Cold War world, his talents might have been more apposite.' See Thatcher, *Downing Street Years*, p. 69.
7. Jimmy Carter, *Keeping Faith: Memoirs of a President* (London: Collins, 1982), p. 144.
8. Rosemary Foot, 'The Cold War and Human Rights', in Melvyn Leffler and Odd Arne Westad (eds), *The Cambridge History of the Cold War: Endings* (Cambridge: Cambridge University Press, 2010), Vol. III, p. 458. For the broader point that the promotion of human right by the United States and Britain had such a dramatic influence upon the subsequent course of international relations see James E. Cronin, *Global Rules: America, Britain and a Disordered World* (New Haven, CT: Yale University Press, 2014); Mark Atwood Lawrence, 'Containing Globalism: The United States and the Developing World in the 1970s', in Niall Ferguson, Charles S. Maier, Erez Manela and Daniel J. Sargent (eds), *The Shock of the Global: The 1970s in Perspective* (Cambridge, MA: Harvard University Press, 2010), pp. 216–19. On how actions within international relations are deemed to be 'legitimate' and why this matters see Ian Clark, *Legitimacy in International Society* (Oxford: Oxford University Press, 2007).
9. Thatcher, *Downing Street Years*, pp. 88, 157; Margaret Thatcher, *Statecraft: Strategies for a Changing World* (London: HarperCollins, 2002), pp. 15–18.
10. Peter Carrington, *Reflect on Things Past* (London: Collins, 1988), p. 274.

11. Ovendale hints at the difference in Thatcher's rhetoric and actions in foreign policy. See Ritchie Ovendale, *Anglo-American Relations in the Twentieth Century* (Basingstoke: Palgrave Macmillan, 1998), pp. 145–6.
12. Philip Ziegler, *Edward Heath: The Authorised Biography* (London: HarperPress, 2010), p. 378.

Select Bibliography

Archives

British National Archives, Kew, United Kingdom

CAB	Cabinet Office files	
	CAB	130
	CAB	133
DEFE	Ministry of Defence files	
	DEFE	24
FCO	Foreign and Commonwealth Office files	
	FCO	36
	FCO	58
	FCO	59
	FCO	82
	FCO	93
	FO	371
PREM	Prime Minister's Office files	
	PREM	16
	PREM	19
T	Treasury files	
	T	364
	T	381

British Olympic Association Archive, University of East London, London, United Kingdom

BOA/ADM/3/3
BOA/M/3/3
BOA/PC/16/1–10

Gerald R. Ford Presidential Library, Ann Arbor, Michigan, United States of America

Henry Kissinger and Brent Scowcroft Files Temporary Parallel File
National Security Adviser: Memoranda of Conversations, 1973–1977
National Security Adviser Outside the System Chronological File 1974–1977
National Security Adviser Presidential Country Files for Europe and Canada
National Security Council Files
Presidential Handwriting Files

Jimmy E. Carter Presidential Library, Atlanta, Georgia, United States of America

Hamilton Jordan's Confidential Files
National Security Affairs Collection
Plains Files
Presidential Correspondence Files
Vertical Files
White House Central Files
Zbigniew Brzezinski Collection

National Archives II, College Park, Maryland, United States of America

Department of State Electronic Telegrams
RG 59 General Records of the Department of State
RG 218 Records of the Joint Chiefs of Staff

Private papers consulted

Cyrus R. Vance and Grace Sloane Vance Papers, Sterling Library, Yale University, USA
David Owen Papers, University of Liverpool, UK
Harold Macmillan Papers, Bodleian Library, Oxford University, Oxford, UK
Harold Wilson Papers, Bodleian Library, Oxford University, Oxford, UK
James Callaghan Papers, Bodleian Library, Oxford University, Oxford, UK

Select Bibliography

Julian Amery Papers, Churchill Archives Centre, Cambridge University, UK
Lord Hailsham Papers, Churchill Archives Centre, Cambridge University, UK
Margaret Thatcher Papers, Churchill Archives Centre, Cambridge University, UK
Michael Foot Papers, Labour Party Archive, Manchester, UK
Peter Jay Private Papers, Churchill Archives Centre, Cambridge University, UK
Tip O'Neill Papers, John J. Burns Library, Boston College, Massachusetts, USA
William Simon Papers, Gerald Ford Library, Ann Arbor, Michigan, USA

Oral histories

British Diplomatic Oral History Project (BDOHP), Churchill Archives Centre, Churchill College, Cambridge University, UK

Anthony Parsons
Charles Powell
Curtis Keeble
David Summerhayes
Denis Greenhill
Donald Maitland
John Killick
John Willson
Juliet Campbell
Michael Alexander
Michael Palliser
Oliver Wright
Peter Jay
Peter Ramsbotham
Robin Renwick
Roderic Lyne

Nuclear History Oral History Project, Center for Strategic and International Studies, Washington DC, United States of America

Gill, David, 'Lord Carrington', in Jenifer Mackby and Paul Cornish (eds), *US–UK Nuclear Cooperation after 50 Years*. Washington DC: CSIS Press, 2008.

Gill, David, 'Sir Michael Quinlan', in Jenifer Mackby and Paul Cornish (eds), *US–UK Nuclear Cooperation after 50 Years*. Washington DC: CSIS Press, 2008.
Robb, Thomas, 'Lord Owen', in Jenifer Mackby and Paul Cornish (eds), *US–UK Nuclear Cooperation after 50 Years*. Washington DC: CSIS Press, 2008.
Robb, Thomas, 'Lord Robertson', in Jenifer Mackby and Paul Cornish (eds), *US–UK Nuclear Cooperation after 50 Years*. Washington DC: CSIS Press, 2008.
Robb, Thomas, 'Sir Kevin Tebbitt', in Jenifer Mackby and Paul Cornish (eds), *US–UK Nuclear Cooperation after 50 Years*. Washington DC: CSIS Press, 2008.
Robb, Thomas, 'Sir Richard Mottram', in Jenifer Mackby and Paul Cornish (eds), *US–UK Nuclear Cooperation after 50 Years*. Washington DC: CSIS Press, 2008.
Smith, Cassandra, 'Harold Brown', in Jenifer Mackby and Paul Cornish (eds), *US–UK Nuclear Cooperation after 50 Years*. Washington DC: CSIS Press, 2008.

Memoirs and diaries

Albright, Madeleine, *Madam Secretary: A Memoir*. London: HarperCollins, 2003.
Brzezinski, Zbigniew, *Power and Principle: Memoirs of the National Security Adviser 1977–1981*. London: Weidenfeld & Nicolson, 1983.
Callaghan, James, *Time & Chance*. London: Collins, 1987.
Carrington, Peter, *Reflect on Things Past*. London: Collins, 1988.
Carter, Jimmy, *Why Not the Best?* New York: Bantam Books, 1976.
Carter, Jimmy, *Keeping Faith: Memoirs of a President*. London: Collins, 1982.
Carter, Jimmy, *An Hour before Daylight: Memories of My Rural Boyhood*. New York: Simon & Schuster, 2001.
Carter, Jimmy, *White House Diary*. New York: Farrar, Straus and Giroux, 2010.
Carter, Jimmy, *A Full Life: Reflections at Ninety*. New York: Simon & Schuster, 2015.
Christopher, Warren, *Chances of a Lifetime: A Memoir*. New York: Scribner, 2001.
Donoughue, Bernard, *Downing Street Diary: With Harold Wilson in No. 10*. London: Jonathan Cape, 2005.

Select Bibliography

Donoughue, Bernard, *Downing Street Diary: Volume 2 – With James Callaghan in No. 10*. London: Jonathan Cape, 2008.
Hattersley, Roy, *Fifty Years On: A Prejudiced History of Britain since the War*. London: Little, Brown, 1997.
Heath, Edward, *The Course of My Life*. London: Hodder & Stoughton, 1997.
Jenkins, Roy, *A Life at the Centre*. London: Macmillan, 1991.
Jordan, Hamilton, *No Such Thing as a Bad Day: A Memoir*. New York: Pocket Books, 2001.
Kissinger, Henry, *Years of Upheaval*. Boston, MA: Little, Brown, 1982.
Kissinger, Henry, *Years of Renewal*. New York: Simon & Schuster, 1999.
Mondale, Walter, *The Good Fight: A Life in Liberal Politics*. New York: Simon & Schuster, 2010.
Muzorewa, Abel, *Rise Up and Walk: An Autobiography*. London: Evans Bros, 1978.
Nixon, Richard, *RN: The Memoirs of Richard Nixon*. London: Grosset & Dunlap, 1978.
Nkomo, Joshua, *Nkomo: The Story of My Life*. London, Methuen, 1984.
Nott, John, *Here Today, Gone Tomorrow: Memoirs of an Errant Politician*. London: Politico's, 2002.
Owen, David, *Time to Declare*. London: Michael Joseph, 1991.
Owen, David, *Nuclear Papers*. Liverpool: Liverpool University Press, 2010.
Powell, Jody, *The Other Side of the Story*. New York: William Morrow, 1984.
Seitz, Raymond, *Over Here*. London: Weidenfeld & Nicolson, 1998.
Simon, William, *A Time for Reflection: An Autobiography*. New York: Regnery, 2003.
Smith, Ian, *Bitter Harvest: The Great Betrayal*, 2nd revised edn. London: Blake, 2001.
Sulzberger, L. C., *An Age of Mediocrity, Memoirs and Diaries: 1963–1972*. New York: Macmillan, 1973.
Thatcher, Margaret, *The Downing Street Years*. London: Harper, 1993.
Thatcher, Margaret, *Statecraft: Strategies for a Changing World*. London: HarperCollins, 2002.

Turner, Stansfield, *Burn before Reading: Presidents, CIA Directors, and Secret Intelligence*. New York: Hyperion, 2006.

Vance, Cyrus, *Hard Choices: Critical Years in America's Foreign Policy*. New York: Simon & Schuster, 1983.

Wass, Douglas, *Decline to Fall: The Making of British Macro-economic Policy and the 1976 IMF Crisis*. Oxford: Oxford University Press, 2008.

Index

Afghanistan, 2, 6, 9, 13, 113, 114–31
Albright, Madeline, 142

Blumenthal, Michael, W., 15, 69, 113
Botha, Frederick, 82
Brezhnev, Leonid, 42, 46, 73, 93, 102, 117, 118, 122
Brown, Harold, 15, 29, 31, 39, 49, 75, 102, 103, 130, 142, 143, 149
Brzezinski, Zbigniew, 15, 17, 18, 20, 21, 22, 25, 29, 30, 32, 33, 37, 38, 43, 45, 47, 49, 64, 66, 67, 74, 75, 80, 81, 91, 113, 115, 120, 128, 129, 142, 143

Callaghan, James, 8, 9, 11, 12, 21, 22, 25, 28–31, 33, 44, 45, 51, 65, 68, 69, 70, 71, 89, 147
  IMF Crisis, 11–12
  nuclear policy, 37–8, 73–6, 85–8
  Rhodesia policy, 57–61, 82–5
  style of government, 21, 22
  the special relationship, 25–6
Campaign for Nuclear Disarmament (CND), 37, 38
Carrington, Peter, 23, 90, 91, 92, 94, 96, 102, 103, 107, 108, 109, 110, 111, 121, 122, 139, 144, 146, 156
Carter, Jimmy, 6, 7, 11, 13–17, 103, 105, 113, 115, 117, 118, 124, 126, 128, 129, 137, 144, 151, 152, 154, 157
  human rights, 7–9, 19, 24, 25, 26, 27, 28, 44, 45, 46, 47, 48, 49
  international economic policy, 70, 71, 72
  Iranian Hostage Crisis, 137–45
  morality, 16, 17, 44, 54, 55, 74, 166
  nuclear policy, 29, 30, 35, 41, 47, 48, 74–6, 85–8, 94, 95
  outsider status, 15, 66

Rhodesia policy, 54, 77, 79, 80, 107, 111
Christopher, Warren, 20, 45, 75, 125, 140, 143, 144, 145
Churchill, Winston, 1

Diggs, Charles, 189
Dobrynin, Anatoly, 19, 41
Donoughue, Bernard, 44, 89

Ford, Gerald, 15, 16, 17, 20, 21, 26, 31, 32, 42, 45, 49, 54, 118, 150, 151
France, 67, 69, 87, 96, 114, 124, 129, 130, 135, 147

Garcia, Diego, 103, 105, 149, 150
Gromyko, Andrei, 127

Haig, Alexander, 91
Healey, Denis, 22, 69, 87, 173
Heath, Edward, 10, 11, 91, 130, 151
Helms, Jesse, 107, 214
Howe, Geoffrey, 96, 146

IMF Crisis, 8, 107, 175–99
India, 67, 123
intelligence cooperation, 2, 3, 4, 6, 8, 11, 23, 28, 49, 103, 139, 151, 154

Jay, Peter, 7, 12, 43, 66, 68, 81, 82, 90, 91, 112

Kissinger, Henry, 4, 10, 11, 17, 25, 53, 54, 130, 142, 144, 151

Macmillan, Harold, 3, 52
Mason, Roy, 50
Mondale, Walter, 16, 17, 18, 26, 27, 28, 41, 58, 66, 124, 131, 143, 145
Mugabe, Robert, 54, 77, 78, 79, 83, 109, 110, 111
Mutual and Balanced Force Reductions (MBFR), 45
Muzorewa, Abel, 58, 60, 62, 76–9, 82, 106, 107, 109, 110, 111

Nixon, Richard, 10, 11, 13, 17, 19, 49
Nkomo, Joshua, 54, 77, 78, 79, 83, 109, 110
North Atlantic Treaty Organization (NATO), 2, 8, 13, 22, 25, 26, 27, 28, 29, 31–41, 48, 63, 65, 67, 68, 72–6, 103, 105, 115, 123, 127, 128, 129, 130, 135, 146, 147, 149, 150, 153, 155

Index

Odom, William, 17
Olympic Games, 131–7
O'Neill, Tip, 51, 101, 105
Owen, David, 11, 22, 28, 44, 56–61, 74, 75, 76, 79, 82, 86, 87, 90

Pakistan, 67, 117, 118, 123, 219
People's Republic of China (PRC), 7, 36, 53, 54, 77, 80, 111
Polaris, 2, 29, 31, 43, 85, 86, 87, 88, 95, 114, 146, 147, 148, 149, 154
Pym, Francis, 96, 130, 146, 149
Ramsbotham, Peter, 24, 25, 30, 33
Reagan, Ronald, 7, 23, 113, 114, 145, 154

Schlesinger, James, 20, 75
Schmidt, Helmut, 8, 41, 65, 70, 71, 72, 73, 74, 91, 94, 95, 126, 129, 132, 133, 140, 141
Scowcroft, Brent, 187
Smith, Ian, 52, 53, 55, 56, 57, 58, 59, 60, 61, 62, 76, 77, 78, 79, 80, 81, 82, 83, 84, 105, 106, 107, 110

Strategic Arms Limitations Talks (SALT), 25, 29, 30, 35, 36, 41–48, 64, 65, 68, 86, 92–7, 100, 102, 105, 113, 117, 118, 148, 149, 152, 153

Trident, 2, 7, 8, 13, 65, 85, 86, 87, 88, 105, 114, 146–51, 154, 155
Turner, Stansfield, 143

United Nations (UN), 44, 52, 53, 56, 59, 61, 62, 78, 123, 138, 139
Union of Soviet Socialist Republics (USSR), 2, 3, 9, 13, 15, 16, 17, 19, 24, 25, 26, 27, 28, 31–5, 40, 41, 43, 45, 47, 54, 67, 68, 73, 75, 90, 91, 93, 94, 95, 96, 102, 114, 115, 116, 117–21, 124, 126–30, 135, 142, 147, 150, 151, 156

Vance, Cyrus, 12, 15, 20, 21, 22, 25, 27, 28, 32, 33, 37, 43, 45, 46, 55, 56, 57, 58, 59, 60–3, 77–9, 83, 93, 94, 96–9, 101, 104, 107, 110, 114, 119, 120, 128, 134, 141–3, 148
Vietnam War, 5, 10, 14, 15, 40, 156

Watergate, 10, 15, 16
West Germany, 8, 37, 69, 72, 73, 76, 86, 96, 114, 124, 129, 130, 135, 137

Whitelaw, Willie, 146
Wilson, Harold, 5, 11, 52

Young, Andrew, 25, 56, 61, 78, 189

EU representative:
Easy Access System Europe
Mustamäe tee 50, 10621 Tallinn, Estonia
Gpsr.requests@easproject.com

www.ingramcontent.com/pod-product-compliance
Lightning Source LLC
Chambersburg PA
CBHW051114230426
43667CB00014B/2579